Essentials of Software Testing

Software testing can be regarded as an art, a craft, and a science. The practical, step-by-step approach presented in this book provides a bridge between these different viewpoints. A single worked example runs throughout, with consistent use of test automation. Each testing technique is introduced in the context of this example, helping students see its strengths and weaknesses. The technique is then explained in more detail, providing a deeper understanding of the underlying principles. Finally the limitations of each technique are demonstrated by inserting faults, giving learners concrete examples of when each technique succeeds or fails in finding faults. Topics addressed include black-box testing, white-box testing, random testing, unit testing, object-oriented testing, and application testing. The authors also emphasise the process of applying the techniques, covering the steps of analysis, test design, test implementation, and interpretation of results. The book's website has programming exercises and Java source code for all examples.

Dr. Ralf Bierig is a lecturer at Maynooth University. He received his undergraduate degree from Furtwangen University in Germany and completed his PhD at The Robert Gordon University in Aberdeen, Scotland. He gained experience as a Senior IT Consultant in the car industry in Germany and worked as a postgraduate researcher in academia in the UK, the USA, Austria, and in Thailand before moving to Ireland. He has taught software testing for four years, and many related topics in computer and information science, e.g. software engineering, web development, interactive information retrieval, interaction design, and human–computer interaction. He is an active researcher in the wider area of interactive information retrieval and human-computer interaction.

Dr. Stephen Brown is a senior lecturer at Maynooth University. He graduated from Trinity College Dublin with BA, BAI, and MSc degrees. He then spent 10 years in industry, with Digital Equipment Corporation, in Ireland, the USA, and the UK. Following a period as a Research Fellow (TCD) on the EU-funded ADVANCE project, he moved to Maynooth where he completed his PhD degree (UCC). He has lectured in many topics, including software testing, software engineering, databases, programming, computing ethics, wireless sensor networking, computer architecture. He is an active researcher in wireless networking.

Dr. Edgar Galván is a senior researcher in the Department of Computer Science, Maynooth University and the co-head of the Naturally Inspired Computation Research Group. Prior to this he held multiple senior positions in University College Dublin, Trinity College Dublin and Inria-Paris Saclay. Dr. Galván has been independently ranked as one of the all-time top 1% researchers in Genetic Programming, according to University College London. He has published more than 80 peer-reviewed publications in top-tier journals and conference venues.

Dr. Joe Timoney joined the Department of Computer Science at Maynooth University in 1999. He teaches on undergraduate programs in Computer Science and in Music Technology. His research interests are based in the areas of Software Engineering and Audio signal processing, with a focus on musical applications. He has supervised a number of PhD students. In 2003 he spent a 3 month research visit at ATR laboratory in Kyoto, Japan, and in 2010 to the College of Computing at Zhejiang University, Hangzhou, China. He also is a keen DIY electronics enthusiast and has built a number of electronic instruments.

Essentials of Software Testing

RALF BIERIG

Maynooth University

STEPHEN BROWN

Maynooth University

EDGAR GALVÁN

Maynooth University

JOE TIMONEY

Maynooth University

CAMBRIDGE
UNIVERSITY PRESS

University Printing House, Cambridge CB2 8BS, United Kingdom

One Liberty Plaza, 20th Floor, New York, NY 10006, USA

477 Williamstown Road, Port Melbourne, VIC 3207, Australia

314–321, 3rd Floor, Plot 3, Splendor Forum, Jasola District Centre, New Delhi – 110025, India

103 Penang Road, #05–06/07, Visioncrest Commercial, Singapore 238467

Cambridge University Press is part of the University of Cambridge.

It furthers the University's mission by disseminating knowledge in the pursuit of education, learning, and research at the highest international levels of excellence.

www.cambridge.org
Information on this title: www.cambridge.org/9781108833349
DOI: 10.1017/9781108974073

© Ralf Bierig, Stephen Brown, Edgar Galván, Joe Timoney 2022

First published 2022

Printed in the United Kingdom by TJ Books Limited, Padstow Cornwall

A catalogue record for this publication is available from the British Library.

ISBN 978-1-108-83334-9 Hardback

Additional resources for this publication at www.cambridge.org/bierig

Contents

Preface

Modern society is heavily reliant on software, and the correct operation of this software is a critical concern. The purpose of this book is to introduce the reader to the essential principles of software testing, enabling them to produce high-quality software. Software testing can be regarded as an art, a craft, and a science – the approach we present provides a bridge between these different viewpoints.

This book is based on many years of lecturing in software engineering and software testing at undergraduate and postgraduate level, as well as industrial experience. Software testing techniques are introduced through worked examples, leading to automated tests. Each technique is then explained in more detail, and then its limitations are demonstrated by inserting faults. The process of applying the techniques is also emphasised, covering the steps of analysis, test design, test implementation, and interpretation of test results.

The worked examples offer the beginner a practical, step-by-step introduction to each technique. The additional details complement these, providing a deeper understanding of the underlying principles. We hope that you will enjoy reading the book as much as we enjoyed writing it.

"For sounds in winter nights, and often in winter days, I heard the forlorn but melodious note of a hooting owl indefinitely far; such a sound as the frozen earth would yield if struck with a suitable plectrum, the very lingua vernácula of Walden Wood, and quite familiar to me at last, though I never saw the bird while it was making it."

Walden
HENRY DAVID THOREAU

Acknowledgements

The authors would like to thank Ana Susac for her painstaking, persistent, and detailed checking of the text and every example in the book. Her assistance has been invaluable. Any mistakes remaining are entirely our own responsibility.

1 Introduction to Software Testing

This chapter discusses the motivations for testing software, and also discusses why exhaustive testing is not generally feasible, and thus various test heuristics must be used. These test heuristics, and the lack of a standard software specification[1] language, are what makes software testing as much an art as a science.

1.1 The Software Industry

The software industry has come a long way since its beginnings in the 1950s. The independent software industry was essentially born in 1969 when IBM announced that it would stop treating its software as a free add-on to its computers, and instead would sell software and hardware as separate products. This opened up the market to external companies that could produce and sell software for IBM machines.

Software products for mass consumption arrived in 1981 with the launch of PC-based software packages. Another dramatic boost came in the 1990s with the arrival of the World Wide Web, and in the 2000s with mobile devices. In 2010 the top 500 companies in the global software industry had revenues of $492 billion, and by 2018 this had risen to $868 billion.[2] The industry is extremely dynamic and continually undergoing rapid change as new innovations appear. Unlike some other industries, for example transportation, it is still in many ways an immature industry. It does not, in general, have a set of quality standards that have been gained through years of experience.

Numerous examples exist of the results of failures in software quality and the costs it can incur. Well-publicised incidents include the failure of the European Space Agency's Ariane 5 rocket, the Therac-25 radiation therapy machine, and the loss of the Mars Climate Orbiter in 1999. A study by the US Department of Commerce's National Institute of Standards and Technology (NIST) in 2002 estimated that the annual cost of inadequate software testing to the US economy was up to $59.5 billion per year.[3]

---

[1] A software specification defines clearly and unambiguously what the software must do.

[2] *Software Magazine*. 2018 Software 500 Companies. Available at: www.rcpbuyersguide.com/top-companies.php.

[3] NIST. *The Economic Impacts of Inadequate Infrastructure for Software Testing*. NIST, 2002.

However, many participants in the industry do apply quality models and measures to the processes through which their software is produced. Software testing is an important part of the software quality assurance process, and is an important discipline within software engineering. It has an important role to play throughout the software development life cycle, whether being used in a *verification* and *validation* context, or as part of a test-driven software development process such as *eXtreme Programming*.

Software engineering as a discipline grew out of the *software crisis*. This term was first used at the end of the 1960s, but it really began to have meaning through the 1970s as the software industry was growing. This reflected the increasing size and complexity of software projects combined with the lack of formal procedures for managing such projects. This resulted in a number of problems:

- projects were running over budget;
- projects were running over time;
- the software products were of low quality;
- the software products often did not meet requirements;
- projects were chaotic; and
- software maintenance was increasingly difficult.

If the software industry was to keep growing, and the use of software was to become more widespread, this situation could not continue. The solution was to formalise the roles and responsibilities of software engineering personnel. These software engineers would plan and document in detail the goals of each software project and how it was to be carried out; they would manage the process via which the software code would be created; and they would ensure that the end result had attributes that showed it was a quality product. This relationship between quality management and software engineering meant that software testing would be integrated into its field of influence. Moreover, the field of software testing was also going to have to change if the industry wanted to get over the software crisis.

While the difference between debugging a program and testing a program was recognised by the 1970s, it was only from this time on that testing began to take a significant role in the production of software. It was to change from being an activity that happened at the end of the product cycle, to check that the product worked, to an activity that takes place throughout each stage of development, catching faults as early as possible. A number of studies comparing the relative costs of early and late defect detection have all reached the same conclusion: the earlier the defect is caught, the lower the cost of fixing it.

The progressive improvement of software engineering practices has led to a significant improvement in software quality. The short-term benefits of software testing to the business include improving the performance, interoperability and conformance of the software products produced. In the longer term, testing reduces the future costs, and builds customer confidence.

Software testing is integrated into many of the software development processes in use today. Approaches such as *test driven development* (TDD) use testing to drive the code development. In this approach, the tests are developed (often with the assistance of the end-user or customer) before the code is written.

1.1.1 Software Testing and Quality

Proper software testing procedures reduce the risks associated with software development. Modern programs are often very complex, having millions of lines of code and multiple interactions with other software systems. And they often implement a solution that has been defined in very abstract terms, described as a vague set of requirements lacking in exactness and detail. Quality problems are further compounded by external pressures on developers from business owners, imposing strict deadlines and budgets to reduce both the time to market and associated production costs. These pressures can result in inadequate software testing, leading to reduced quality. Poor quality leads to increased software failures, increased development costs, and increased delays in releasing software. More severe outcomes for a business can be a loss of reputation, leading to reduced market share, or even to legal claims.

The international standard ISO/IEC 25010[4] defines a product quality model with eight quality characteristics (Table 1.1).

Table 1.1 Software quality attributes in ISO/IEC 25010.

Attribute	Characteristics
Functional suitability	Functional completeness, functional correctness, functional appropriateness
Performance efficiency	Time behaviour, resource utilisation, capacity
Compatibility	Coexistence, interoperability
Usability	Appropriateness, recognisability, learnability, operability, user error protection, user interface aesthetics, accessibility
Reliability	Maturity, availability, fault tolerance, recoverability
Security	Confidentiality, integrity, non-repudiation, authenticity, accountability
Maintainability	Modularity, reusability, analysability, modifiability, testability
Portability	Adaptability, installability, conformance, replaceability

Attributes that can be measured objectively, such as performance and functionality, are easier to test than those that require a subjective opinion, such as learnability and installability.

1.1.2 Software Testing and Risk Management

Software testing can be viewed as a risk-management activity. The more resources that are spent on testing, the lower the probability of a software failure, but the higher

---

[4] ISO/IEC 25010:2011 Systems and software engineering – Systems and software Quality Requirements and Evaluation (SQuaRE) – System and software quality models.

the testing cost. One factor in risk management is to compare the expected cost of failure against the cost of testing. The expected cost is estimated as follows:

$$\text{expected cost} = \text{risk of failure} \times \text{cost of failure}$$

For a business, there are short- and long-term costs associated with failure. The short-term costs are primarily related to fixing the problem, but may also be from lost revenue if product release is delayed. The long-term costs are primarily the costs of losing reputation and associated sales.

The cost of testing needs to be proportional to income and the cost of failure (with the current state of the art, it is arguable that all software is subject to failure at some stage). The effectiveness of testing can generally be increased by the testing team being involved early in the process. Direct involvement of customers/users is also an effective strategy. The expected cost of failure is controlled through reducing the probability of failure through rigorous engineering development practices and quality assurance (testing is part of the quality assurance process).

Software testing can be addressed as an optimisation process: getting the best return for the investment. Increased investment in testing reduces the cost of software failures, but increases the cost of software development. The key is to find the best balance between these costs. This interaction between cost of testing and profit is demonstrated in Figure 1.1.

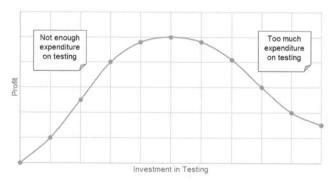

Figure 1.1 Cost of testing vs. profit.

1.2   Mistakes, Faults, and Failures

Leaving aside the broader relationship between software testing and the attributes of quality for the moment, the most common application of testing is to search for defects present in a piece of software and/or verify that particular defects are not present in that software. The term software defect is often expanded into three categories: mistakes, faults, and failures.

1.   **Mistakes**: these are made by software developers. These are conceptual errors and can result in one or more faults in the source code.

2. **Faults**: these are flaws in the source code, and can be the product of one or more mistakes. Faults can lead to failures during program execution.

3. **Failures**: these are symptoms of a fault, and consist of incorrect, or out-of-specification behaviour by the software. Faults may remain hidden until a certain set of conditions are met which reveal them as a failure in the software execution. When a failure is detected by software, it is often indicated by an *error code*.

1.2.1 Mistakes

Mistakes can be made in a number of different ways. For example:

1. A misunderstanding in communication, such as confusing metric with imperial measurements.
2. A misinterpretation or misreading of the specification by a software developer, such as swapping the order of parameters by mistake.
3. Assuming defaults: for example, in Java integers have a default value of 0, but in C++ there is no default value.

1.2.2 Software Faults

It is helpful to have a classification of the types of faults. The classification can be used for a number of purposes:

1. When analysing, designing, or coding software: as a checklist of faults to avoid.
2. When developing software tests: as a guide to likely faults.
3. When undergoing software process evaluation or improvement: as input data.

There are a number of different ways to categorise these software faults, but no single, accepted standard exists. The significance of faults can vary depending on the circumstances. One representative categorisation[5] identifies the following 10 fault types:

Algorithmic A unit of the software does not produce an output corresponding to the given input under the designated algorithm.

Syntax Source code is not in conformance with the programming language specification.

Computation and precision The calculated result using the chosen formula does not conform to the expected accuracy or precision.

Documentation Incomplete or incorrect documentation.

Stress or overload The system fails to operate correctly when the applied load exceeds the specified maximum for the system.

---

[5] S.L. Pfleeger and J.M. Atlee, *Software Engineering: Theory and Practice*, 4th ed. Pearson Higher Education, 2010.

Capacity and boundary   The system fails to operate correctly when data stores are filled beyond their capacity.

Timing or coordination   The timing or coordination requirements between inter-acting, concurrent processes are not met. These faults are a significant problem in real-time systems.[6] where processes have strict timing requirements and may have to be executed in a carefully defined sequence.

Throughput or performance   The developed system does not meet its specified throughput or other performance requirements.

Recovery   The system does not recover to the expected performance even after a fault is detected and corrected.

Standards and procedure   A team member does not follow the standards deployed by the organisation, which will lead to the problem of other members having to understand the logic employed or to find the data description needed for solving a problem.

It is very difficult to find industry figures relating to software faults, but one example is a study by Hewlett Packard[7] on the frequency of occurrence of various fault types, which found that 50% of the faults analysed were either *algorithmic* or *computation and precision* errors.

1.2.3   Software Failures

Classifying the severity of failures that result from particular faults is more difficult because of their subjective nature, particularly with failures that do not result in a program crash. One user may regard a particular failure as being very serious, while another may not feel as strongly about it. Table 1.2 shows an example of how failures can be classified by their severity.

Table 1.2 Sample classification of software failures.

Severity level	Behaviour
1 (most severe)	Failure causes a system crash and the recovery time is extensive; or failure causes a loss of function and data and there is no workaround.
2	Failure causes a loss of function or data but there is a manual workaround to temporarily accomplish the tasks.
3	Failure causes a partial loss of function or data where the user can accomplish most of the tasks with a small amount of workaround.
4 (least severe)	Failure causes cosmetic and minor inconveniences where all the user tasks can still be accomplished.

Hardware failures show a typical *bathtub* curve, where there is a high failure rate initially, followed by a period of relatively low failures, but eventually the failure rate rises again. The early failures are caused by manufacturing issues, and handling

---

[6] A real-time system is one with well-defined time constraints.
[7] Pfleeger and Atlee, *Software Engineering.*

and installation errors. As these are ironed out, during the main operational life of a product, the failure rate stays low. Eventually, however, hardware ages and wears out, and the failure rates rise again. Most consumer products follow this curve.

Software failures demonstrate a similar pattern, but for different reasons as software does not physically wear out. A typical curve for the failure rate of software is shown in Figure 1.2.

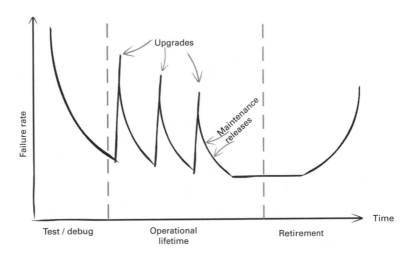

Figure 1.2 Failure rate for a software product over its life cycle.

During initial development, the failure rate is likely to fall rapidly during the test and debug cycle. After the first version is released, during the operational lifetime of the software, there may be periodic upgrades, which tend to introduce new failures, exposing latent faults in the software or introducing new faults. These upgrades may, for example, include additional features, changes required for integration with other software, or modifications required to support changes in the execution environment (such as operating system updates). Subsequent maintenance activity progressively lowers the failure rate again, reflecting an overall increase in code quality. Finally, the software is retired when it is no longer actively developed; this is particularly relevant to open-source software, where the original developer may stop maintaining their contribution. Eventually changes to the environment, or to software dependencies, may lead to failure again.[8]

The bathtub model is relevant to modern, Agile development projects with continuous integration of software features. New features are added on a regular basis, and software is frequently redesigned (referred to as refactoring). The changes introduced by this rapid rate of upgrading are likely to lead to new faults being introduced. Most

---

[8] For example, Python 3 was not fully compatible with Python 2, and Python 2 libraries that were not updated stopped working with libraries that were updated.

software is eventually replaced, or ceases to be maintained as a supported version, leaving existing users with an eventual rise in the failure rate.[9]

1.2.4   Need for Testing

There are a number of reasons why software has faults, or is perceived to have faults. For example, it is difficult to:

- collect the user requirements correctly;
- specify the required software behaviour correctly;
- design software correctly;
- implement software correctly; and
- modify software correctly.

There are two engineering approaches to developing correct systems: one is *forward engineering*, the other is based on *feedback*.

The ideal software development project, as shown in Figure 1.3, starts with the user and ends with a correct implementation. The development is completely reliable: each activity creates the correct outputs based on its inputs (specification) from the previous activity. The end product thereby matches its specification and meets the user's needs.

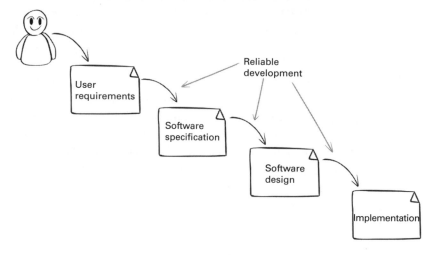

Figure 1.3 Ideal project progression using forward engineering.

In practice, however, all the development steps are subject to mistakes and ambiguities, leading to less-than-ideal results. To resolve this, each of the steps must be subject to a check to ensure that it has been carried out properly, and to provide an opportunity to fix any mistakes before proceeding. The verification and fixing following unreliable development at each step is shown in Figure 1.4.

---

[9] For example, support for the Windows 7 operating system ended at the beginning of 2020, leaving existing users with no security upgrades. A progressive rise in the failure rate of these systems can be expected until they are replaced with Windows 10.

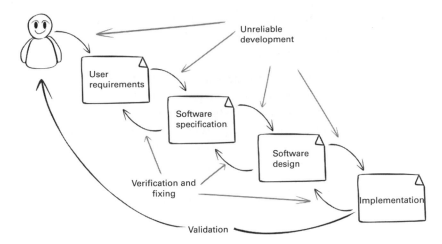

Figure 1.4 Realistic project progression with verification and validation.

For software products, in addition to checking that each individual step has been done correctly, it has been found in practice that a second form of checking is necessary: making sure that the implementation meets users' needs. The first form is referred to as verification, the second as validation.

1.3 The Role of Specifications

A *software specification* identifies the precise and detailed behaviour that the software is required to provide. It gives a *model* of what the software is supposed to do. These specifications play a key role in testing. In order to be tested, the correct behaviour of software must be known. This implies the need for detailed specifications (or software requirements[10]).

To support thorough testing of the code, specifications must describe both *normal* and *error* behaviour. Normal behaviour is the expected behaviour (or output) of the software when the inputs are not in error. Error behaviour is the expected results of the software when one or more inputs are in error, or will cause an error in processing.

Attempts have been made to develop test approaches based on *reasonable* behaviour of software – often deduced from the name of the method. This fails as not every developer and tester will have exactly the same expectations of reasonable behaviour, especially for error cases. Some examples include the following:

- If an invalid input is provided, should the method ignore it, return an invalid value, raise an exception, or write to an error log?
- If a temperature is calculated, should it be returned in degrees Celsius (°C), kelvin (K), or degrees Fahrenheit (°F)?

[10] Note the difference between software requirements and user requirements. Software requirements state what the software must do. User requirements state what the user wants to be able to do.

- Is zero to be treated as a positive number, a negative number or neither?
- Can an angle have a value of 0°? Can a shape have an area of 0 cm^2? Or even a negative area?

In general terms, the expected behaviour of a program in handling errors in the input data is to indicate that this has occurred – for example by returning an error code, or raising an exception. But in order to test the software, the exact details of this must be defined. These specify exactly what an error in the input is, and how such errors should be notified to the caller. In summary, in order to test software properly, detailed specifications are necessary.[11]

Note that often a tester will need to convert a specification from a *written English* or natural-language form to one that is more concise and easier to create tests from.

1.4   Manual Test Example

Consider a program check for an online shop that determines whether a customer should get a price discount on their next purchase, based on their bonus points to date, and whether they are a gold customer.

Bonus points accumulate as customers make purchases. Gold customers get a discount once they have exceeded 80 bonus points. Other customers only get a discount once they have more than 120 bonus points. All customers always have at least one bonus point.

The program returns one of the following:

- FULLPRICE, which indicates that the customer should be charged the full price.
- DISCOUNT, which indicates that the customer should be given a discount.
- ERROR, which indicates an error in the inputs (bonusPoints is invalid if it is less than 1).

The inputs are the number of bonusPoints the customer has, and a flag indicating whether the customer is a gold customer or not (true or false, respectively). For the sake of simplicity, we will ignore illegal input values at the moment (where the first parameter is not a number, or the second parameter is not a Boolean).

Output from some demonstration runs of the program, using the command line,[12] are shown in Figure 1.5. All console output will be shown like this.

These results look correct: a regular customer with 100 points is charged the full price, a gold customer with 100 points is given a discount, and −10 is an invalid number of points.

So does this method work correctly? Does it work for every possible input? Next, we will consider the theory of software testing to try to answer these questions.

---

[11] One exception is in stability testing, where tests ensure that the software does not crash.

[12] See Section 14.4.2 for details of how to run the examples.

```
$ check 100 false
FULLPRICE
$ check 100 true
DISCOUNT
$ check -10 false
ERROR
```

Figure 1.5 Manual test example.

1.5   The Theory of Software Testing

A test consists of executing the software under test with the selected input values, gathering the output values, and verifying that these output values are correct (i.e. are as specified).

The goal of developing a theory of software testing is to be able to identify the ideal tests – that is the minimum set of test data required to ensure that software works correctly for all inputs. The fundamental result in this area[13] can be summarised as follows:

- For a test to be successful, all test data within the test set must produce the results as defined by the specification.
- The test data selection criteria is reliable if it consistently produces test sets that are successful, or it consistently produces test sets that are not successful.
- If a set of test data is chosen using a criterion that is reliable and valid, then the successful execution of that test data implies that the program will produce correct results over its entire input domain.
- Leading to the result: the only criterion that can be guaranteed to be reliable and valid is one that selects each and every value in the program domain (i.e. exhaustively tests the program).

1.6   Exhaustive Testing

Based on this theory result, the most obvious form of testing is to test for every possible input and output. This is referred to as *exhaustive testing*, and is explored next.

1.6.1   Exhaustive Test Data

The parameter goldCustomer, from the example discussed previously, can have two possible values: true or false. The parameter bonusPoints is defined as a 64-bit integer (a Java long) so the parameter bonusPoints can have 2^{64} possible

---

[13] J. Goodenough and S. Gerhart. Toward a theory of test data selection. *Proc. Int. Conf. Reliable Software*, ACM, 1975.

values. This means that the total number of possible combinations of input values is 2^{65}, or 3.6893488×10^{19}. This is a very large number even for this simple example. Exhaustive testing requires executing this number of tests.

1.6.2   Feasibility of Exhaustive Testing

There are two key problems with this approach:

- Test execution time: executing this number of tests would take too long. For example, on a PC that can execute 60,000 tests per second, it would take approximately 600,000,000,000,000 seconds, or more than 19 million years to test this simple program.
- Test design time: just executing the code with all these different inputs is not enough to test the software. The test has to ensure that every answer is correct. So for each of these 2^{65} sets of input values, the correct output value would have to be worked out so it can be verified in each test.

Implications

Considering other examples, a class might easily hold 64 bytes of data (class attributes). These 64 bytes represents 2^{512} possible states, leading to 2^{512} tests. A database might hold one million records of 128 bytes each. This represents approximately $2^{1,000,000,000}$ possible values, leading to the same number of tests. Testing with large numbers of combinations is *intractable*.

In addition, identifying the correct output for each test is a more difficult problem than it sounds. Doing this manually takes too long. And writing a program to do this introduces a new problem – the *test oracle* problem. The requirements for a test oracle are the same as the requirements for the software being tested – so how do you make sure the test oracle is correct?

1.7   Test Heuristics

It would be desirable to test all possible inputs, combinations of inputs and sequences of inputs to the system. This would include both valid and invalid inputs. But, as shown, this is infeasible in practice as it would take too long.

Therefore, we need to significantly reduce the number of tests without significantly reducing the effectiveness of the testing. For both time and cost efficiencies, good tests should: (1) have a high probability of finding faults; (2) not duplicate one another; (3) be independent in what they measure to prevent faults concealing each other; and (4) test as much of the code as possible. Satisfying all these criteria is difficult in practice and a subject of much research.

The fundamental basis of all testing techniques is selecting a subset of the possible input parameters. Therefore, the quality of a test technique is determined by how effective this subset is in finding faults. Unfortunately, there is no well-established theory of faults, so test techniques tend to be *heuristic* techniques, based on fundamental principles and practice.

1.7.1 Random Testing

The simplest form of heuristic is *random testing*. This allows us to test with a number of different inputs selected at random, and scales well to provide a large number of inputs. This is invariably automated, and simple code for a random test of the method check() is shown in Listing 1.1.

Listing 1.1 Random test for check().

```
1   public static void checkRandomTest(long loops) {
2
3       Random r = new Random();
4       long bonusPoints;
5       boolean goldCustomer;
6       String result;
7
8       for (long i = 0; i < loops; i++) {
9         bonusPoints = r.nextLong();
10        goldCustomer = r.nextBoolean();
11        result = Check.check( bonusPoints, goldCustomer );
12        System.out.println("check("+bonusPoints+","+goldCustomer
             + ")->" + result);
13      }
14
15  }
```

Executing this program with loops = 1,000,000 results in check() being called one million times with different random inputs, and generates a large amount of output. A short extract from the output is shown in Figure 1.6. This example took about seven seconds to execute, mainly due to writing the output to the screen – without the output, the execution time is under 100 milliseconds.

```
check(8110705872474193638,false)->DISCOUNT
check(-4436660954977327983,false)->ERROR
check(973191624493734389,false)->DISCOUNT
check(4976473102553651620,false)->DISCOUNT
check(-7826939567468457993,true)->ERROR
check(6696033593436804098,false)->DISCOUNT
check(8596739968809683320,true)->DISCOUNT
check(-8776587461410247754,true)->ERROR
check(-947669412182307441,true)->ERROR
check(5809077772982622546,true)->DISCOUNT
```

Figure 1.6 Random test output.

This code *exercises* the program and demonstrates that it does not crash, but it does not *test* the program: the output result is not checked each time. In addition, half of the random values for bonusPoints are less than zero and create an ERROR, and most of the other inputs create the output DISCOUNT. The probability of getting FULLPRICE as an output is approximately 1 in 100,000,000 – this output does not even appear once in the sample shown above.

This example illustrates the three key problems with random testing:

1. The *test oracle* problem – how to tell if the result is correct. Doing this manually would be very tedious and take too long. And writing a program to do it does not make sense – how would it be tested? In fact, we have already written a program to do this, and are trying to test it!

2. The *test data* problem – this code is generating random values, not random data. This results typically in both generating too many error input values and missing some required input values.

3. The *test completion* problem – in this example the random tests run for 1,000,000 iterations, but there is no real basis for this number. Perhaps 1000 tests would have provided adequate assurance of correctness; or perhaps 1,000,000,000 would be required.

Note that these problems exist with all forms of testing – but in random testing their solutions are invariably automated, which requires further analysis. Later in the book some solutions to these problems are explored.

1.7.2   Black-Box and White-Box Testing

These are two general categories of heuristic for selecting a subset of the input parameters. One is to generate input values based on *exercising* the specification. This is referred to as *black-box* testing (or *specification-based testing*). The other is to generate input values based on *exercising* the implementation (most techniques use the source code). This is referred to as *white-box* testing (or *structure-based testing*).

Exercising the specification means to have generated enough tests to ensure that every different type of processing, contained in the specification, has been performed. This not only means that every different category of output has been generated, but also that every different category of output has been generated for every different input cause.

Exercising the implementation means to have generated enough tests so that every component that makes up the implementation has been demonstrated to produce a valid result when executed. At its simplest, each line of source code is regarded as a separate component. But, as you will see in the following chapters, there are more sophisticated ways of identifying components that provide for fuller coverage of a program's possible behaviours.

In all tests, just *exercising* the code or the specification is not enough. A test must not only do this, it must also *verify* that the actual results match the expected results. The test result is a pass if and only if this verification succeeds.

This book introduces a number of essential techniques for selecting test data and demonstrates their use in unit testing (testing a single method), object-oriented testing (testing an entire class), and application testing (testing an entire application). Once the reader has developed an understanding of these techniques, they can then consider applying the following techniques: experience-based testing and fault insertion.

1.7.3 Experience-Based Testing

This is an ad-hoc approach, also known as error guessing or expert opinion, in which the tester uses their experience to develop tests. The goal is usually to try to find faults in the code. The tests may be based on a range of experiences, including end-user experience, operator experience, business or risk experience, legal experience, maintenance experience, programming experience and general problem domain experience, and so on.

Its strengths are that intuition can frequently provide an accurate basis for finding faults, and the technique tends to be quite efficient. However, it relies heavily on the experience of those developing the tests, and the ad-hoc nature of the approach means that it is difficult to ensure any degree of rigour or completeness in the testing.

1.7.4 Fault Insertion

Another philosophically different approach to testing is based on inserting faults into the software or input data, and checking that they are found. This has its foundations in hardware testing, where typically a connection will be artificially held at a low or high voltage representing a *stuck at 1* or *stuck at 0* condition. The hardware is then run, typically through simulation, to ensure that the fault is detected and handled correctly by the hardware. The fault represents a data fault – all data that is transmitted down that connection will be subject to the fault.

When used in software testing, faults can be inserted either into the code or into known good data. When inserted into *data*, the purpose is similar as for hardware testing – to ensure that the fault is detected and handled correctly by the software. When inserted into *code*, the purpose is different: it can be used to measure the effectiveness of the testing, or to demonstrate that a particular fault is not present. The terms weak and strong *mutation testing* are used here: weak mutation testing is when the fault is manually evaluated through review, and strong mutation testing is when the fault is automatically evaluated by running existing tests to see if they can find it. See further reading in Section 14.3.

1.8 When to Finish Testing

Given that the theory of testing only identifies one end point, that of complete exhaustive testing, the decision of when testing is finished can be made from a number of different viewpoints:

- from a budgetary point of view, when the time or budget allocated for testing has expired;

- from an activity point of view, when the software has passed all of the planned tests; and
- from a risk management point of view, when the predicted failure rate meets the quality criteria.

Ultimately, the decision has to take all these viewpoints into account – it is rare for software to pass all of its tests prior to release. Two techniques to assist in making this decision are *risk of release* and *usage-based criteria*. During testing, usage-based criteria give priority to the most frequent sequences of program events. The risk of release predicts the cost of future failures, based on the chance of these failures occurring, and the estimated cost of each.

Ethical and legal issues may be involved in making this decision, especially where the software is a part of mission-critical or safety-critical systems.[14] Appropriate criteria for software test completion are also an important factor if a software failure results in litigation.[15]

1.9   Static and Dynamic Testing

The previous examples have all used dynamic testing, where the code has first been executed and then the output verified. An alternative approach is static verification (also known as static analysis or static testing), where the code is verified without executing it.

There are two approaches to static verification: review-based techniques and proving programs mathematically. Both of these may be manual, semi-automated, or fully automated.

1.9.1   Review-Based Techniques

Code may be reviewed with different levels of formality. The least formal is *pair programming*, where two programmers work in tandem, with one writing the code while the other continuously reviews their work. This has been shown to be very effective, and is a core element of many modern software engineering processes (e.g. Agile). The most formal is a *code review* or a *walkthrough*, where a review team is presented with the specifications (product requirements, design documents, software requirements, etc.) and the code in advance. This is followed up with a formal meeting at which a code walkthrough is performed, checking that the code meets its requirements. Typically a code inspection checklist is used and a formal report produced

---

[14] Safety-critical or life-critical systems may pose a threat to health or life if they fail. Mission-critical systems may pose a threat to a mission if they fail. Examples include software for space exploration, the aerospace industry, and medical devices.

[15] The topic is explored in more detail in D. Kellegher and K. Murray. *Information Technology Law in Ireland*. Bloomsbury Professional, 2007.

at the end of the meeting, which is the basis of remedial work to the code. This is a typical and highly effective method in software engineering, especially for high-quality requirements. Automated code analysis tools can also be used: these might find potential security flaws, identify common mistakes in the code, or confirm that the software conforms to a particular coding standard.

1.9.2 Program Proving

Research has developed mathematical techniques, known as *formal methods* or *formal verification*, based heavily on set theory, that can be used to prove that a program meets its specifications. This can be done manually, though it is very time-consuming and requires a high level of expertise. It can be semi-automated, where a tool evaluates the code and provides *proof obligations* to be manually proven. Or, due to recent research advances, the proof can be fully automated. The programmer (or designer) produces formal requirements for the code, using mathematical notation, and the finished code is then run through a program prover to prove that the code matches its requirements (or to find counter-examples that demonstrate where it fails to do so). The programmer will also be required to produce internal specifications in the code, and one of the most challenging of these are *loop invariants*. This requires less skill and experience than manual proofs, but is significantly more challenging than dynamic testing.

The benefits of a proof are very significant: a program can be proven to work *in all circumstances*. The low-level program proof can also be incorporated with higher-level design proofs (such as model checking), providing an integrated proof framework for a full computer-based system.

There are a number of languages and tools for program proving in development at the moment – however, it is arguable whether any of them are quite ready for industrial use. For example, JML[16] provides support for Java programs. See Section 14.3 for suggested further reading on this topic.

1.10 Testing in the Software Development Process

Having discussed why software needs testing, and summarised how testing might be done, it is useful to consider where testing fits into the software development process.

Software of any degree of complexity has three key characteristics:

1. user requirements, stating the needs of the software users;
2. a functional specification, stating what the software must do to meet those needs; and
3. a number of modules that are integrated together to form the final system.

---

[16] www.openjml.org

Verifying each of these leads to different levels of testing:

Unit testing   An individual unit of software is tested to make sure it works correctly. This unit may be a single component or a compound component formed from multiple individual components. For example, a component might be a function or method, a class, or a subsystem. The unit may also be a single graphical user interface (GUI) component (such as a button), or a collection of them (e.g. a window). Unit testing almost invariably makes use of the *programming* interface of the unit. Test data is selected to ensure that the unit satisfies its specification.

Regression testing   When a new unit has been added, or an existing unit modified, the tests for the previous version of the software are executed to ensure that nothing has been broken. This may be done for individual units, a subsystem, or for the full software system.

Integration testing   Two or more units (or subsystems) are tested to make sure they interoperate correctly. The testing may make use of the programming interface (typically for simple components), or possibly the *system* interface (for subsystems). Test data is selected to exercise the interactions between the integrated units.

Subsystem testing   Where a large system is constructed from multiple subsystems, each subsystem may be tested individually to make sure it works correctly. The testing uses the *subsystem* interface: this may be a GUI for an application, web interface for a web-server, network interface for a network server, etc. Test data is selected to ensure the subsystem satisfies its specification.

System testing   The entire software system is tested as a whole to make sure it works correctly.[17] The testing uses the *system* interface: this may be a GUI for an application, web interface for a web-server, network interface for a network server, etc. Test data is selected to ensure the system satisfies the specification. Desktop, mobile, and web-based application testing are all forms of system testing that are tested via the user interface.

Acceptance testing   The entire software system is tested as a whole to make sure it meets users' needs or solves users' problems, or passes a set of tests developed by users. This is frequently used before payment when software is developed under contract.

Each of these test activities can use black-box or white-box techniques to develop tests; however, white-box techniques are seldom used except in unit testing.

The focus of this book is on dynamic software verification, with a particular emphasis on using the essential test design techniques for unit testing (including object-oriented testing) and application testing. Recommendations for further reading are provided in Chapter 14.

---

[17] A simple form of system testing is called *smoke testing*, coming from hardware development where the first step in testing is to turn it on and see if it produces any smoke.

1.11   Software Testing Activities

Independent of the type of software testing being performed, there are a number of activities that need to be undertaken. This book uses the following seven-step approach[18]:

1. **Analysis** – the specification and the software implementation are analysed to extract the information required for designing the tests.
2. **Test coverage items** – these are the criteria that the tests are required to address (or *cover*), and are derived using the results of the analysis.
3. **Test cases** – these specify the data required to address the test coverage items.
4. **Test design verification** – the test cases are reviewed to ensure that every test coverage item has been included.
5. **Test implementation** – tests are usually implemented using automated test tool libraries, though in some cases a manual test procedure may be defined.
6. **Test execution** – the tests are executed: the code being tested is called, using the selected input data values, and it is checked that the results are correct.
7. **Test results** – the test results are examined to determine whether any of the tests have failed. In a formal test process, this may result in the production of test incident reports.

The worked examples throughout the book demonstrate the application of these activities. In practice, an experienced tester may perform many of the steps mentally without documenting the results. Software in mission-critical or safety-critical systems requires a high level of quality, and the test processes for these would usually generate significant amounts of documentation. This documentation supports detailed reviews of the test activities as part of the overall software quality assurance process. In this book, all the results are fully documented as a learning guide.

1.11.1   Analysis

All test design requires some form of analysis to be undertaken. This may either be analysis of the source code, or analysis of the specification – including both the user requirements and the software specifications. These sources of test information are referred to as the *test basis*. The results of the analysis are sometimes referred to as *test conditions*, and are used to determine test coverage items. In practice, the analysis results may not be fully documented, if at all – but there is value in doing so, as it allows the test coverage items to be reviewed more accurately for completeness.

---

[18] Many software processes may define their own specific set of activities.

1.11.2   Test Coverage Items

Test coverage items are particular items to be *covered* by a test. They are generated by reviewing the results of the analysis using the test design technique that has been selected.[19]

Some examples of test coverage items are:

- a particular value, or range of values, for a parameter to take;
- a particular relationship between two parameters to be achieved;
- a particular line of code to be executed; and
- a particular path in the code to be taken.

A test case may cover multiple test coverage items. A goal of most test techniques is to reduce the number of test cases by covering as many coverage items as possible in each. This is for the simple reason of reducing the time it takes to execute the tests. For a small number of tests this is not important, but large software systems may have tens of thousands of tests, and the execution time may run into multiple days.

Any values used in defining a test coverage item should be as generic as possible, referencing constants by name, and stating relationships rather than actual values where possible. This allows maximum flexibility in designing the test cases, allowing a single test case to cover as many coverage items as possible.

Each test coverage item requires an identifier, so that it can be referenced when the test design is being verified. This identifier must be unique for each test item. To achieve this, as the test coverage items are specific to each test technique, this book uses a prefix based on the test technique being used (e.g. EP1 as an identifier for test coverage item 1, using *equivalence partitions* as shown in Chapter 2).

In simple testing, all the inputs are passed as arguments to the code, and the output is returned as a value. In practice, it is not unusual for there to be both *explicit* arguments (passed in the call to the code) and *implicit* inputs (for example, in Java, class attributes read by the code; or, in C, global variables). Also, there may be both an *explicit* return value and other *implicit* outputs (such as, in Java, class attributes modified by the code). These should all be included in the test coverage items.

Error Hiding

Test coverage items are usually divided into two categories: *normal* and *error* cases. It is important to separate these as multiple input normal coverage items may be incorporated into the same test case; multiple input error coverage items may not. This is because of *error hiding*. Most software does not clearly differentiate between all the possible error causes; therefore, in order to test that each input error is identified and handled correctly, only one such error may be tested at a time. In this book, an asterisk (*) is used to signify input error test coverage items and error test cases.

---

[19] Not every text differentiates clearly between what is being tested for (the *test coverage items*), what values are needed to perform the test (the *test data*), and the tests themselves (*test cases*). However, the distinction is important, and this book clearly delineates the different terms.

A simple example is shown in Snippet[20] 1.1.

Snippet 1.1 Example of error hiding

```
1    // return true if both x and y are valid
2    //         (within the range 0..100)
3    // otherwise return false to indicate an error
4    public static boolean valid(int x, int y) {
5        if (x < 0 || x > 100) return false;
6        if (y < 0 || y > 1000) return false;
7        return true;
8    }
```

A test with the inputs x = 500 and y = 500 does not verify that errors in both parameters are identified. The code on line 5 will correctly detect the first error case and return false. The fault on line 6 is not detected – where y is incorrectly compared with 1000 instead of 100 as specified in the comment on line 1.

To find faults like this, two separate tests are required:

- a test with x = 50 and y = 500; and
- a test with x = 500 and y = 50.

This ensures that each error value is tested individually, so that an earlier fault does not hide a subsequent fault.

1.11.3 Test Cases

The test data for each test case is based on matching uncovered test coverage items.

For *normal* test coverage items, in order to reduce the number of tests, each test case should cover as many test coverage items as possible. For *error* test coverage items, each test case must only cover exactly one test coverage item. Selecting data to minimise the number of tests is a skill – initially the important factor is to make sure to cover all the test coverage items. Reducing the number of test cases is a secondary optimisation. With practice, it becomes easier to see these optimisations as one is selecting the test data.

The specification for a test case includes the following information:

- an identification of the test item: for example, the method name and version number from the version control system;
- a unique identifier for the test case (e.g. T1 for Test Case 1);
- a list of the test coverage items covered by each test case; and
- the test data, consisting of:

  - input values – these should be specific values; and
  - expected results – these are *always* derived from the specification, *never* from the source code.

---

[20] In this book, short segments of code used to demonstrate a point are presented as snippets of code.

The test case specifications define the tests to be implemented.

It is crucial that every test case for a particular test item has a unique identifier.[21] A particular test case may cover test coverage items derived using different techniques, so it is not useful to include the technique name as a prefix to the test case identifiers. One possible approach, used in this book, is to number the tests for a test item in sequence as they are designed.

The test case specification may include additional related information. For example, in object-oriented testing, setting input values may require calling a number of different methods, and so the names of the methods and the order in which they are to be called must also be specified.

The list of test coverage items covered by each test case should be used as a guide for determining when enough tests have been created. Each test coverage item must be covered if possible (sometimes impossible test coverage may be created, which must be clearly identified).

1.11.4   Test Design Verification

The process of performing the analysis, defining test coverage items, and developing test cases and test data is referred to as *test design*.

During test design, when developing the test data, it is good practice to document both the test coverage items that are covered by each test case, and the test cases that cover each test coverage item. This allows the test design to be easily reviewed, ensuring that every test coverage item is efficiently covered.

Formal reviews can be used to ensure the quality of the test designs. For a test review to be effective, the reviewer needs to see the outputs of the previous steps: analysis, test coverage items, and test cases. However, in practice, much of this work is frequently done mentally and not documented in detail.

1.11.5   Test Implementation

Tests may be implemented as code (for automated testing), or as procedures (for manual testing). This book only addresses automated software testing.

Recent trends are to automate as many tests as possible. However, there is still a place for manual testing. This requires a *test procedure* to be documented for executing the test. The documentation must describe how to set up the correct environment, how to execute the code, the inputs to be provided, and the expected results.

Unit tests are invariably automated; integration tests usually are; system tests are where possible. Implementing an automated test involves writing code to invoke the test item with the specified input parameters, and comparing the *actual results* with the

---

[21] This is primarily to aid debugging, so that a test may be re-executed reliably.

expected results. It is good practice to use method names in the test code that reflect the matching test case identifier. Each specified test case should be implemented separately – this allows individual failures to be clearly identified. Tests may be grouped into *test suites* (or test sets) that allow a tester to select a large number of tests to be run as a block.

1.12 Test Artefacts

Testing produces a number of artefacts, as shown in Figure 1.7. These reflect the significant effort required to design and implement tests.

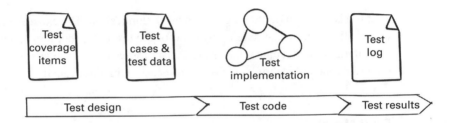

Figure 1.7 Test artefacts.

- The test design activity needs to produce the following information:

    – The test coverage items – these are the specific items that the test data must exercise.

    – The test cases and test data – this includes the test identifiers, values for the input data, values for the expected results, and the test coverage items covered by each test case.

- The test code activity produces the test implementation. This is based on the test cases.

- The test results are produced by executing the test implementation, producing a test log.

In this book, test cases are specified using the template shown in Table 1.3. There is no standard for this format, but it is important to be consistent to allow test specifications to be reviewed easily. The suggested layout is as follows:

- The ID column provides a unique Test Case ID for each test (this needs to be unique to the test item).

- The TCI column documents the test coverage items that this test case covers. It is recommended to identify the new test coverage items covered by this test case separately from those already covered by previously defined test cases.

- The Inputs gives the required input data values for each parameter.

- The Expected Results documents the output values that are expected based on the specification of the software being tested. This may be abbreviated as Exp. Results in tables in this book. For Java, this is usually the *return value* from the method called.

Table 1.3 Test case specification template.

ID	TCI	Inputs	Exp. results
		(Column for each)	return value
(ID)	(List here)	(Values here)	(Values here)

It is a key goal in developing tests to avoid duplication. The experienced tester may be able to do this while developing data for the test cases, but it is recommended (at least initially) to document the required data for each test case as it is designed, and then subsequently identify and discard test cases with duplicate data.

1.13   Fault Models

As exhaustive testing is not feasible, every test approach is a compromise, designed to find particular classes of faults. These are referred to as *fault models*. Each type of testing is designed around a particular fault model. The initial types shown in the book have simple fault models, and the later ones address progressively more complex fault models. An understanding of the classes of faults *introduced* by the software developers into the code can lead to a more effective emphasis on those tests most likely to find the faults.

1.14   Using this Book

This book is intended for an introductory audience and can be used for a number of undergraduate and postgraduate courses. It is also suitable as an introduction to testing for researchers and professionals. It should be read in sequence: later chapters make use of material presented earlier in the book.

1.14.1   Book Structure

This book introduces the essential elements of software testing, providing the reader with the knowledge required to perform basic *unit testing*, *object-orientated testing*, and *system testing* in an automated test environment. Both the practice and the principles of systematic software testing are covered. Further reading for more advanced techniques is provided in Section 14.3.

- The introduction describes the motivation for testing, discusses exhaustive and random testing, and describes the basic steps required to test software.
- Six fundamental test techniques, covering black-box and white-box testing, are introduced by examples of unit testing. Each is fully worked from analysis of the problem through to automated test implementation. Following the worked example, the principles of each technique are then addressed in more detail.
- The fundamental elements of testing of object-oriented software are introduced. This is a very substantial topic, and this book addresses some of the underlying principles and provides a number of examples.
- Unit testing is addressed before application testing as user interfaces tend to be more complex to analyse than programming interfaces; this distracts from learning the principles of test techniques and test automation. Application testing is introduced through the example of testing a web-based software application system over its user interface.
- The book ends with a more detailed look at software test automation, random testing, and a discussion on the role of software testing in the software development process.

1.14.2   Order of Testing

Usually, unit testing is followed by integration testing, and then by system[22] testing. Within unit testing, black-box testing is invariably used first, followed by white-box testing, in order to selectively increase coverage measures, such as the percentage of statements executed. This approach maximises test coverage, while reducing the duplication of tests.

This book follows the same ordering with one exception: integration testing is not detailed in this book.

1.14.3   Documenting Test Design

In practice, most testers will not document their tests to the degree of detail shown in this book, except in situations in which high software quality is required. However, the tester must do the same mental work to develop tests systematically, and while learning to test it is good practice to write down all the intermediate results as shown in this book.

1.14.4   The Programming Language

The Java programming language (Java 11) has been used for all examples. The principles shown and the approach used for Java serves as an example for testing in other procedural or object-oriented languages.

---

[22] System testing for user applications is often referred to as application testing.

1.14.5   Level of Detail

This book focuses on the principles of software functional testing and how to apply them in practice. Some topics (e.g. object-oriented testing, system testing) are not covered in as much detail as other topics due to their extensive scope. Non-functional testing techniques, such as performance testing (e.g. load testing, stress testing, stability testing), are not covered in any detail in this book.

1.14.6   Examples

A number of examples are presented, both of software to be tested and of automated tests. These examples are intended to show how testing principles are used, and should not be taken as an example of good coding practice. In many cases comments and Javadoc specifications have been omitted in the interests of space.

1.14.7   Software Test Tools

The key goal of the book is that the reader should understand the principles of software testing, and be able to apply them in practice. The software test tools used in this book have been selected as good examples for demonstrating test automation. They have not been selected as the most popular or up-to-date examples of each, and they may or may not be the best tools to use in particular real-world testing situations. This book does not endorse or recommend any particular tool. Only an essential subset of the tool features are covered in this book: the reader should refer to the tool-specific documentation for more details.

1.15   Notes on Terminology

There is little consistent use of the terms associated with software testing. The reader will find many books, research papers, white papers, test automation documentation, and web pages that use different or even conflicting terms. This book is consistent with the terminology used in the ISO International Standard 29119.[23] In particular, in this book the terms *test coverage item*, *test case*, and *test implementation* are used to distinguish between the test goals, the data needed to achieve those goals, and the code which implements the test, respectively.

---

[23] ISO/IEC/IEEE 29119:2016 Software and systems engineering – Software testing (parts 1–5).

2   Equivalence Partitions

This chapter introduces the simplest black-box testing technique of equivalence partitions (often referred to as EPs), using a worked unit test example. The tests are developed using the steps identified previously: analysis, test coverage items (TCIs), test cases, test design verification, test implementation, test execution, and examination of test results.

2.1   Testing with Equivalence Partitions

The goal of this technique is to verify that the software works correctly by using at least one *representative* input value for each different type of processing. This technique should also ensure that at least one representative output value for each different type of processing is produced. To identify these values, *equivalence partitions* are used. The chapter starts with a fully worked example and concludes with a more detailed examination of the topic.

Definition: an *equivalence partition* is a range of discrete values for an input or an output for which the specification states *equivalent processing*.

2.2   Example

The program `check` as described in Section 1.4 uses a class `OnlineSales` to implement its core functionality. This class contains a static method `giveDiscount()`, which is defined below.[1] Test techniques will be introduced using static methods that do not require an object to be instantiated through a constructor. Once the basic techniques have been described, the chapter on testing object-oriented software (Chapter 9) examines using these techniques to test instance methods.

---

[1]   Javadoc is used for specifications in this book.

Status giveDiscount(long bonusPoints, boolean goldCustomer)
Inputs
  bonusPoints: the number of bonusPoints the customer has accumulated
  goldCustomer: true for a Gold Customer
Outputs
  return value:
    FULLPRICE if bonusPoints $\leq$ 120 and not a goldCustomer
    FULLPRICE if bonusPoints $\leq$ 80 and a goldCustomer
    DISCOUNT if bonusPoints > 120
    DISCOUNT if bonusPoints > 80 and a goldCustomer
    ERROR if any inputs are invalid (bonusPoints < 1)

Status is defined as follows:

```
enum Status { FULLPRICE, DISCOUNT, ERROR };
```

For simplicity, this example does not use Java exceptions to indicate an error: see Section 11.8 for an example of how to test code that does.

2.2.1   Analysis: Identifying the Equivalence Partitions

The first step in developing the tests is an analysis of the specification in order to identify the equivalence partitions.

The analysis is shown in two stages: first, identifying the *natural ranges* for each parameter, and then identifying the *specification-based ranges* (or equivalence partitions) based on the principle of equivalent processing.

Natural Ranges

The natural ranges are based on the types of the input parameters and of the return value(s). To help with this analysis, we suggest the application of *value lines* for each input and output.

A value line is a graphical representation of a range of values. The minimum value is always placed to the left, and the maximum value to the right. These value lines assist in ensuring that there are no gaps or overlaps in the equivalence partitions once they have been identified.

The parameter bonusPoints is of the type long, and has one natural range with 2^{64} values.[2] The value line for bonusPoints, representing this range of possible values, is shown in Figure 2.1. This indicates that bonusPoints may hold any value from Long.MIN_VALUE to Long.MAX_VALUE.

Figure 2.1 Value line showing the natural range of bonusPoints.

---

[2] This example is based on Java, which uses 64 bits for the long data type.

Boolean values are best treated as two separate ranges with one value each, as there is no natural ordering of the values `true` and `false`. The Boolean parameter `goldCustomer` has two natural ranges, each with one value as shown in Figure 2.2.

Figure 2.2 Value line showing the natural ranges of `goldCustomer`.

Enumerated values are best treated in the same way as Boolean values, with multiple separate ranges and one value in each range. Even though some languages do define an ordering for enumerated values – Java provides the `ordinal()` method – the different enumerated values often reflect different types of processing, and it is most effective to treat each value as a separate range. The enumerated type for the return value from `giveDiscount()` has three defined values, and therefore has three natural ranges, each with one value as shown in Figure 2.3.

| FULLPRICE | DISCOUNT | ERROR |

Figure 2.3 Value line showing the natural ranges of the return value.

Having used value lines to assist in identifying the natural ranges for the inputs and outputs of `giveDiscount()`, it is useful to document these as shown in Table 2.1.

Table 2.1 Natural ranges.

Parameter	Natural range
bonusPoints	Long.MIN_VALUE..Long.MAX_VALUE
goldCustomer	true
	false
return value	FULLPRICE
	DISCOUNT
	ERROR

The double-dot (..) notation indicates that the parameter may have any value in the range, including the minimum and maximum values shown. This is equivalent to the mathematical notation of the inclusive interval [`Long.MIN_VALUE`, `Long.MAX_VALUE`] as used throughout the book.

Specification-Based Ranges

The specification-based ranges may now be identified by *walking* the value lines from left to right and identifying the values at which a change of processing may take place.

For the input `bonusPoints`, the first value at the left is `Long.MIN_VALUE`. Walking along the value line, according to the specification, all the subsequent values up to and including the value 0 are treated equivalently: they are all processed as errors. This produces the first specification-based range on the value line, as shown in Figure 2.4.

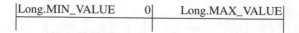

Figure 2.4 First specification-based range for bonusPoints.

Value lines are conceptual models that do not require to be drawn to scale, as you can see in Figure 2.4. The width of each range should be chosen to allow the values to be clearly entered; it does not represent the number of values in the range.

The next value after 0 is 1, which can now be entered as shown in Figure 2.5.

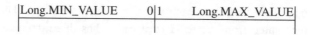

Figure 2.5 Start of the second range.

Walking along the value line from 1, all the subsequent values up to and including value 80 are treated equivalently. Value 81, however, will not always be treated differently, but it may be, and thus the processing is not equivalent for both 80 and 81. This produces the second specification-based range on the value line, as shown in Figure 2.6.

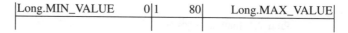

Figure 2.6 Second specification-based range for bonusPoints.

The next value after 80 is 81, which can now be entered as shown in Figure 2.7.

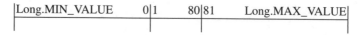

Figure 2.7 Start of the third range.

Walking along the value line from 81, all the subsequent values up to and including 120 are treated equivalently. This produces the third specification-based range on the value line, as shown in Figure 2.8.

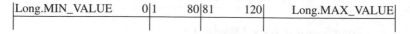

Figure 2.8 Third specification-based range for bonusPoints.

The next value after 120 is 121, which can now be entered as shown in Figure 2.9. All the values from 121 to Long.MAX_VALUE are treated equivalently again, and so this produces the fourth and final specification-based range for bonusPoints.

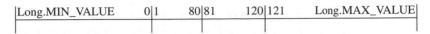

Figure 2.9 Fourth specification-based range for bonusPoints.

Next, we consider the input parameter `goldCustomer`, which is a Boolean. The natural ranges were identified in Figure 2.2. There are two equivalence partitions, matching the natural ranges, as the processing in each may be different. The specification-based ranges are shown in Figure 2.10.

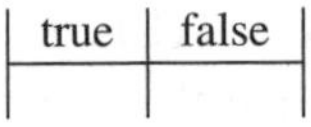

Figure 2.10 Specification-based ranges for goldCustomer.

Finally, for the `return value`, the specification states that each of the natural ranges is the result of a different type of processing and as with `goldCustomer` this produces an identical value line for the specification-based ranges as for the natural ranges, as shown in Figure 2.11.

| FULLPRICE | DISCOUNT | ERROR |

Figure 2.11 Specification-based ranges for the return value.

Each specification-based range shown on the value lines is an equivalence partition (a range of values with equivalent processing). The input and output equivalence partitions, for both valid and error partitions, can now be derived from the value lines, and documented as shown in Tables 2.2 and 2.3.

Table 2.2 Input equivalence partitions for giveDiscount( ).

Parameter	Equivalence partition
`bonusPoints`	`(*) Long.MIN_VALUE..0`
	`1..80`
	`81..120`
	`121..Long.MAX_VALUE`
`goldCustomer`	`true`
	`false`

Table 2.3 Output equivalence partitions for giveDiscount( ).

Parameter	Equivalence partition
`return value`	`FULLPRICE`
	`DISCOUNT`
	`ERROR`

Some of the equivalence partitions are associated with error processing, and are indicated with an asterisk (*). In this example it is straightforward to identify these. However, it may be much harder to do this correctly for other specifications. In normal test development, this analysis is probably not written down, and an experienced developer will identify the equivalence partitions directly. But, when learning how to test, it is recommended that you fully document the results of the analysis as shown above. This helps to ensure that you are following the technique correctly.

2.2.2   Test Coverage Items

The next step is to generate TCIs from the equivalence partitions. A TCI is something to be tested for. Each equivalence partition is a TCI, as shown in Table 2.4.

Unique identifiers are used for each TCI in order to keep track of which test cases (with test data) cover each TCI, and to make sure nothing is missed. In this example, the first TCI has been labelled EP1, the second EP2, and so on.

An asterisk (*) is used after the identifier to indicate TCIs for errors – this is important as only one TCI representing an input error can be used for a test case at any time. The equivalence partitions for each parameter should be grouped together and presented in order, as we can see in the table.

A blank Test Case column is also included on the right-hand side of the table – this will be completed later, to indicate which test case covers each TCI.

Table 2.4 TCIs for giveDiscount( ).

TCI	Parameter	Equivalence partition	Test case
EP1*	bonusPoints	Long.MIN_VALUE..0	
EP2		1..80	
EP3		81..120	To be completed later
EP4		121..Long.MAX_VALUE	
EP5	goldCustomer	true	
EP6		false	
EP7	return value	FULLPRICE	
EP8		DISCOUNT	
EP9		ERROR	

Notes:

1.   The TCIs are specific to a particular (testing) technique – it is useful to prefix the identifier with the technique name (EP is used as an abbreviation for equivalence partition).
2.   An asterisk (*) indicates a TCI for an input error. Each input error must be tested separately.
3.   The Test Case column is completed later.

2.2.3   Test Cases

The next step is to work out data values to use for each TCI. For equivalence partitions, the goal is to cover as many TCIs as possible with each test case. There are two stages. First, select equivalence values for each input and output using the equivalence partitions as identified. Then build the test case table.

Test input data is selected from arbitrary values within the equivalence partitions: for short ranges, a central value is selected. For longer ranges, a convenient value is selected, but not the start or end value. It is important that boundary values are not selected: picking a value from the centre is more likely to expose faults due to incorrect processing of the entire partition, which is the goal of equivalence partition testing.[3] This makes debugging of any faults easier, as the causes of failures are easier to identify if they are a good match for the fault model of the test technique.

For non-continuous ranges, such as Boolean or enumerated values, each equivalence partition only has a single value. Table 2.5 shows the data values selected for this example.

Table 2.5 Equivalence values.

Parameter	Equivalence partition	Equivalence value
bonusPoints	Long.MIN_VALUE..0	−100
	1..80	40
	81..120	100
	121..Long.MAX_VALUE	200
goldCustomer	true	true
	false	false
return value	FULLPRICE	FULLPRICE
	DISCOUNT	DISCOUNT
	ERROR	ERROR

To create the test case table, complete each column as described below, and shown in Table 2.6. Give each test case a unique identifier – here we have started with T1.1. Select the first non-error equivalence partition for each parameter: this gives EP2 for bonusPoints and EP5 for goldCustomer. Enter the TCI identifier for each into the TCI Covered column – note that EP2,5 is shorthand notation for EP2 and EP5, used to save space. Enter the selected data values for each parameter in the Inputs columns.

Table 2.6 EP test case: T1.1 input values.

ID	TCI covered	Inputs		Exp. results
		bonusPoints	goldCustomer	return value
T1.1	EP2,5	40	true	

---

[3] As you will see in the next chapter, exposing faults in processing the boundary values correctly is the goal of boundary value analysis testing.

Now use the specification to determine the correct output. In this example, this is the return value, and the correct value according to the specification is referred to as the *expected results*. This is abbreviated here to Exp. Results. From the specification, if bonusPoints is 40 and goldCustomer is true, then the expected results are the return value FULLPRICE. Place this value into the expected results column and add the matching TCI (EP7) to the TCI Covered column, as shown in Table 2.7.

Table 2.7 EP test case: T1.1 output value.

ID	TCI covered	Inputs		Exp. results
		bonusPoints	goldCustomer	return value
T1.1	EP2,5,7	40	true	FULLPRICE

Complete the test cases for all the other normal TCIs, working in order where possible. For each additional test case, data is selected to cover as many additional normal coverage items as possible. For test case T1.2, use EP3 and EP6 as inputs. And test case T1.3, use the remaining uncovered input TCI: EP4. See Table 2.8 for the completed non-error test cases.

Table 2.8 Normal test cases for giveDiscount( ).

ID	TCI covered	Inputs		Exp. results
		bonusPoints	goldCustomer	return value
T1.1	EP2,5,7	40	true	FULLPRICE
T1.2	EP3,6,[7]	100	false	FULLPRICE
T1.3	EP4,[6],8	200	false	DISCOUNT

T1.2 produces the same output as T1.1 – this is documented by placing EP7 in square brackets, as shown in the table for T1.1. And test case T1.3 must reuse one of the already tested values for goldCustomer – here the value false has been selected.

Finally, complete the error TCIs: each input error TCI *must* have its own unique test case – there can only be one input error TCI covered by any one test case. This is due to *error hiding*, as explained in Section 1.11.2. Table 2.9 shows the final result with all test cases with their chosen input data values and their expected results.

It is important to include the TCI Covered column. This allows the tester to confirm that all the TCIs have been addressed, and it also allows the test auditor to verify for completeness.

Combinations of input values are not considered: for example, it is *not* part of equivalence partition testing to test for bonusPoints equal to 40 with goldCustomer both true and false. Chapter 4 presents a systematic approach to testing combinations.

Table 2.9 EP test cases for giveDiscount( ).

ID	TCI covered	Inputs		Exp. results
		bonusPoints	goldCustomer	return value
T1.1	EP2,5,7	40	true	FULLPRICE
T1.2	EP3,6,[7]	100	false	FULLPRICE
T1.3	EP4,[6],8	200	false	DISCOUNT
T1.4*	EP1*,9	−100	false	ERROR

Notes:

1. Each input error TCI is tested separately.
2. The test cases and their test data are not necessarily specific to a particular technique – it makes it easier to reuse test cases if the technique abbreviation is not included in the ID of the test case.
3. Minimising the number of test cases can require multiple iterations. A target to aim for is the maximum number of partitions of any input or output: in this example it is 4 (for the bonusPoints parameter) – but this is not always achievable.

2.2.4   Verification of the Test Cases

Verification consists of two steps: first, completing the TCI table, and then reviewing your work.

Completing the TCI Table

The Test Case column in the TCI table (shown in Table 2.4) can now be completed, as shown in Table 2.10. This is completed by reading the TCI Covered column in Table 2.9.

Table 2.10 Completed TCI table.

TCI	Parameter	Equivalence partition	Test case
EP1*	bonusPoints	Long.MIN_VALUE..0	T1.4
EP2		1..80	T1.1
EP3		81..120	T1.2
EP4		121..Long.MAX_VALUE	T1.3
EP5	goldCustomer	true	T1.1
EP6		false	T1.2
EP7	return value	FULLPRICE	T1.1
EP8		DISCOUNT	T1.3
EP9		ERROR	T1.4

Reviewing Your Work

The design verification consists of a review to ensure that:

1. Every TCI is covered by at least one test case with suitable test data (this confirms that the test cases are complete).

2. Every new test case covers at least one additional TCI (this confirms that there are no unnecessary test cases). Ideally, each test case should cover as many new TCIs as possible (up to three in this example: two input TCIs and one output TCI).

In this example, we can see from Table 2.10 that every TCI is covered, and from Table 2.9 that every equivalence partition test case covers additional TCIs, as follows:

- T1.1 covers EP2, EP5, and EP7 for the first time.
- T1.2 covers EP3 and EP6 for the first time. It also covers EP7 again, but this is unavoidable as that is the result of these inputs.
- T1.3 covers EP4 and EP8 for the first time. It also covers EP6, but this is also unavoidable.
- T1.4 is an error test case and it covers the single input error TCI EP1*. It also covers the output TCI EP9. Although the selected input value of `goldCustomer` is `false`, it does not cover EP6 – this is an error TCI, and because of *error hiding*, EP6 is not verified by this test case.

2.3   Test Implementation and Results

2.3.1   Manual Test Output

The results of manually running a small example program (which uses the method `giveDiscount()` to do the calculations) with this test data are shown in Figure 2.12.

```
$ check 40 true
FULLPRICE
$ check 100 false
FULLPRICE
$ check 200 false
DISCOUNT
$ check -100 false
ERROR
```

Figure 2.12 Random test output.

By comparing the actual results against the specification, it can be determined that the method `giveDiscount()` works correctly for the equivalence partitions identified. However, in practice running each test case manually, typing in the input data, and checking the result values is tedious, error-prone, and very slow. Software testing needs to be easy, error-free, and fast. This is especially useful in modern software development practices, where software may have ongoing changes made as functionality is incrementally added, requiring frequent re-tests of the software. For this reason, software testing is usually automated and we will only show automated testing in future examples.

2.3.2 Automated Test Implementation

The manually executed test cases are now implemented for automated execution. TestNG[4] is used as a demonstrative example in this book – there are many other test frameworks.

A test framework typically includes a *test runner* that runs the tests and collects the test results. Because of this, no `main()` method is required in the test class. Tests need to be identified for the runner: in TestNG, Java Annotation is used, which allows method information to be determined at runtime.

Test case T1.1 (see Table 2.6) has the inputs `40L`[5] and `true`, and the expected results are the `return value FULLPRICE`. Using these values, the automated implementation is shown in Listing 2.1.

Listing 2.1 Test T1.1 implemented in TestNG.

```
1  package example;
2
3  import static org.testng.Assert.*;
4  import org.testng.annotations.*;
5  import example.OnlineSales.Status;
6  import static example.OnlineSales.Status.*;
7
8  public class OnlineSalesTest {
9
10     // T1.1
11     @Test
12     public void testT1_1() {
13         assertEquals( OnlineSales.giveDiscount(40L,true), FULLPRICE );
14     }
15
16  }
```

Key features to note are:

1. The `import` statements ensure that the correct TestNG methods and the enum `OnlineSales.Status` can be accessed – lines 3–6.

2. The test method `testT1_1()` is annotated with `@Test` to allow the TestNG test runner to identify it at runtime, and invoke the method to execute the test – lines 11 and 12.

3. Assertions are used to check that the output from the method being tested is correct. The call to `assertEquals()` on line 13 calls `giveDiscount()` with the input values for test case T1.1, and then checks that the return value is as expected. In TestNG, the code:

   ```
   assertEquals( <actual-value>, <expected-value> )
   ```

   raises an exception if the values are not equal, and the TestNG framework catches this and records it as a failed test. If the `@Test` method runs to completion, without any exceptions, then this is recorded as a passed test.

---

[4] See https://testng.org for full details.
[5] The Java notation 40L is used for a long constant with the value 40.

In this example:

- The <actual-value> is the return value from calling
  OnlineSales.giveDiscount(40L,true)
- The <expected-value> is the constant FULLPRICE

The code[6] for test case T1.2 is now added as shown in Listing 2.2. Note that there is significant duplication: the method testT1_1() is exactly the same as the method testT1_2(), except for the different data values used.

Listing 2.2 Tests T1.1 and T1.2.

```
1   public class OnlineSalesTest {
2
3       // T1.1
4       @Test
5       public void testT1_1() {
6           assertEquals( OnlineSales.giveDiscount(40L,true), FULLPRICE );
7       }
8
9       // T1.2
10      @Test
11      public void testT1_2() {
12          assertEquals( OnlineSales.giveDiscount(100L,false), FULLPRICE );
13      }
14
15  }
```

To reduce the code duplication and allow the same test code to be used with different data, parameterised (or data-driven) tests can be used. In TestNG this facility is called a *data provider*. Listing 2.3 shows the implementation of tests T1.1–T1.4 using parameterised tests. Again, the package and import statements are not shown for brevity.[7]

Listing 2.3 OnlineSalesTest with equivalence partitions.

```
1   public class OnlineSalesTest {
2
3       // EP test data
4       private static Object[][] testData1 = new Object[][] {
5       // test, bonusPoints, goldCustomer, expected output
6           { "T1.1", 40L, true, FULLPRICE },
7           { "T1.2", 100L, false, FULLPRICE },
8           { "T1.3", 200L, false, DISCOUNT },
9           { "T1.4", -100L, false, ERROR },
10      };
11
12      // Method to return the EP test data
13      @DataProvider(name = "dataset1")
14      public Object[][] getTestData() {
15          return testData1;
16      }
```

---

[6] The package and import statements are omitted for brevity.

[7] The expected results are referenced in the code examples as expected output to emphasise that the expected results are the output from the test item.

```
17
18      // Method to execute the EP tests
19      @Test(dataProvider = "dataset1")
20      public void test_giveDiscount( String id, long bonusPoints,
21          boolean goldCustomer, Status expected)
22      {
23          assertEquals(
24          OnlineSales.giveDiscount(bonusPoints, goldCustomer),
25              expected );
26      }
27
28  }
```

Key features to note are:

1. Using the same test method with multiple sets of test data (for the test cases T1.1 through T1.4) requires both a test and a data provider for the test:

    *   On line 19, the @Test annotation specifies the name of the data provider (dataset1) required for the test method test_giveDiscount().
    *   On line 13, the @DataProvider annotation defines the method getTestData() as a data provider with the name dataset1.

2. The test data is specified on lines 6–9 in the array testData1 using the data from Table 2.9. The test case IDs are provided as a string in the test data to allow failed tests to be easily identified. The data provider – getTestData() – returns this array on line 15. Note that the array could have been defined within the method, or even within the return statement. It is clearer, however, to initialise data arrays at the top of the test class.

3. The TestNG test runner first finds the method marked with the @Test annotation, and then finds the method annotated as a @DataProvider with the matching name (dataset1). The data provider is called, which returns an array of test data. The test method is called repeatedly with each row of test data from the array in turn.

2.3.3 Test Results

Running these tests against the class OnlineSales produces the results shown in Figure 2.13. All the tests have passed. The actual results produced by the software have matched the expected results derived from the specification.

```
PASSED: test_giveDiscount("T1.1", 40, true, FULLPRICE)
PASSED: test_giveDiscount("T1.2", 100, false, FULLPRICE)
PASSED: test_giveDiscount("T1.3", 200, false, DISCOUNT)
PASSED: test_giveDiscount("T1.4", -100, false, ERROR)
===============================================
Command line suite
Total tests run: 4, Passes: 4, Failures: 0, Skips: 0
===============================================
```

Figure 2.13 EP test results for OnlineSales.giveDiscount().

2.4   Equivalence Partitions in More Detail

2.4.1   Fault Model

The equivalence partition fault model is where entire ranges of values are not processed correctly. These faults can be associated with incorrect decisions in the code, or missing sections of functionality.

By testing with at least one value from every equivalence partition, where every value should be processed in the same way, equivalence partition testing attempts to find these faults.

2.4.2   Description

Equivalence partitions are based on selecting representative values of each parameter from the equivalence partitions. Each equivalence partition for each of the parameters is a TCI. Both the inputs and the output should be considered. The technique invariably involves generating as few test cases as possible: each new test case should select data from as many uncovered partitions as possible. Test coverage items for errors should be treated separately to avoid error hiding. The goal is to achieve 100% coverage of the equivalence partitions.

2.4.3   Analysis: Identifying Equivalence Partitions

Parameters

Methods (and functions) have *explicit* and *implicit* parameters. Explicit parameters are passed in the method call. Implicit parameters are not: for example, in a C program they may be global variables; in a Java program they may be attributes. Both types of parameter must be considered in testing. A complete specification should include all inputs and outputs.

Value Ranges

All inputs and outputs have both natural ranges of values and specification-based ranges of values. The natural range is based on the type. The specification-based ranges, or partitions, are based on the specified processing. It often helps in analysing ranges to use a diagram – see Figure 2.14. This figure shows a Java int, which is a 32-bit value, having a minimum value of -2^{31} and a maximum value of $2^{31} - 1$ (or `Integer.MIN_VALUE` and `Integer.MAX_VALUE`), giving the natural range:

- **int** `[Integer.MIN_VALUE..Integer.MAX_VALUE]`

Integer.MIN_VALUE	Integer.MAX_VALUE

Figure 2.14 Natural range for a Java int.

Natural ranges for a number of other common types are:

- **byte** [Byte.MIN_VALUE..Byte.MAX_VALUE]
- **short** [Short.MIN_VALUE..Short.MAX_VALUE]
- **long** [Long.MIN_VALUE..Long.MAX_VALUE]
- **char** [Character.MIN_VALUE..Character.MAX_VALUE]

Natural ranges for types with no natural ordering are treated slightly differently – each value is a separate range containing one value:

- **boolean** [true] [false]
- **enum Colour {Red, Blue, Green}** [Red] [Blue] [Green]

Compound types, such as arrays and classes are more complicated to analyse, though the principles are the same.

Equivalence Partitions

An equivalence partition is a range of values for a parameter for which the specification states equivalent processing.

Consider a method, boolean isNegative(int x), which accepts a single Java int as its input parameter. The method returns true if x is negative, otherwise false. From this specification, two equivalence partitions for the parameter x can be identified:

1. Integer.MIN_VALUE..−1
2. 0..Integer.MAX_VALUE

These specification-based ranges are called equivalence partitions. According to the specification, any value in the partition is processed equivalently to any other value. See Figure 2.15.

| Integer.MIN_VALUE | −1 | 0 | Integer.MAX_VALUE |

Figure 2.15 Equivalence partitions.

Both input and output parameters have natural ranges and equivalence partitions.

A Java boolean is an enumerated type with the values true and false. Each enumerated value is a separate range. In this example, the two different values are produced by different processing, and so the return value has two equivalence partitions:

1. true
2. false

Selecting Equivalence Partitions

Some guidelines for identifying equivalence partitions are as follows:

- Every value for every parameter must be in one equivalence partition.

- There are no values between partitions.
- The natural range of the parameter provides the upper and lower limits for partitions where not specified otherwise.

Equivalence partitions are used in testing as, according to the specification, any one value can be selected to represent any other value. So, instead of having a separate test for *every* value in the partition, a single test can be executed using a *single* value from the partition. It is equivalent to any other value, and can be picked from anywhere in the partition. Traditionally a value in the middle of the partition is picked. Equivalence partitions are useful for testing the fundamental operation of the software: if the software fails using equivalence partition values, then it is not worth testing with more sophisticated techniques until the faults have been fixed.

2.4.4   Test Coverage Items

Each partition for each input and output is a TCI. It is good practice to give each TCI for each test item a unique identifier. It is often useful to use the prefix 'EP' for equivalence partition TCIs. Note that the values selected from the partitions are part of test cases, as we have shown in the test case tables – for example, see Table 2.9.

2.4.5   Test Cases

Input test cases are selected based on TCIs that are not yet covered. Ideally, each normal test cases will include as many additional normal TCIs as possible. Each test case that represents an error must only include one error TCI.

Values of expected results are derived from the specification. However, the tester must ensure that all the TCIs related to the output parameters are covered. It may be necessary to read the specification *backwards* to determine input values that will result in an output value being in the required equivalence partition.

Hint: it is usually easier to identify test cases by going through the TCIs in order, selecting the next uncovered TCI for each parameter, and then selecting an equivalence partition value for the test data. There is no reason to use different values from the same partition – in fact it is easier to review the test case for correctness if one particular value is chosen from each partition and then used throughout.

2.4.6   Pitfalls

The technique calls for a minimal number of test cases. Do not provide tests for every combination of inputs. Do not provide a separate test case for each TCI.

After completing the test cases, check whether there are any unnecessary test cases. Also, check whether a reorganisation can reduce the number of test cases. Table 2.11 shows an example of each of these situations for the worked example in Section 2.2.3.

Table 2.11 Non-optimal EP test cases for giveDiscount( ).

ID	TCI covered	Inputs		Exp. results
		bonusPoints	goldCustomer	return value
X1.1	EP2,5,7	040	true	FULLPRICE
X1.2	EP2,6[7]	040	false	FULLPRICE
X1.3	EP[3]6,8	100	false	FULLPRICE
X1.4	EP4[6]8	200	false	DISCOUNT
X1.5	EP[4,6,8]	1000	false	DISCOUNT
X1.6	EP1*,9	−100	false	ERROR

1.   Duplicate test case: X1.5 covers exactly the same TCIs as X1.4, and either one of these can be deleted.
2.   Unnecessary test cases: X1.2 can be deleted, as X1.1 and X1.3 cover all the TCIs.
3.   The result of these improvements is as shown previously in Table 2.9.

2.5   Evaluation

Testing with equivalence partitions provides a minimum level of black-box testing. At least one value has been tested from every input and output partition, using a minimum number of test cases. These tests are likely to ensure that the basic data processing aspects of the code are correct. But they do not exercise the different decisions made in the code.

This is important, as decisions are a frequent source of mistakes in the code. These decisions generally reflect the boundaries of input partitions or the identification of combinations of inputs requiring particular processing. These issues will be addressed in later techniques.

2.5.1   Limitations

The software has passed all the equivalence partition tests – so is it fault-free? As discussed earlier, only exhaustive testing can answer this question, and faults may remain. Some limitations of equivalence partition testing are explored below by making changes to *inject* faults into the source code.

Source Code

The source code for the method giveDiscount() in class OnlineSales is shown in Listing 2.4.

Listing 2.4 OnlineSales.java – method giveDiscount().

```
1  package example;
2
3  import static example.OnlineSales.Status.*;
4
5  public class OnlineSales {
6
```

```
7        public static enum Status { FULLPRICE, DISCOUNT, ERROR
                };
8
9        /**
10        * Determine whether to give a discount for online
              sales.
11        * Gold customers get a discount above 80 bonus points.
12        * Other customers get a discount above 120 bonus
              points.
13        *
14        * @param bonusPoints How many bonus points the
              customer has accumulated
15        * @param goldCustomer Whether the customer is a Gold
              Customer
16        *
17        * @return
18        * DISCOUNT - give a discount<br>
19        * FULLPRICE - charge the full price<br>
20        * ERROR - invalid inputs
21        */
22        public static Status giveDiscount(long bonusPoints,
                boolean goldCustomer)
23        {
24                Status rv = FULLPRICE;
25                long threshold = 120;
26
27                if (bonusPoints <= 0)
28                        rv = ERROR;
29
30                else {
31                        if (goldCustomer)
32                                threshold = 80;
33                        if (bonusPoints > threshold)
34                                rv = DISCOUNT;
35                }
36
37                return rv;
38        }
39
40 }
```

Fault 1

Equivalence partition tests are designed to find faults associated with entire ranges of values. If we inject a fault on line 33, which in effect disables the processing that returns DISCOUNT, we expect to see at least one test fail. This fault is shown in Listing 2.5. Note that the original operator '>' in Listing 2.4 has been changed to '==' in Listing 2.5 on line 33.

Listing 2.5 Fault 1.

```
22    public static Status giveDiscount(long bonusPoints, boolean
          goldCustomer)
23    {
24        Status rv = FULLPRICE;
```

```
25          long threshold = 120;
26
27          if (bonusPoints <= 0)
28              rv = ERROR;
29
30          else {
31              if (goldCustomer)
32                  threshold = 80;
33              if (bonusPoints == threshold) // fault 1
34                  rv = DISCOUNT;
35          }
36
37          return rv;
38      }
```

EP Testing against Fault 1

The results of running the equivalence partition tests against the code with Fault 1 are shown in Figure 2.16. Note that one of the tests has failed – the fault has been detected.

```
PASSED: test_giveDiscount("T1.1", 40, true, FULLPRICE)
PASSED: test_giveDiscount("T1.2", 100, false, FULLPRICE)
PASSED: test_giveDiscount("T1.4", -100, false, ERROR)
FAILED: test_giveDiscount("T1.3", 200, false, DISCOUNT)
java.lang.AssertionError: expected [DISCOUNT] but found [FULLPRICE]
===============================================
Command line suite
Total tests run: 4, Passes: 3, Failures: 1, Skips: 0
===============================================
```

Figure 2.16 EP test results for `OnlineSales.giveDiscount()` with Fault 1.

Fault 2

Equivalence partition tests are not designed to find faults at the values at each end of an equivalence partition. If we inject a fault that moves the boundary value for the processing that returns `DISCOUNT`, then we do not expect to see any failed tests. This fault is shown in Listing 2.6. Note that the original operator '>' in Listing 2.4 has been changed to '>=' in this fault in Listing 2.6 on line 33.

Listing 2.6 Fault 2.

```
22      public static Status giveDiscount(long bonusPoints, boolean
                goldCustomer)
23      {
24          Status rv = FULLPRICE;
25          long threshold = 120;
26
27          if (bonusPoints <= 0)
28              rv = ERROR;
29
30          else {
```

```
31              if (goldCustomer)
32                  threshold = 80;
33              if (bonusPoints >= threshold) // fault 2
34                  rv=DISCOUNT;
35          }
36
37          return rv;
38      }
```

EP Testing against Fault 2

The results of running the equivalence partition tests against the code with Fault 2 are shown in Figure 2.17. Note that none of the tests have identified the fault.

```
PASSED: test_giveDiscount("T1.1", 40, true, FULLPRICE)
PASSED: test_giveDiscount("T1.2", 100, false, FULLPRICE)
PASSED: test_giveDiscount("T1.3", 200, false, DISCOUNT)
PASSED: test_giveDiscount("T1.4", -100, false, ERROR)
Total tests run: 4, Passes: 4, Failures: 0, Skips: 0
=================================================
```

Figure 2.17 EP test results for `OnlineSales.giveDiscount()` with Fault 2.

Demonstrating Fault 2

The results of executing the code with Fault 2, using specially selected input values, are shown in Figure 2.18.

```
$ check 80 true
DISCOUNT
$ check 120 false
DISCOUNT
```

Figure 2.18 Manual demonstration of Fault 2.

Note that the wrong result is returned for both of the inputs (80,true) and (120,false). The correct result is FULLPRICE in each case, but DISCOUNT has been returned.

2.5.2   Strengths and Weaknesses

Strengths

- It provides a good basic level of testing.
- It is well suited to data processing applications where input variables may be easily identified and take on distinct values allowing easy partitions.
- It provides a structured means for identifying basic TCIs.

Weaknesses

*   Correct processing at the edges of partitions is not tested.
*   Combinations of inputs are not tested.

2.6   Key Points

*   Equivalence partition testing is used to test basic software functionality.
*   Each range of values with equivalent processing is a TCI.
*   A representative value from each partition is selected as test data.

2.7   Notes for Experienced Testers

An experienced tester may be able to reduce the number of formal steps that we have shown. For example, an expert will most certainly not need value lines for identifying the equivalence partitions (as TCIs) for Boolean and enumerated data types. Experienced testers may also not need them for variables such as integers if the number of equivalence partitions is small. In these cases, such a tester may proceed to directly developing the table with the TCIs and ignore some or all of the value lines. If the test item (e.g. a function) only has a few variables and those are very simple, the tester may also directly develop the test case table with test data. However, in cases where high quality is required (embedded systems, life-critical systems, etc.) even an experienced tester may need to document these steps for quality review, or in the case of a legal challenge to the quality of the software.

3 Boundary Value Analysis

Equivalence partition testing uses representative values from each range of values for which the specification states equivalent processing. Programmers often make mistakes at the boundary values of these ranges, which will not be caught by equivalence partition testing, as has been demonstrated in Chapter 2. This chapter introduces the black-box testing technique of boundary value analysis (BVA), starting with a worked example and concluding with a more detailed examination of the topic.

3.1 Testing with Boundary Value Analysis

Boundary values are the minimum and maximum values for each equivalence partition. Having identified the partitions, identifying the boundary values is straightforward. The goal is to verify that the software works correctly at these boundaries.

Definition: a *boundary value* is the value at the boundary (or edge) of an equivalence partition. Each equivalence partition has exactly two boundary values.

3.2 Example

Testing of the method `OnlineSales.giveDiscount(bonusPoints, goldCustomer)` continues in this chapter. To summarise, this method returns:

FULLPRICE if bonusPoints $\leq$ 120 and not a goldCustomer
FULLPRICE if bonusPoints $\leq$ 80 and a goldCustomer
DISCOUNT if bonusPoints $>$ 120
DISCOUNT if bonusPoints $>$ 80 and a goldCustomer
ERROR if any inputs are invalid (bonusPoints $<$ 1)

3.2.1 Analysis: Identifying the Boundary Values

Boundary value analysis uses the equivalence partitions previously identified for `giveDiscount()` in Chapter 2. These are repeated here in Figures 3.1–3.3.

Figure 3.1 Specification-based range for bonusPoints.

Figure 3.2 Specification-based range for goldCustomer.

Figure 3.3 Specification-based range for the return value.

The boundary values are the minimum and maximum values of each equivalence partition, as shown in Table 3.1. This table highlights again that Boolean and enum parameters have single-valued equivalence partitions.

Table 3.1 Boundary values for giveDiscount ( ).

Parameter	Minimum value	Maximum value
bonusPoints	Long.MIN_VALUE	0
	1	80
	81	120
	121	Long.MAX_VALUE
goldCustomer	true	
	false	
return value	FULLPRICE	
	DISCOUNT	
	ERROR	

3.2.2 Test Coverage Items

Each boundary value is a test coverage item (TCI). The input boundary values and test cases – for now left empty – are shown in Table 3.2. Approach this systematically: unless there is a good reason not to, consider boundary values in increasing order (or in the order in which the values are defined). Identify TCIs for errors clearly (in this book we use an asterisk '*', for example BV1*).

3.2.3 Test Cases

Test cases are now created with test input data that is selected from the boundary values. The expected results are determined from the specification. For each additional

Table 3.2 BVA TCIs for `giveDiscount()`.

TCI	Parameter	Boundary value	Test case
BV1*	bonusPoints	Long.MIN_VALUE	
BV2*		0	
BV3		1	
BV4		80	
BV5		81	
BV6		120	To be completed later
BV7		121	
BV8		Long.MAX_VALUE	
BV9	goldCustomer	true	
BV10		false	
BV11	return value	FULLPRICE	
BV12		DISCOUNT	
BV13		ERROR	

test case, data is selected to cover as many additional normal TCIs as possible. Each TCI that represents an error must have its own unique test case. The input test data must cover every input boundary value, and also ensure that every output boundary value is included in the expected results.

Table 3.3 BVA test cases for `giveDiscount()`.

ID	TCI covered	Inputs		Exp. results
		bonusPoints	goldCustomer	return value
T2.1	BV3,9,11	1	true	FULLPRICE
T2.2	BV4,10,[11]	80	false	FULLPRICE
T2.3	BV5,[10,11]	81	false	FULLPRICE
T2.4	BV6,[10,11]	120	false	FULLPRICE
T2.5	BV7,[10],12	121	false	DISCOUNT
T2.6	BV8,[10,12]	Long.MAX_VALUE	false	DISCOUNT
T2.7	BV1*,13	Long.MIN_VALUE	false	ERROR
T2.8	BV2*,[13]	0	false	ERROR

Notes:

1. Boundary value analysis may appear to duplicate all the equivalence partition TCIs, but it does not. The boundary values are not reasonable values to use for equivalence partitions as they are special edge values and not representative of the entire range.
2. As for equivalence partitions, minimising the number of test cases can be an iterative process. The target number of test cases is the largest number of boundary values for a parameter (here, it is 8 for `bonusPoints`).
3. The technique is achieved if every TCI is covered.

At the expense of approximately twice the number of tests, the minimum and maximum value of each equivalence partition has been tested at least once, using a minimum number of test cases. However, combinations of different values have not been exhaustively tested. We will do this in Chapter 4. Also, none of these test cases are duplicates of those developed for equivalence partitions, and so all of these require new test implementations.

3.2.4   Verification of the Test Cases

Completing the TCI Table

The Test Case column in the TCI table (Table 3.2) can now be completed and the results are in Table 3.4. This is completed by reading the TCI Covered column from Table 3.3.

Table 3.4 Completed TCI table for `giveDiscount()`.

TCI	Parameter	Boundary value	Test case
BV1*	bonusPoints	Long.MIN_VALUE	T2.7
BV2*		0	T2.8
BV3		1	T2.1
BV4		80	T2.2
BV5		81	T2.3
BV6		120	T2.4
BV7		121	T2.5
BV8		Long.MAX_VALUE	T2.6
BV9	goldCustomer	true	T2.1
BV10		false	T2.2
BV11	return value	FULLPRICE	T2.1
BV12		DISCOUNT	T2.5
BV13		ERROR	T2.7

Reviewing Your Work

We can review our work for correctness by ensuring the following:

1. Every BVA TCI is covered by at least one test case to confirm completeness.
2. Every new BVA test case covers at least one additional TCI to confirm that there are no unnecessary tests. Ideally, each test case should cover as many new TCIs as possible – in Table 3.4 we have a maximum of two new TCIs as inputs and a maximum of one new TCI for the output.
3. There should be no duplicate tests while taking the equivalence partition test cases into consideration.

In this example, we can see from Table 3.4 that every TCI is covered, and from Table 3.3 that every equivalence partition test case covers additional TCIs, as follows:

- T2.1 covers BV3, BV9, and BV11 for the first time.
- T2.2 covers BV4 and BV10 for the first time. It also covers BV11 again, but this is unavoidable as that is the result of these inputs.

- T2.3 covers BV5 for the first time. It also covers BV10 and BV11 again, but this is also unavoidable.
- T2.4 covers BV6 for the first time. It also, unavoidably, covers BV10 and BV11 again.
- T2.5 covers BV7 and BV12. It also, unavoidably, covers BV10 again.
- T2.6 covers BV8. It also, unavoidably, covers BV10 and BV12 again.
- T2.7 is an error test case, and it covers the single input error TCI BV1*. It also covers the output TCI BV13. Note that although the selected input value of `goldCustomer` is false, it does *not* cover BV10.
- T2.8 is also an error test case, and it covers BV2*. It also unavoidably covers BV13. As in the previous test case, it does *not* cover BV10.

T2.3 is not a duplicate of any of the equivalence partition test cases. Even though it appears to cover the equivalence partition TCIs EP3, EP6, and EP7, it is *not* a duplicate. It is required that equivalence partition test cases select values near the centre of the partition – BVA selects values at the boundaries of the partitions. The same is true for the other BVA test cases where the boundary values are in the same partitions as those covered by the equivalence partition test cases.[1]

3.3   Test Implementation and Results

3.3.1   Implementation

You can write a separate test class for the BVA tests, but it is usual practice to keep extending the existing test class. The full test implementation, including the previously developed equivalence partition tests, is shown in Listing 3.1. For brevity, the include statements are omitted.

Listing 3.1 `OnlineSalesTest` for BVA testing.

```
15  public class OnlineSalesTest {
16
17      // EP and BVA test data
18      private static Object[][] testData1 = new Object[][] {
19          // test, bonusPoints, goldCustomer, expected output
20          { "T1.1",       40L,          true,      FULLPRICE },
21          { "T1.2",      100L,         false,      FULLPRICE },
22          { "T1.3",      200L,         false,       DISCOUNT },
23          { "T1.4",     -100L,         false,          ERROR },
24          { "T2.1",        1L,          true,      FULLPRICE },
25          { "T2.2",       80L,         false,      FULLPRICE },
26          { "T2.3",       81L,         false,      FULLPRICE },
27          { "T2.4",      120L,         false,      FULLPRICE },
28          { "T2.5",      121L,         false,       DISCOUNT },
```

---

[1] The only exception to this would be if all the inputs were two-valued, such as Boolean values, which is not happening here.

```
29          { "T2.6", Long.MAX_VALUE,      false,      DISCOUNT },
30          { "T2.7", Long.MIN_VALUE,      false,      ERROR },
31          { "T2.8",              0L,      false,      ERROR },
32      };
33
34      // Method to return the test data
35      @DataProvider(name = "dataset1")
36      public Object[][] getTestData() {
37          return testData1;
38      }
39
40      // Test method
41      @Test(dataProvider = "dataset1")
42      public void test_giveDiscount( String id, long bonusPoints,
43              boolean goldCustomer, Status expected)
44      {
45          assertEquals(
46          OnlineSales.giveDiscount(bonusPoints, goldCustomer),
47              expected );
48      }
49
50  }
```

3.3.2 Test Results

The results of running the full set of tests (equivalence partition and BVA) is shown in Figure 3.4. All the tests have passed.

```
PASSED: test_giveDiscount("T1.1", 40, true, FULLPRICE)
PASSED: test_giveDiscount("T1.2", 100, false, FULLPRICE)
PASSED: test_giveDiscount("T1.3", 200, false, DISCOUNT)
PASSED: test_giveDiscount("T1.4", -100, false, ERROR)
PASSED: test_giveDiscount("T2.1", 1, true, FULLPRICE)
PASSED: test_giveDiscount("T2.2", 80, false, FULLPRICE)
PASSED: test_giveDiscount("T2.3", 81, false, FULLPRICE)
PASSED: test_giveDiscount("T2.4", 120, false, FULLPRICE)
PASSED: test_giveDiscount("T2.5", 121, false, DISCOUNT)
PASSED: test_giveDiscount("T2.6", 9223372036854775807, false, DISCOUNT)
PASSED: test_giveDiscount("T2.7", -9223372036854775808, false, ERROR)
PASSED: test_giveDiscount("T2.8", 0, false, ERROR)
===============================================
Command line suite
Total tests run: 12, Passes: 12, Failures: 0, Skips: 0
===============================================
```

Figure 3.4 BVA and EP test results for giveDiscount().

3.4   Boundary Value Analysis in More Detail

3.4.1   Fault Model

The BVA fault model is where the boundary values of ranges of values are not identified properly. This leads to incorrect processing near the boundary or edge of the
equivalence partition. These faults tend to be associated with minor typos in the source
code, where the wrong comparison operator has been used. By testing with two values
from every equivalence partition – the minimum and the maximum values – BVA tests
are able to find these kinds of faults.

3.4.2   Description

Programming faults are often related to the incorrect processing of boundary conditions, so an obvious extension to equivalence partitions is to select two values from
each partition: the bottom and the top. This doubles the number of tests, but is more
likely to find boundary-related programming faults. Each boundary value for each
parameter is a TCI. As for equivalence partitions, the number of test cases is min-
imised by selecting data that includes as many uncovered TCIs as possible in each new
test case. Error test cases are always considered separately – only one error boundary
value is included per error test case. The goal is to achieve 100% coverage of the
boundary values.

3.4.3   Analysis: Identifying Boundary Values

Each equivalence partition has an upper and a lower boundary value. Experience
has shown that many software failures are due to the incorrect handling of limits.
Boundary values therefore increase the sophistication over just using equivalence
partitions, but at the cost of doubling the number of test cases and tests that need
to be run.

For the example method `isNegative(int x)`, the boundary values for x are
as follows:

1.   `Integer.MIN_VALUE`
2.   `−1`
3.   `0`
4.   `Integer.MAX_VALUE`

The boundary values for the return value are the same as the equivalence partitions
as it is a Boolean type – each equivalence partition is a range with only one data value:

1.   `true`
2.   `false`

Some rules for picking boundary values:

- Every parameter has a boundary value at the top and bottom of every equivalence partition.
- For a contiguous data type, the successor to the value at the top of one partition must be the value at the bottom of the next. In the example above, the upper value −1 from the first partition is directly followed by the lower value 0 from the next partition.
- The natural range of the parameter provides the ultimate maximum and minimum values.

Boundary values *do not* overlap, and there must be *no gap* between partitions. A convenient shorthand for specifying partitions and their boundary values is as follows:

x: `[Integer.MIN_VALUE..-1] [0..Integer.MAX_VALUE]`
return value: `[true] [false]`

3.4.4 Test Coverage Items

Each boundary value for each partition for each input and output is a TCI. It is good practice to give each TCI for each test item a unique identifier. It is often useful to use the prefix 'BV' (for boundary value) for the TCIs. In equivalence partition testing, the tester has to decide on representative values from each partition: in BVA testing, the tester uses the already identified upper and lower values for each partition.

3.4.5 Test Cases

Input test data is selected based on TCIs that are not yet covered. Ideally, each normal test case will include as many additional normal TCIs as possible. Each error test case must only include one error TCI.

Expected return values are derived from the specification. However, the tester must ensure that all the TCIs related to the output parameters are covered. It may be necessary to read the specification *backwards* to determine input values that will result in a return value having the required boundary value.

Hint: it is usually easier to identify test cases by going through the TCIs in order, and selecting the next uncovered boundary value for each parameter.

3.4.6 Pitfalls

As for equivalence partition testing, BVA should use a minimal number of tests. Do not provide test cases for every combination of input boundary values, and do not provide a separate test case for each TCI.

3.5   Evaluation

Boundary value analysis enhances the testing provided by equivalence partitions. Experience indicates that this is likely to find significantly more errors than equivalence partitions.

Boundary value analysis tests two additional values from every input and output partition, the minimum and maximum. These tests provide some basic assurance that the correct decisions are made in the code. Boundary value analysis provides exactly the same TCIs as equivalence partitions for Boolean and for enumerated parameters.

Snippet 3.1 shows a simple example of a boundary value fault. Line 3 contains a fault in the if statement. Instead of the expression $(!x <= 100)$, which is what the developer intended, the expression $(!(x < 100))$ has been used.

Snippet 3.1 Fault in boundary value handling

```
1    // Return true if x is greater than 100
2    public void greater(int x) {
3        if (!(x < 100)) return true;
4        else return false;
5    }
```

Boundary value analysis does not explore the decisions in detail, and in particular does not explore decisions associated with different combinations of inputs. Combinations of inputs will be addressed in the next chapter.

3.5.1   Limitations

The software has passed all the equivalence partition and BVA tests – so is it correct? As discussed earlier, only exhaustive testing can answer this question, and faults may remain.

We will now explore the limitations of BVA testing by deliberately *injecting* faults into the source code.

BVA Testing against Fault 2

The results of running the equivalence partition and BVA tests against the code with Fault 2 are shown in Figure 3.5.

The fault is found by one of the BVA tests. This is expected as the fault was inserted at the processing of a boundary value. All the tests are run, even though one of them has failed.

Fault 3

Equivalence partition and BVA tests are not designed to find faults associated with the correct processing of combinations of values from the input partitions. If we inject a

```
PASSED: test_giveDiscount("T1.1", 40, true, FULLPRICE)
PASSED: test_giveDiscount("T1.2", 100, false, FULLPRICE)
PASSED: test_giveDiscount("T1.3", 200, false, DISCOUNT)
PASSED: test_giveDiscount("T1.4", -100, false, ERROR)
PASSED: test_giveDiscount("T2.1", 1, true, FULLPRICE)
PASSED: test_giveDiscount("T2.2", 80, false, FULLPRICE)
PASSED: test_giveDiscount("T2.3", 81, false, FULLPRICE)
PASSED: test_giveDiscount("T2.5", 121, false, DISCOUNT)
PASSED: test_giveDiscount("T2.6", 9223372036854775807, false, DISCOUNT)
PASSED: test_giveDiscount("T2.7", -9223372036854775808, false, ERROR)
PASSED: test_giveDiscount("T2.8", 0, false, ERROR)
FAILED: test_giveDiscount("T2.4", 120, false, FULLPRICE)
java.lang.AssertionError: expected [FULLPRICE] but found [DISCOUNT]


===================================================
Command line suite
Total tests run: 12, Passes: 11, Failures: 1, Skips: 0
```

Figure 3.5 BVA and EP test results for `giveDiscount()` with Fault 2.

fault that causes a combination of input values to be incorrectly processed, then we do not expect to see any failed tests.[2]

A fault is inserted as shown in Listing 3.2 on line 32.

Listing 3.2 Fault 3.

```
22    public static Status giveDiscount(long bonusPoints, boolean
          goldCustomer)
23    {
24        Status rv = FULLPRICE;
25        long threshold = 120;
26
27        if (bonusPoints <= 0)
28            rv = ERROR;
29
30        else {
31            if (goldCustomer)
32                threshold = 120; // fault 3
33            if (bonusPoints > threshold)
34                rv = DISCOUNT;
35        }
36
37        return rv;
38    }
```

By changing the value from 80 to 120 on line 32, the code no longer works correctly when `goldCustomer` is `true` and `bonusPoints` is in the range 81..120. This combination of input values has not been tested by equivalence partition or BVA.

---

[2] If we do, it is by chance.

BVA Testing against Fault 3

The results of running the equivalence partition and BVA tests against Fault 3 are shown in Figure 3.6.

```
PASSED: test_giveDiscount("T1.1", 40, true, FULLPRICE)
PASSED: test_giveDiscount("T1.2", 100, false, FULLPRICE)
PASSED: test_giveDiscount("T1.3", 200, false, DISCOUNT)
PASSED: test_giveDiscount("T1.4", -100, false, ERROR)
PASSED: test_giveDiscount("T2.1", 1, true, FULLPRICE)
PASSED: test_giveDiscount("T2.2", 80, false, FULLPRICE)
PASSED: test_giveDiscount("T2.3", 81, false, FULLPRICE)
PASSED: test_giveDiscount("T2.4", 120, false, FULLPRICE)
PASSED: test_giveDiscount("T2.5", 121, false, DISCOUNT)
PASSED: test_giveDiscount("T2.6", 9223372036854775807, false, DISCOUNT)
PASSED: test_giveDiscount("T2.7", -9223372036854775808, false, ERROR)
PASSED: test_giveDiscount("T2.8", 0, false, ERROR)
=================================================
Command line suite
Total tests run: 12, Passes: 12, Failures: 0, Skips: 0
=================================================
```

Figure 3.6 BVA and EP test results for `giveDiscount()` with Fault 3.

The fault is not discovered by our tests. In a small example like this, depending on the data values selected, the equivalence partition and BVA tests might have found this combination of values that expose this fault. But in general, and for larger examples, neither equivalence partition nor BVA provide a systematic way to find and test all combinations.

Demonstrating the Fault

The results of executing the code with Fault 3, using specially selected input values, are shown in Figure 3.7. Here, the wrong result is returned for the inputs (`100`,`true`). The correct result is `DISCOUNT` and not `FULLPRICE` as returned.

```
$ check 100 true
FULLPRICE
```

Figure 3.7 Manual demonstration of Fault 3.

3.5.2   Strengths and Weaknesses

Strengths

- Test data values are directly provided by the technique.
- Tests focus on areas where faults are more likely to be created by the developer.

Weaknesses

- It doubles the number of TCIs compared to equivalence partitions.
- Combinations of values from different input partitions are not tested.

3.6   Key Points

- Boundary value analysis is used to ensure correct processing with data values at the start and end of every equivalence partition.
- Each BVA value is a TCI.
- Each BVA value is used in a test case.

3.7   Notes for Experienced Testers

The boundary values will often be read directly from the specification and added to the test code by an experienced tester. However, this does not allow the test design process to be easily reviewed, and may therefore not be good practice in a mission-critical development environment.

The example shown demonstrates what is referred to as two-point boundary values: at each boundary between partitions, the value just below it and just above it are selected (at the top of the lower range and at the bottom of the upper range). Experienced testers may decide to use what is referred to as three-point boundary values (at the top of a partition one additional value is used just below the upper boundary value; at the bottom of a partition one additional value is used just above the lower boundary value).

4 Decision Table Testing

The techniques presented previously have not considered different *combinations* of input values that can lead to undetected faults in the code. This chapter introduces the black-box technique of decision table testing.

4.1 Testing Combinations with Decision Tables

There are a number of techniques for identifying combinations of inputs for testing software. Decision tables provide a systematic approach for identifying all the possible combinations of input values based on equivalence partitions. The chapter starts with a worked example and ends with a more detailed examination of the topic.

Definition: a *decision table* is a model of the functional requirements that maps combinations of input values (causes) to their matching output values (effects) through rules.

4.2 Example

Testing of the method `OnlineSales.giveDiscount(bonusPoints, goldCustomer)` continues in this chapter. To summarise the specification, this method returns:

FULLPRICE if `bonusPoints` $\leq$ 120 and not a `goldCustomer`
FULLPRICE if `bonusPoints` $\leq$ 80 and a `goldCustomer`
DISCOUNT if `bonusPoints` > 120
DISCOUNT if `bonusPoints` > 80 and a `goldCustomer`
ERROR if any inputs are invalid (`bonusPoints` < 1)

This specification forms the test basis.

4.2.1 Analysis

The first step in the analysis is to restate the specification in terms of *causes* and *effects*. These are Boolean expressions relating to possible values, or ranges of values, of the inputs and outputs associated with different types of processing.

These causes and effects are then used to generate a decision table that relates the causes (inputs) to the effects (outputs) through *rules*. This provides a systematic way of identifying all the combinations, which are the test coverage items (TCIs) for testing.

This example only considers normal inputs and not error inputs. If different combinations of error inputs result in different outputs, then we use a separate table.

Causes

Non-error causes can be derived from the input equivalence partitions, identified from the specification in Chapter 2, and shown in Table 4.1.

Table 4.1 Input equivalence partitions for `giveDiscount()`.

Parameter	Equivalence partition
bonusPoints	(*) Long.MIN_VALUE..0
	1..80
	81..120
	121..Long.MAX_VALUE
goldCustomer	true
	false

The next step is to develop Boolean expressions that define the non-error causes. We develop these causes by working through the input parameters in order, and examining the partitions for each from left to right (i.e. increasing values). This provides a systematic approach and limits mistakes.

Non-error partitions for `bonusPoints` can be turned into the following causes[1]:

- The partition `Long.MIN_VALUE..0` is an error partition, and is not used.
- The partition `1..80` is a normal partition, and can be identified by the Boolean expression `bonusPoints` $\leq$ `80` being `true` (as error values less than 1 are not being considered).
- The partition `81..120` is also a normal partition, and can be identified by the previously derived expression `bonusPoints` $\leq$ `80` being `false`, and the expression `bonusPoints` $\leq$ `120` being `true`.
- The partition `121..Long.MAX_VALUE` is a normal partition, and can be identified by the previously derived expressions `bonusPoints` $\leq$ `80` being `false` and `bonusPoints` $\leq$ `120` being `false`.

Having fewer causes is better as this reduces the size of the decision table. N partitions should lead to no more than $\log_2(N)$ expressions – for example, 10 partitions could realistically be turned into about three or four expressions. For the example above, a third expression `bonusPoints` > `120` is not required as the negation of `bonusPoints` $\leq$ `120` caters for this situation.

---

[1] Refer to Chapter 2 for details of how the partitions are derived.

A consistent approach to developing the Boolean expressions both reduces mistakes, and eases their review; in our example, we use the $\leq$ operator to generate such a consistent logical style.

In a similar way, the causes for `goldCustomer` are derived:

- The partition `true` is a normal partition, and can be identified by the expression `goldCustomer` being `true`.
- The partition `false` is a normal partition, and can be identified by the expression `goldCustomer` being `false`.

Please note:

- `goldCustomer` is already a Boolean expression, so it is redundant to state `goldCustomer == true` and `goldCustomer == false` as separate causes.
- Avoid double negatives: it is much easier to work with positive expressions. The expression `goldCustomer` being `true` is much easier to understand than the expression not `goldCustomer` being `false`.
- Handling Boolean and enum types is generally very straightforward

To summarise, the analysis has lead to the following non-error caused:

- `bonusPoints` $\leq$ 80
- `bonusPoints` $\leq$ 120
- `goldCustomer`

We recommend following our approach, as this will lead to similar results every time. Other approaches may lead to a logically equivalent set of causes that may look quite different. It takes practice to develop causes that are easy to use and review. It is in general bad practice to include logical operators in the causes.

Effects

The output equivalence partitions, identified from the specification in Chapter 2, are repeated in Table 4.2 for convenience.

Table 4.2 Output equivalence partitions for giveDiscount( ).

Parameter	Equivalence partition
return value	FULLPRICE
	DISCOUNT
	ERROR

Working through the output partitions in order allows the non-error effects for `bonusPoints` to be systematically developed:

- The partition FULLPRICE is a normal partition, and can be identified by the expression return value == FULLPRICE[2] being true.
- The partition DISCOUNT is a normal partition, and can be identified by the expression return value == DISCOUNT being true.
- The partition ERROR is an error partition, and can be discounted.

For output enum values it is clearer to identify each explicitly, as shown here. It would be equally valid to identify the partition DISCOUNT by the expression return value == FULLPRICE being false, but this does not reduce the size of the table, and makes further development of the test much more difficult. Minimising the number of effects is not important.

Here is the full set of all non-error effects for this method:

- return value == FULLPRICE
- return value == DISCOUNT

The causes and effects form the test conditions.

Feasible Combinations of Causes

In order to build the decision table, all the combinations of causes must be identified. Often, all the combinations of the causes are not logically possible. In this example, it is not possible for bonusPoints $\leq$ 80 to be true and bonusPoints $\leq$ 120 to be false at the same time.

You can build the table in many ways, but our advice is to first identify all possible combinations of causes through an intermediary table. Here, all combinations can be listed; all those that are infeasible can then be removed. All remaining combinations can then be moved to a final table. With enough practise, the need for such an intermediary step will eventually fade.

Start with an empty table and list all the causes in the first column. It helps to order the causes based on the variables they address, for example the two causes about bonusPoints are next to each other. Next, create 2^N columns for the combinations, where there are N causes. In our example, we have three causes, and therefore create space for eight combinations (see Table 4.3). It is good practice to document the non-error condition in the table title – here it is bonusPoints $>$ 0 – as a reminder that error causes are excluded.

Table 4.3 Empty combinations table, bonusPoints $>$ 0.

Causes	Combinations
bonusPoints $\leq$ 80	
bonusPoints $\leq$ 120	
goldCustomer	

---

[2] The alternative syntax getDiscount() == FULLPRICE can also be used.

We complete the combination columns systematically, starting with all T (for true) at the left-hand side of the table, and ending with all F (for false) at the right-hand side. The sequence of T/F values to use for different numbers of causes is[3]:

1 cause produces 2 combinations:	T, F
2 causes produce 4 combinations:	TT, TF, FT, FF
3 causes produce 8 combinations:	TTT, TTF, TFT, TFF,
	FTT, FTF, FFT, FFF
4 causes produce 16 combinations:	TTTT, TTTF, TTFT, TTFF
	TFTT, TFTF, TFFT, TFFF,
	FTTT, FTTF, FTFT, FTFF,
	FFTT, FFTF, FFFT, FFFF

Using the value sequence for eight combinations, our completed combinations table is shown in Table 4.4.

Table 4.4 Complete combinations table where `bonusPoints > 0`.

Causes	Combinations							
bonusPoints ≤ 80	T	T	T	T	F	F	F	F
bonusPoints ≤ 120	T	T	F	F	T	T	F	F
goldCustomer	T	F	T	F	T	F	T	F

Infeasible combinations can now be identified – these are greyed out in Table 4.5:

- The combination T,F is infeasible for the causes `bonusPoints ≤ 80` and `bonusPoints ≤ 120`. If `bonusPoints` is greater than 120 it must also be greater than 80.

Table 4.5 Combinations of causes for `giveDiscount()` where `bonusPoints > 0`.

Causes	Combinations							
bonusPoints ≤ 80	T	T	T	T	F	F	F	F
bonusPoints ≤ 120	T	T	F	F	T	T	F	F
goldCustomer	T	F	T	F	T	F	T	F

The columns that contain impossible combinations of causes can now be removed, leaving only the feasible combinations of causes, as shown in Table 4.6.

In practice, only one table needs to be used, and developed step-by-step as shown in Tables 4.3–4.6. The infeasible columns can be crossed out, instead of being removed, as shown in Table 4.7.

---

[3] This is similar to a hardware truth table, where 1 and 0 are used in place of T and F.

Table 4.6 Feasible combinations of causes for `giveDiscount()` where `bonusPoints > 0`.

Causes	Combinations					
bonusPoints ≤ 80	T	T	F	F	F	F
bonusPoints ≤ 120	T	T	T	T	F	F
goldCustomer	T	F	T	F	T	F

Table 4.7 Feasible combinations of causes for `giveDiscount()` where `bonusPoints > 0`.

Causes	Combinations							
bonusPoints ≤ 80	T	T	T̶	T̶	F	F	F	F
bonusPoints ≤ 120	T	T	F̶	F̶	T	T	F	F
goldCustomer	T	F	T̶	F̶	T	F	T	F

Decision Table

A software test decision table maps each combination of causes to its specified effect. Using all feasible combinations of causes (Table 4.6) as a basis, a decision table is initialised with all causes and effects. Columns are numbered for the rules. The effects rows are initially left blank, as shown in Table 4.8.

Table 4.8 Initial decision table for `giveDiscount()` where `bonusPoints > 0`.

		Rules					
		1	2	3	4	5	6
Causes							
	bonusPoints ≤ 80	T	T	F	F	F	F
	bonusPoints ≤ 120	T	T	T	T	F	F
	goldCustomer	T	F	T	F	T	F
Effects							
	return value == FULLPRICE						
	return value == DISCOUNT						

The rules must be (a) complete, and (b) independent. One rule, and exactly one rule, must be selected by any feasible combination of the input causes.

The effects for each rule can now be completed from the specification. Starting with Rule 1, which applies when:

- bonusPoints ≤ 80 is true
- bonusPoints ≤ 120 is true
- goldCustomer is true

This means that `bonusPoints` is less than or equal to 80 (but greater than 0), and `goldCustomer` is true. According to the specification, the expected results are the `return value FULLPRICE` for these input values. We now include this as an effect, as shown in Table 4.9.

Table 4.9 Decision table in progress for `giveDiscount()` where `bonusPoints > 0`.

		Rules					
		1	2	3	4	5	6
Causes							
	bonusPoints ≤ 80	T	T	F	F	F	F
	bonusPoints ≤ 120	T	T	T	T	F	F
	goldCustomer	T	F	T	F	T	F
Effects							
return value == FULLPRICE		T					
return value == DISCOUNT		F					

It is good practice to complete both the T and F values for the effects: T for `FULLPRICE` and F for `DISCOUNT`. In more complex examples, multiple effects may be the result of the same rule. Also, when reviewing the table later, blank entries can be confused with an incomplete table.

We now continue in the same style and add the effects for all remaining rules (Table 4.10).

Table 4.10 Decision table for `giveDiscount()` where `bonusPoints > 0`.

		Rules					
		1	2	3	4	5	6
Causes							
	bonusPoints ≤ 80	T	T	F	F	F	F
	bonusPoints ≤ 120	T	T	T	T	F	F
	goldCustomer	T	F	T	F	T	F
Effects							
return value == FULLPRICE		T	T	F	T	F	F
return value == DISCOUNT		F	F	T	F	T	T

For small decision tables, no optimisation is required. Optimisations to reduce the size of large tables are discussed in Section 4.4.3.

Verifying the Decision Table

We verify the decision table by reading each rule in turn, and checking it against the specification. For reference, the specification is repeated here:

`giveDiscount(bonusPoints,goldCustomer)` returns:

FULLPRICE if `bonusPoints` $\leq$ 120 and not a `goldCustomer`

FULLPRICE if `bonusPoints` $\leq$ 80 and a `goldCustomer`

DISCOUNT if `bonusPoints` > 120

DISCOUNT if `bonusPoints` > 80 and a `goldCustomer`

ERROR if any inputs are invalid (`bonusPoints` < 1)

Considering the rules:

- Rule 1 states that when `bonusPoints` is less than or equal to 80 (and greater than 0), and `goldCustomer` is `true`, then the expected `return value` is FULLPRICE. This is correct.
- Rule 2 states that when `bonusPoints` is less than or equal to 80 (and greater than 0), and `goldCustomer` is `false`, then the expected `return value` is FULLPRICE. This is correct.
- Rule 3 states that when `bonusPoints` is greater than 80 and less than or equal to 120, and `goldCustomer` is `true`, then the expected `return value` is DISCOUNT. This is correct.
- Rule 4 states that when `bonusPoints` is greater than 80 and less than or equal to 120, and `goldCustomer` is `false`, then the expected `return value` is FULLPRICE. This is correct.
- Rule 5 states that when `bonusPoints` is greater than 120, and `goldCustomer` is `true`, then the expected `return value` is DISCOUNT. This is correct.
- Rule 6 states that when `bonusPoints` is greater than 120, and `goldCustomer` is `false`, then the expected `return value` is DISCOUNT. This is correct.

The full decision table is shown to be correct.

4.2.2 Test Coverage Items

Each rule in the decision table is a TCI, as shown in Table 4.11. As before, the Test Case column is left empty until the test cases (with the test data) have been completed. Each TCI is given a unique identifier (here, DT indicates a coverage item derived from a decision table).

4.2.3 Test Cases

In decision table testing, each TCI must be covered by a separate test case. It is, by definition, not possible to have multiple combinations in the same test case.

Test data is selected by picking input values that satisfy the causes, and output values that match the effects, for each rule to be tested. Using the previously selected equivalence partition values for the input parameters allows duplicate tests to be easily

Table 4.11 Decision table TCIs for `giveDiscount()`
where `bonusPoints > 0`.

TCI	Rule	Test case
DT1	1	
DT2	2	
DT3	3	
DT4	4	To be completed later
DT5	5	
DT6	6	

identified and removed, and also makes the task of reviewing the tests easier. For reference, the previously selected equivalence partition values are shown in Table 4.12.

Table 4.12 Equivalence values.

Parameter	Equivalence partition	Equivalence value
`bonusPoints`	`Long.MIN_VALUE..0`	−100
	`1..80`	40
	`81..120`	100
	`121..Long.MAX_VALUE`	200
`goldCustomer`	true	true
	false	false
`return value`	FULLPRICE	FULLPRICE
	DISCOUNT	DISCOUNT
	ERROR	ERROR

The development of test data for the first test case is shown in Table 4.13. We initially consider the test cases as being candidate test cases as we expect to duplicate some test cases from equivalence partition testing. The test case ID's are temporary at this stage (marked with an X instead of a T).

Test coverage item DT1 requires that `bonusPoints` is less than or equal to 80, so the value 40 is selected from Table 4.12. This test case also requires that `goldCustomer` is true which is therefore chosen. The expected results are the `return value` – this is identified in the Effects section of the decision table for rule 1: FULLPRICE.

Table 4.13 Initial decision table test cases for `giveDiscount()` where `bonusPoints > 0`.

ID	TCI covered	Inputs		Exp. results
		bonusPoints	goldCustomer	return value
X3.1	DT1	40	true	FULLPRICE

The completed test cases required to achieve full decision table coverage are shown in Table 4.14.

Table 4.14 Candidate decision table test cases for `giveDiscount()` where `bonusPoints > 0`.

ID	TCI covered	Inputs		Exp. results
		bonusPoints	goldCustomer	return value
X3.1	DT1	40	true	FULLPRICE
X3.2	DT2	40	false	FULLPRICE
X3.3	DT3	100	true	DISCOUNT
X3.4	DT4	100	false	FULLPRICE
X3.5	DT5	200	true	DISCOUNT
X3.6	DT6	200	false	DISCOUNT

Removing Duplicate Test Cases

From the candidate test cases, shown in Table 4.14, we can identify a few duplicates – new test cases that have equivalent test data to previously defined test cases. They can be removed. We are able to identify a number of such duplicate test cases:

- X3.1 duplicates test case T1.1.
- X3.2 duplicates test case T2.2, even though the data values differ:
  - The data values are different, as X3.2 is based on equivalence partition values (40,false) and T2.2 is based on boundary value analysis (BVA) values (80,false).
  - However, T2.2 matches the same rule in the decision table: Rule 2 (bonusPoints $\leq$ 80 and !goldCustomer).
  - So X3.2 would be a duplicate test case for decision table testing.
- X3.4 duplicates test case T1.2.
- X3.6 duplicates of test case T1.3.

By selecting the same values as before for each partition, we have made the task of identifying duplicate tests much easier. Alternatively, testers may remove duplicates only during the test implementation, or even refrain from removing them at all.

After removing duplicates, we can now add the decision tables tests to create the complete set of test cases (see Table 4.15) with test case IDs assigned in our typical notation (e.g. T3.1).

4.2.4 Verification of the Test Cases

We now verify that each TCI is covered by a test case, and that each test case also covers a different TCI.

Table 4.15 Final decision table test cases for `giveDiscount()` where `bonusPoints > 0`.

ID	TCI covered	Inputs		Exp. results
		`bonusPoints`	`goldCustomer`	return value
T3.1	DT3	100	true	DISCOUNT
T3.2	DT5	200	true	DISCOUNT

Completing the TCIs Table

We now complete the Test Case column in the TCIs table (Table 4.11) as shown in Table 4.16 by reading the TCI Covered column from the test case table in Table 4.15.

Table 4.16 Decision table TCIs for `giveDiscount()` where `bonusPoints > 0`.

TCI	Rule	Test case
DT1	1	T1.1
DT2	2	T2.2
DT3	3	T3.1
DT4	4	T1.2
DT5	5	T3.2
DT6	6	T1.3

Reviewing Your Work

We can review our work for correctness by ensuring that:

1. every decision table TCI is covered by at least one[4] test case (this confirms that the tests are complete);
2. every decision table test case covers a different TCI (this confirms that there are no unnecessary tests);
3. there are no duplicate tests (taking previously developed tests into consideration).

In this example, we can see from Table 4.16 that every TCI is covered, and from Table 4.15 that every test case covers a different TCI. Comparing the test data for the equivalence partition, BVA, and decision tables tests (Tables 2.9, 3.3, and 4.15), we can see that there are no duplicate tests.

4.3   Test Implementation and Results

4.3.1   Implementation

The full test implementation, including the previously developed equivalence partition and BVA tests, is shown in Listing 4.1. Full decision table testing is not achieved unless these previously developed tests are included.

---

[4] As discussed previously, T2.2 covers DT2 even though the data values are different.

Listing 4.1 `OnlineSalesTest` for decision table testing.

```
11  public class OnlineSalesTest {
12
13      private static Object[][] testData1 = new Object[][] {
14          // test, bonusPoints, goldCustomer, expected output
15          { "T1.1",            40L,          true,    FULLPRICE },
16          { "T1.2",           100L,         false,    FULLPRICE },
17          { "T1.3",           200L,         false,     DISCOUNT },
18          { "T1.4",          -100L,         false,        ERROR },
19          { "T2.1",             1L,          true,    FULLPRICE },
20          { "T2.2",            80L,         false,    FULLPRICE },
21          { "T2.3",            81L,         false,    FULLPRICE },
22          { "T2.4",           120L,         false,    FULLPRICE },
23          { "T2.5",           121L,         false,     DISCOUNT },
24          { "T2.6", Long.MAX_VALUE,         false,     DISCOUNT },
25          { "T2.7", Long.MIN_VALUE,         false,        ERROR },
26          { "T2.8",             0L,         false,        ERROR },
27          { "T3.1",           100L,          true,     DISCOUNT },
28          { "T3.2",           200L,          true,     DISCOUNT },
29      };
30
31      @DataProvider(name = "testset1")
32      public Object[][] getTestData() {
33          return testData1;
34      }
35
36      @Test(dataProvider = "testset1")
37      public void test_giveDiscount( String id, long bonusPoints,
              boolean goldCustomer, Status expected) {
38          assertEquals( OnlineSales.giveDiscount(bonusPoints,
              goldCustomer), expected );
39      }
40
41  }
```

4.3.2   Test Results

The results of running the full set of tests (equivalence partition, BVA, and decision tables) are shown in Figure 4.1. All the tests pass.

4.4   A More Detailed Look at Testing with Decision Tables

4.4.1   Fault Model

The fault model for the combinations identified by decision tables is where combinations of input values are not processed correctly. This leads to incorrect outputs. The faults tend to be associated with an incorrect algorithm, or missing code, which does not identify or process the different combinations properly.

By testing every combination of values from the input partitions, decision table testing attempts to find these faults.

```
PASSED: test_giveDiscount("T1.1", 40, true, FULLPRICE)
PASSED: test_giveDiscount("T1.2", 100, false, FULLPRICE)
PASSED: test_giveDiscount("T1.3", 200, false, DISCOUNT)
PASSED: test_giveDiscount("T1.4", -100, false, ERROR)
PASSED: test_giveDiscount("T2.1", 1, true, FULLPRICE)
PASSED: test_giveDiscount("T2.2", 80, false, FULLPRICE)
PASSED: test_giveDiscount("T2.3", 81, false, FULLPRICE)
PASSED: test_giveDiscount("T2.4", 120, false, FULLPRICE)
PASSED: test_giveDiscount("T2.5", 121, false, DISCOUNT)
PASSED: test_giveDiscount("T2.6", 9223372036854775807, false, DISCOUNT)
PASSED: test_giveDiscount("T2.7", -9223372036854775808, false, ERROR)
PASSED: test_giveDiscount("T2.8", 0, false, ERROR)
PASSED: test_giveDiscount("T3.1", 100, true, DISCOUNT)
PASSED: test_giveDiscount("T3.2", 200, true, DISCOUNT)
=================================================
Command line suite
Total tests run: 14, Passes: 14, Failures: 0, Skips: 0
=================================================
```

Figure 4.1 Decision table test results for `giveDiscount()`.

4.4.2   Description

The previous two techniques (equivalence partition and BVA) reduce the number of tests by not considering combinations. Decision table testing provides additional coverage by identifying as few tests as possible to cover all the possible combinations that have an impact on the output.

The test objective is to achieve 100% coverage of the rules in the decision table (representing combinations).

4.4.3   Analysis: Developing Decision Tables

Some programs do simple data processing just based on the individual input values. Other programs exhibit different behaviour based on the combinations of input values. Handling complex combinations incorrectly can be a source of faults that need testing.

The analysis of combinations involves identifying all the different combinations of input *causes* to the software and their associated output *effects*. The causes and effects are described as logical statements (or predicates), based on the specification. These expressions specify the conditions required for a particular variable to cause a particular effect.

To identify a minimum subset of possible combinations that will test all the different behaviours of the program, a decision table is created. The inputs (*causes*) and outputs (*effects*) are specified as Boolean expressions (using predicate logic). Combinations of the causes are the inputs that will generate a particular response from the program. These causes and effects are combined in a decision table that describes their relationship. Test coverage items are then constructed that will cover all feasible combinations of cause and effect. For N independent causes, there are 2^N

different combinations. The decision table specifies how the software should behave for each combination. The decision table can be reduced by removing infeasible cause combinations.

Causes and Effects

Causes and effects are expressed as Boolean expressions, as shown in the examples below.

Example A   Consider the method `boolean isNegative(int x)` as described previously.

    There is a single *cause*:

       1.   `x < 0` (which can be `true` or `false`)

and a single *effect*:

       1.   the `return value` (which can be `true` or `false`).

Please note:

- For *mutually exclusive* expressions, such as `x < 0` and `x >= 0`, only one form of the expression is needed, as it can take on the value `true` or `false`.
- For Boolean variables, the two expressions `variable == true` and `variable == false` are *not* needed. The single expression variable (in this example, it is the `return value`) can take on the value `true` or `false`.

Example B   Consider the method `boolean isZero(int x)`, which returns `true` if x is zero, and otherwise returns `false`.

    There is a single *cause*:

       1.   `x==0`

and a single *effect*:

       1.   the `return value`.

Example C.   Consider the method int largest (int x, int y), which returns the largest of the two input values.

    The *causes* are:

       1.   `x > y`
       2.   `x < y`

and the *effects* are:

       1.   `return value == x`
       2.   `return value == y`

Please note:

- Where there are three possible situations (here, `x < y`, `x == y`, and `x > y`) you need at least two expressions to cover them:

       1.   If `x > y`, then `x < y` is `false`.
       2.   If `x < y`, then `x > y` is `false`.
       3.   If `x == y`, then `x > y` and `x < y` are both `false`.

- Where the effect is for an output (here the `return value`) to take on one of the input values, it is important to list all the possibilities, as they are not mutually exclusive. In this case, when `x` is equal to `y`, the output is equal to both `x` and `y`.

Example D   Consider the method `boolean inRange(int x, int low, int high)`, which returns `true` when `low ≤ x ≤ high`. Note that the `return value` is undefined if `high < low`, and we cannot test in this condition.

It is not optimal, but it would be possible to create three causes as follows:

1.   `x < low`
2.   `low ≤ x ≤ high`
3.   `x > high`

However, mutually exclusive rules (where only one can be true) make for large decision tables, which are difficult to handle. A preferred set of *causes* is as follows:

1.   `x < low`
2.   `x ≤ high`

These causes can be interpreted as shown in Table 4.17.

Table 4.17 Interpretation of combinations.

`x < low`	`x ≤ high`	**Interpretation**
T	T	x out of range, `x < low`
T	F	not possible, x cannot be both smaller than low and greater than high
F	T	x in range, `x ≥ low` and `x ≤ high`
F	F	x out of range, `x > high`

This both reduces the number of causes and allows for better use of combinations of causes (as they are no longer completely mutually exclusive).

There is only one *effect* for the Boolean `return value` (which can be `true` or `false`):

1.   `return value`

Please note:

- It is redundant to use the effect `return value == true`. The expression `return value` is a Boolean expression, and the T and F in the decision table indicates when it is `true` or `false`.
- For a Boolean `return value`, it is also redundant to use two effects:

1.   `return value`
2.   `!(return value)`

Only a single rule is required:

1.   return value[5]

*   An example of what happens if you do not follow these guidelines in shown in Table 4.25.

Valid Combinations of Causes

Before developing a decision table, the infeasible combinations of input causes should be removed. The decision table then only contains feasible combinations, thus reducing work wasted by removing these later.

> **Example E**   The method boolean condInRange(int x, int low, int high, boolean flag) returns true if the flag is true and low $\leq$ x $\leq$ high. It returns false otherwise. As before, if high < low, the output is undefined, and we cannot test for this.
>
> The causes are:
> 1.   flag
> 2.   x < low
> 3.   x $\leq$ high
> and the effect is:
> 1.   return value

The full set of input combinations is shown in Table 4.18.

Table 4.18 All combination of causes for condInRange().

Causes	All combinations							
flag	T	T	T	T	F	F	F	F
x < low	T	T	F	F	T	T	F	F
x $\leq$ high	T	F	T	F	T	F	T	F

The highlighted combinations are infeasible, as x cannot be both less than low and greater than high, and can be removed, as shown in Table 4.19.

Table 4.19 Feasible combinations of causes for condInRange().

Causes	All combinations					
flag	T	T	T	F	F	F
x < low	T	F	F	T	F	F
x $\leq$ high	T	T	F	T	T	F

---

[5] An alternate notation is to use the name of the method in place of the expression return value. In this example, you could the expression inRange() instead.

- In both cases, where $x < low$, then x must be less than high, so $x \leq high$ must be true.

Decision Tables

A *decision table*[6] is used to map the causes and effects through *rules*. Each rule states that under a particular combination of input *causes*, a particular set of output *effects* should result. Only one rule may be *active* at a time: the decision table is invalid if any input matches more than one rule.

To generate the decision table, each cause is listed in a separate row, and each combination of causes listed in a separate column creates a different effect. Each column is referred to as a rule in the table – each rule is a different TCI (and a different test case).

The decision tables for the three previous examples are shown in the following. The letter 'T' is used as shorthand for true and 'F' for false.

Table 4.20 shows the decision table for is Negative():

- Rule 1 states that if $x < 0$, then the return value is true.
- Rule 2 states that if $!(x < 0)$, then the return value is false.

Table 4.20 Decision table for isNegative().

		Rules	
		1	2
Causes			
	x < 0	T	F
Effects			
	return value	T	F

Table 4.21 shows the decision table for isZero():

- Rule 1 states that if $x == 0$, then the return value is true.
- Rule 2 states that if $!(x == 0)$, then the return value is false.

Table 4.21 Decision table for isZero().

		Rules	
		1	2
Causes			
	x == 0	T	F
Effects			
	return value	T	F

[6] In mathematics, these tables are referred to as truth tables, as they only contain the values true and false, but the term decision tables is widely used in software testing as they define the decisions to be made by the software. Cause–effect graphs can also be used here.

Table 4.22 shows the decision table for largest ().

- Rule 1 states that if (x > y) and !(x < y), then the `return value` is x.
- Rule 2 states that if !(x > y) and (x < y), then the `return value` is y.
- Rule 3 states that if !(x > y) and !(x < y), implying that (x == y), then the `return value` is equal to both x and y.

Table 4.22 Decision table for largest ( ).

		Rules		
		1	2	3
Causes				
	x > y	T	F	F
	x < y	F	T	F
Effects				
	return value == x	T	F	T
	return value == y	F	T	T

Table 4.23 shows the decision table for inRange ( ).

- Rule 1 states that if (x < low) and (x ≤ high), then the `return value` is `false`.
- Rule 2 states that if !(x < low) and (x ≤ high), then the `return value` is `true`.
- Rule 3 states that if !(x < low) and !(x ≤ high), then the `return value` is `false`.

Table 4.23 Decision table for inRange ( ).

		Rules		
		1	2	3
Causes				
	x < low	T	F	F
	x ≤ high	T	T	F
Effects				
	return value	F	T	F

Table 4.24 shows the decision table for `condInRange()`. The rules should be interpreted as follows:

- Rule 1: if (flag) and (x < low) and (x ≤ high), then `return value` is `false`.

- Rule 2: if (flag) and !(x < low) and (x ≤ high), then the return value is true.
- Rule 3: if (flag) and !(x < low) and !(x ≤ high), then the return value is false.
- Rule 4: if !(flag) and (x < low) and (x ≤ high), then the return value is false.
- Rule 5: if !(flag) and !(x < low) and (x ≤ high), then the return value is false.
- Rule 6: if !(flag) and !(x < low) and !(x ≤ high), then the return value is false.

Table 4.24 Decision table for condInRange().

		Rules					
		1	2	3	4	5	6
Causes							
	flag	T	T	T	F	F	F
	x < low	T	F	F	T	F	F
	x ≤ high	T	T	F	T	T	F
Effects							
	return value	F	T	F	F	F	F

Table 4.25 shows for comparison a poor implementation of the decision table for condInRange():

- There is an unnecessary number of causes, leading to a larger table.
- The use of the effects return value == true and return value == false leads to hard-to-understand double-negatives, as well as being redundant.
- The table has many more invalid combinations.
- Overall, the table is much harder to generate and use.

Table 4.25 Poor decision table for condInRange().

	Rules															
	1	2	3	4	5	6	7	8	9	10	11	12	13	14	15	16
Causes																
flag	T	T	T	T	T	T	T	T	F	F	F	F	F	F	F	F
x < low	T	T	T	T	F	F	F	F	F	T	T	T	T	F	F	F
low ≤ x ≤ high	T	T	F	F	T	T	F	F	T	T	F	F	T	T	F	F
x > high	T	F	T	F	T	F	T	F	T	F	T	F	T	F	T	F
Effects																
return value == true				F		T	F					F		F	F	
return value == false					T		F	T					T		T	T

Even if you remove the invalid combinations, the table is not being used for its purpose, which is to generate the combinations, and it still contains unnecessary duplication. Note that Table 4.24 contains exactly the same information in a much more concise form.

Handling Large Tables

When the number of rules exceeds 16, the tables become too large to handle easily. Two techniques[7] for reducing the size of large tables are presented here:

- sub-tables
- pairwise testing

Sub-Tables

Table 4.24 can be reduced in size by splitting the problem into two separate tables: one with *flag* always true, and one with *flag* always false. Each table will be half the size of the original table – see Tables 4.26 and 4.27.

Table 4.26 Decision table for `condInRange()` with flag `true`.

		Rules		
		1	2	3
Causes				
	x < low	T	F	F
	x ≤ high	T	T	F
Effects				
	return value	F	T	F

Table 4.27 Decision table for `condInRange()` with flag `false`.

		Rules		
		1	2	3
Causes				
	x < low	T	F	F
	x ≤ high	T	T	F
Effects				
	return value	F	F	F

Recall that we have already used this technique to remove error rules. If there are interesting combinations of causes that produce errors, then these can be presented in a separate table (with error rules only).

---

[7] The other standard technique of using *don't-care conditions* is not covered in this book. It is considered an advanced technique and is difficult to implement correctly.

Pairwise Testing

Large decision tables can be reduced by limiting the number of rules. Instead of including every combination of causes, we can instead include only just the combinations for every pair of causes. The technique involves identifying every possible pair of combinations, and then combining these pairs into as few rules as possible.

To demonstrate pairwise testing, we can reduce Table 4.24 into Table 4.28.

Table 4.28 Pairwise decision table for `condInRange()`.

		Rules				
		1	2	3	4	5
Causes						
	`flag`	T	T	T	F	F
	`x < low`	T	F	F	T	F
	`x ≤ high`	T	T	F	T	F
Effects						
	`return value`	F	T	F	F	F

All the possible pairs of causes are included at least once in the decision table:

- `flag` and `x < low` – Rule 1
- `flag` and `!(x < low)` – Rule 2
- `!flag` and `x < low` – Rule 4
- `!flag` and `!(x < low)` – Rule 5
- `flag` and `x ≤ high` – Rule 1
- `flag` and `!(x ≤ high)` – Rule 3
- `!flag` and `x ≤ high` – Rule 4
- `!flag` and `!(x ≤ high)` – Rule 5
- `x < low` and `x ≤ high` – Rule 1
- `!(x < low)` and `x ≤ high` – Rule 2
- `!(x < low)` and `!(x ≤ high)` – Rule 3

Pairs of causes where `(x < low)` and `(x ≤ high)` are not possible and are therefore not included in the pairwise decision table (as they were also not included in the all-combinations decision table).

The larger the original table, the larger the potential reduction with this technique. For example, the 16 rules of Table 4.29 can be reduced to 6 rules, as shown in Table 4.30.

Each row represents a cause. For each pair of causes, every possible combination of {T,T},{T,F},{F,T},{F,F} occurs at least once.[8] For example:

---

[8] Software tools can help to automatically produce the required sets of pairs.

Table 4.29 Full combination table for four causes.

								Rules							
1	2	3	4	5	6	7	8	9	10	11	12	13	14	15	16
T	T	T	T	T	T	T	T	F	F	F	F	F	F	F	F
T	T	T	T	F	F	F	F	T	T	T	T	F	F	F	F
T	T	F	F	T	T	F	F	T	T	F	F	T	T	F	F
T	F	T	F	T	F	T	F	T	F	T	F	T	F	T	F

Table 4.30 Pairwise combination table for four causes.

		Rules			
1	2	3	4	5	6
T	T	F	F	T	F
T	F	T	F	T	F
T	T	F	T	F	F
T	F	T	T	F	F

- row1 and row2 – Rule 1
- row1 and row3 – Rule 1
- row1 and row4 – Rule 1
- row2 and row3 – Rule 1
- row2 and row4 – Rule 1
- row3 and row4 – Rule 1
- row1 and !row2 – Rule 2
- row1 and !row3 – Rule 5
- row1 and !row4 – Rule 2
- etc.

There is extensive debate about the effectiveness of pairwise testing. While the method may not find N-way faults (associated with a combination of N different causes), some research suggests that the additional benefits of higher-order (three-way, four-way, N-way) combinations may not be cost-effective. The obvious benefit is in reducing the number of test cases. Pairwise testing also reduces the time for test design (fewer tests to design), implementation (fewer tests to code), and execution (fewer tests to run).

4.4.4 Test Coverage Items

Each rule in the decision table is a TCI. If a test item includes multiple decision tables (for example, in a class) then it is useful to signify each rule/TCI with a unique identifier (i.e. a different name).

Usually a decision table will not include error situations, due to the number of rules required to describe all of these. Errors would only be included in a separate table for clarity, and only when different combinations of causes result in different errors.

4.4.5   Test Cases

Input test data for the test cases is selected based on rules not yet covered. Each test case will cover exactly one TCI (or rule). The expected results values are derived from the specification (using the decision table).

Hint: it is usually easiest to identify test data by going through the rules in order, and selecting a value for each parameter that matches the required causes. It is easier to remove duplicates and review the test design for correctness if you use as few different values as possible for each parameter. So it is recommended to reuse the equivalence partition values.

4.4.6   Pitfalls

Decision table testing can go wrong in a number of ways:

*   Ensure that the causes are complete and do not overlap, otherwise the table may be incomplete or inconsistent.
*   Use simple logical expressions for causes (i.e. with no Boolean operators, such as the && or || operators). Otherwise it is difficult to ensure all the combinations are created by the table.
*   The rules must be unique, you must ensure that no two rules can be true at the same time (i.e. every rule must have a different combination of causes). Otherwise the table is invalid and cannot be used to derive test cases.
*   Ensure that there are no possible combinations of input values that cause no rules to be matched.

4.5   Evaluation

Decision table testing approaches black-box testing from a slightly different viewpoint compared to equivalence partition and BVA testing. Instead of considering each input individually, it considers combinations of input values that are expected to have an effect on the processing or the output. This provides increased coverage of decisions in the code relating to categorising the inputs, or deciding what action to take based on a combination of input values.

This is important, as complex decisions are a frequent source of mistakes in the code. These decisions generally reflect the correct identification of a complex situation, and if not correctly implemented can result in the wrong processing taking place.

4.5.1   Limitations

The software has passed all the equivalence partition, BVA, and decision tables tests – so is it correct? As discussed earlier, only exhaustive testing can provide a conclusive result, so after decision table testing faults may remain. Some benefits and limitations of decision table testing are now explored by injecting faults into the source code.

Decision Table Testing against Fault 3

The results of running the equivalence partition, BVA, and decision tables tests against Fault 3 are shown in Figure 4.2. The fault is found by one of the decision table tests.

```
PASSED: test_giveDiscount("T1.1", 40, true, FULLPRICE)
PASSED: test_giveDiscount("T1.2", 100, false, FULLPRICE)
PASSED: test_giveDiscount("T1.3", 200, false, DISCOUNT)
PASSED: test_giveDiscount("T1.4", -100, false, ERROR)
PASSED: test_giveDiscount("T2.1", 1, true, FULLPRICE)
PASSED: test_giveDiscount("T2.2", 80, false, FULLPRICE)
PASSED: test_giveDiscount("T2.3", 81, false, FULLPRICE)
PASSED: test_giveDiscount("T2.4", 120, false, FULLPRICE)
PASSED: test_giveDiscount("T2.5", 121, false, DISCOUNT)
PASSED: test_giveDiscount("T2.6", 9223372036854775807, false, DISCOUNT)
PASSED: test_giveDiscount("T2.7", -9223372036854775808, false, ERROR)
PASSED: test_giveDiscount("T2.8", 0, false, ERROR)
PASSED: test_giveDiscount("T3.2", 200, true, DISCOUNT)
FAILED: test_giveDiscount("T3.1", 100, true, DISCOUNT)
java.lang.AssertionError: expected [DISCOUNT] but found [FULLPRICE]
================================================
Command line suite
Total tests run: 14, Passes: 13, Failures: 1, Skips: 0
================================================
```

Figure 4.2 Decision table test results for `giveDiscount()` with Fault 3.

Fault 4

A new fault is now inserted in the code to demonstrate a limitation of decision table testing, as shown in Listing 4.2.

The inserted fault (lines 35 and 36) adds extra functionality that is not in the specification and is unlikely to be found by any type of black-box testing.

Decision Table Testing against Fault 4

The results of running the equivalence partition, BVA, and decision tables tests against this fault are shown in Figure 4.3. As expected, the fault is not found – the inserted fault bears no relationship to the specification, and therefore is unlikely to be found by any black-box testing technique.

Listing 4.2 Fault 4.

```
22          Status rv = FULLPRICE;
23          long threshold = 120;
24
25          if (bonusPoints <= 0)
26              rv = ERROR;
27
28          else {
29              if (goldCustomer)
30                  threshold = 80;
31              if (bonusPoints > threshold)
32                  rv = DISCOUNT;
33          }
34
35          if (bonusPoints == 43) // Fault 4
36              rv = DISCOUNT;
37
38          return rv;
39      }
40
41  }
```

```
PASSED: test_giveDiscount("T1.1", 40, true, FULLPRICE)
PASSED: test_giveDiscount("T1.2", 100, false, FULLPRICE)
PASSED: test_giveDiscount("T1.3", 200, false, DISCOUNT)
PASSED: test_giveDiscount("T1.4", -100, false, ERROR)
PASSED: test_giveDiscount("T2.1", 1, true, FULLPRICE)
PASSED: test_giveDiscount("T2.2", 80, false, FULLPRICE)
PASSED: test_giveDiscount("T2.3", 81, false, FULLPRICE)
PASSED: test_giveDiscount("T2.4", 120, false, FULLPRICE)
PASSED: test_giveDiscount("T2.5", 121, false, DISCOUNT)
PASSED: test_giveDiscount("T2.6", 9223372036854775807, false, DISCOUNT)
PASSED: test_giveDiscount("T2.7", -9223372036854775808, false, ERROR)
PASSED: test_giveDiscount("T2.8", 0, false, ERROR)
PASSED: test_giveDiscount("T3.1", 100, true, DISCOUNT)
PASSED: test_giveDiscount("T3.2", 200, true, DISCOUNT)
================================================
Command line suite
Total tests run: 14, Passes: 14, Failures: 0, Skips: 0
================================================
```

Figure 4.3 Decision table test results for giveDiscount() with Fault 4.

Demonstrating the Fault

The results of executing the code with Fault 4, using specially selected input values, are shown in Figure 4.4. Note that the wrong result is returned for the inputs (43, true). The correct result is FULLPRICE.

```
$ check 43 true
DISCOUNT
```

Figure 4.4 Manual demonstration of Fault 4.

4.5.2 Strengths and Weaknesses

Strengths

- Decision tables exercise combinations of input data values.
- The expected results are created as part of the analysis process.

Weaknesses

- The decision tables can sometimes be very large. Different approaches exist to reduce the tables.
- A more detailed specification may lead to increased causes and effects, and consequently large and complex tables.

Decision table testing is complementary to equivalence partition and BVA testing. There is little published evidence as to the effectiveness of decision table testing, but experience in programming indicates that this is likely to cover different errors from equivalence partitions and boundary values.

4.6 Key Points

- Decision table testing ensures that the software works correctly with combinations of input values.
- Test coverage items and test cases are based on rules in the decision table.
- The data for the test cases is selected from the equivalence partition test values.

4.7 Notes for Experienced Testers

Experienced testers may produce the causes and effects in their mind and create decision tables directly with support from the specification. They may also implement tests directly from the decision table. However, in cases where high quality is required (embedded systems, life-critical systems, etc.), even an experienced tester may need to document these steps for quality review, or in the case of a legal challenge to the quality of the software.

5 Statement Coverage

In this chapter, white-box testing is introduced, and its most basic form, *statement coverage*, is presented.

5.1 Introduction to White-Box Testing

In the previous chapters, basic black-box test techniques have been described. These provide a basic level of testing *against the specification*. However, faults may remain in unexecuted components of the code. In order to try to find these, tests based on the implementation (code) instead of the specification are used – these techniques are referred to as *white-box testing* or *structure-based testing*. These test techniques identify particular parts of the code, and test that the correct result is produced when these are exercised. Test coverage items are derived from the *implementation*, but the *specification* is used to provide the expected results for each test case.

The expected results must always be derived from the specification and not from the source code. It is easy to make the mistake of using the source code when it is in front of you, and the output is obvious from the code. However, using the source code to derive the expected results only verifies that you have understood the code properly, and not that the code works.

In practice, the coverage of the code components achieved by executing the black-box tests is usually measured automatically, and then white-box tests are developed *only* for components not already covered. That is the approach taken in this book.

Refer to Chapter 8 for a more detailed discussion on white-box testing, and how it complements black-box testing.

5.2 Testing with Statement Coverage

Statement coverage testing (or more formally *testing with statement coverage criteria*) ensures that every line, or *statement*, of the source code is executed during tests, while verifying that the output is correct.

Definition: a *statement* is a line in the source code that can be executed.[1]

---
[1] Not all lines can be executed: blank lines, comments, opening and closing braces, etc.

5.2.1 Statement Coverage Measurement

The lines in the source code that have been executed can be measured automatically[2] for most programming languages. This supports the measurement of statement coverage during testing.

In this chapter, tests are developed to ensure that all the statements are executed during testing, helping to find faults related to unexecuted code.

5.3 Example

We continue testing the method `OnlineSales.giveDiscount()` with Fault 4 inserted as shown in Listing 5.1. This fault was not found by any of the black-box test techniques. As a reminder, the specification and source code are repeated next.

The specification can be summarised as follows – `OnlineSales.giveDiscount()` returns:

FULLPRICE if `bonusPoints` $\leq$ 120 and not a `goldCustomer`
FULLPRICE if `bonusPoints` $\leq$ 80 and a `goldCustomer`
DISCOUNT if `bonusPoints` > 120
DISCOUNT if `bonusPoints` > 80 and a `goldCustomer`
ERROR if any inputs are invalid (`bonusPoints` < 1)

The source code with Fault 4 is repeated for reference in Listing 5.1.

Listing 5.1 Fault 4.

```
22        Status rv = FULLPRICE;
23        long threshold = 120;
24
25        if (bonusPoints <= 0)
26            rv = ERROR;
27
28        else {
29            if (goldCustomer)
30                threshold = 80;
31            if (bonusPoints > threshold)
32                rv = DISCOUNT;
33        }
34
35        if (bonusPoints == 43) // Fault 4
36            rv = DISCOUNT;
37
38        return rv;
39    }
40
41 }
```

---

[2] In this book, the Java/JaCoCo tool is used to measure statement coverage during test execution – see www.jacoco.org for details.

5.3.1   Analysis: Identifying Unexecuted Statements

For code that has already been tested using black-box techniques, the first step in achieving full statement coverage is to examine the coverage results of these existing tests.

Running the full set of existing tests (equivalence partition, boundary value analysis (BVA), and decision tables) against Fault 4 with code coverage measurement enabled produces the test report, a coverage summary report, and a source code coverage report. The test report is as shown previously in Figure 4.3 – all the tests pass. Figure 5.1 shows the (JaCoCo) coverage summary for class OnlineSales that was achieved by executing these tests.[3]

Figure 5.1 Decision table coverage summary for `giveDiscount()` with Fault 4.

For statement coverage we are only interested in the Lines column and the Missed column to its left in the report. We are also only concerned with the method we are testing, shown in the row `giveDiscount(long,boolean)`. Lines shows the number of lines in the method: 11. Missed shows the number of missed (unexecuted) lines in the method: 1. The tests have missed 1 out of 11 lines in the method, and have not achieved full statement coverage.

The next step is to determine which lines have not been executed. We do this by examining the source code coverage report, as shown in Figure 5.2. Note that this shows the full file for OnlineSales.java, including lines that have been omitted from the source code listings elsewhere in the book (to make it easier to read the source code by focusing on the essential elements).

The highlighting of individual lines of code is interpreted as follows:

- Lines that have been executed during testing are highlighted in light grey (green on the screen) and medium grey (yellow on the screen).
- Lines that have not been executed are highlighted in dark grey (red on the screen).

We are only interested in the lines in the method `giveDiscount()` on lines 22–41. Other highlighted lines in the report refer to source code in the class OnlineSales which is not part of this method. The JavaDoc specification is also included, as this is part of the source file – these lines have been left out elsewhere for simplicity.

[3] The report contains other pages with which we are not concerned here.

```
  📄 JaCoCo Coverage Report > ⊞ example > 📄 OnlineSales.java          ⊘ Sessions

  OnlineSales.java

   1.  package example;
   2.  // Note: this version contains Fault 4
   3.  import static example.OnlineSales.Status.*;
   4.
   5.  public class OnlineSales {
   6.
   7.      public static enum Status { FULLPRICE, DISCOUNT, ERROR };
   8.
   9.      /**
  10.       * Determine whether to give a discount for online sales.
  11.       * Gold customers get a discount above 80 bonus points.
  12.       * Other customers get a discount above 120 bonus points.
  13.       *
  14.       * @param bonusPoints How many bonus points the customer has accumulated
  15.       * @param goldCustomer Whether the customer is a Gold Customer
  16.       *
  17.       * @return
  18.       * DISCOUNT - give a discount<br>
  19.       * FULLPRICE - charge the full price<br>
  20.       * ERROR - invalid inputs
  21.       */
  22.      public static Status giveDiscount(long bonusPoints, boolean goldCustomer)
  23.      {
  24.          Status rv = FULLPRICE;
  25.          long threshold=120;
  26.
  27. ◆       if (bonusPoints<=0)
  28.              rv = ERROR;
  29.
  30.          else {
  31. ◆           if (goldCustomer)
  32.                  threshold = 80;
  33. ◆           if (bonusPoints>threshold)
  34.                  rv=DISCOUNT;
  35.          }
  36.
  37. ◇       if (bonusPoints==43) // fault 4
  38.              rv = DISCOUNT;
  39.
  40.          return rv;
  41.      }
  42.
  43.  }
```

Figure 5.2 Decision table test coverage details for `giveDiscount()` with Fault 4.

The coverage of the method `giveDiscount()` achieved by black-box testing is as follows:

- Line 38 is marked in dark grey, indicating that it has not been executed.
- Line 37 is medium grey, indicating that it has been partially executed. This counts as executed for statement coverage, and is explored in more detail when we discuss branch coverage in the next chapter.
- Lines 24, 25, 27, 28, 31–34, and 40 are light grey, indicating that they have been fully executed.

Remember, we are testing the method `giveDiscount()` and *not* the entire class – the coverage shows that some of the compiler-generated code for the class has not been executed. This is of relevance when we consider object-oriented testing in Chapter 9.

By examining the source code and the coverage results, we can identify the following: the unexecuted lines of code, the conditions that must be met to cause these lines to be executed, and the required input values to meet these conditions.

In this example, from Figure 5.2, we can identify the unexecuted statements: line 38.

By a careful examination of the source code, we can identify the condition that will cause line 38 to execute – `bonusPoints == 43` must be true on line 37, which means that `bonusPoints` must have the value 43 at this point in the code execution.

As `bonusPoints` is an input parameter, it is easy to identify the required input: `bonusPoints` must have the value 43. When the condition is the result of a calculation in the code, more detailed analysis is required. These results are summarised in Table 5.1.

Table 5.1 Unexpected statements in `giveDiscount()`.

ID	Line number	Condition
1	38	`bonusPoints == 43`

5.3.2   Test Coverage Items

Each unexecuted line of source code (or statement) is a test coverage item (TCI), as shown in Table 5.2. Lines that cannot be executed are ignored (for example, comments and blank lines). This shows that only one extra TCI is required to provide full source code coverage (when executed along with the full set of black-box tests). There is little value in identifying all the previously executed statements and which test covers them, especially for large numbers of statements.

The TCIs and test cases are all marked as being extra to indicate that on their own they do not provide full statement coverage. The complementary tests required to provide full statement coverage must be documented: in this example it is all the equivalence partition, BVA, and decision tables tests as developed previously.

The Test Case column in Table 5.2 is completed later. If it is required for review purposes, you can also include in this table exactly which black-box test case causes each statement to be executed, but this level of detail is seldom necessary in practice, and would require each black-box test to be run and measured separately.

Table 5.2 Extra statement coverage TCIs for `giveDiscount()`.

TCI	Line number	Test case
SC1	38	To be completed

5.3.3   Test Cases

Test cases are developed to ensure that all the unexecuted statements are now executed. Experience allows a minimum set of tests to be developed, but the emphasis is on ensuring full coverage.

The analysis has identified the condition required for each uncovered statement to be executed, and this assists in developing the test data.

In this example, as we have already worked out, to execute the code on line 38 the parameter bonusPoints must have the value 43. According to the specification, if bonusPoints is 43, then the result will always be FULLPRICE, irrespective of the value of the goldCustomer parameter. This allows any value to be picked for goldCustomer, as shown in Table 5.3.

Table 5.3 Extra statement coverage test cases for giveDiscount().

ID	TCI	Inputs		Exp. results
		bonusPoints	goldCustomer	return value
T4.1	SC1	43	false	FULLPRICE

- Unlike in black-box testing, there is no differentiation between error and non-error cases for white-box testing.

5.3.4   Verification of the Test Cases

As described previously, verification consists of two steps: first completing the test cases table, and then reviewing your work.

Completing the Test Coverage Items Table

Reading the TCI column from the test cases in Table 5.3 allows us to complete the Test Case column in the TCI table, as shown in Table 5.4.

Table 5.4 Extra statement coverage TCI for giveDiscount().

TCI	Line	Test case
SC1	38	T4.1

Reviewing Your Work

The design verification consists of a review to ensure that:

1. Every TCI is covered by at least one test case (this confirms that the tests are complete).
2. Every new test case covers additional TCIs (this confirms that there are no unnecessary tests).

3. There are no duplicate tests (taking the equivalence partition, BVA, and decision tables tests into consideration).

In this example, we can see from Table 5.4 that every TCI is covered, and from Table 5.3 that every statement coverage test case covers additional TCIs. Comparing the test cases for the equivalence partition, BVA, decision tables, and statement coverage tests (Tables 2.9, 3.3, 4.15, and 5.3), we can see that there are no duplicate tests.

5.4 Test Implementation and Results

5.4.1 Implementation

The full test implementation is shown in Listing 5.2. This includes the previously developed equivalence partition, BVA, and decision tables tests, as these are required to provide full statement coverage.[4]

Listing 5.2 `OnlineSalesTest` for statement coverage testing.

```
1   public class OnlineSalesTest {
2
3       private static Object[][] testData1 = new Object[][] {
4           // test, bonusPoints, goldCustomer, expected output
5           { "T1.1",        40L,        true,  FULLPRICE },
6           { "T1.2",       100L,        false, FULLPRICE },
7           { "T1.3",       200L,        false,  DISCOUNT },
8           { "T1.4",      -100L,        false,     ERROR },
9           { "T2.1",         1L,        true,  FULLPRICE },
10          { "T2.2",        80L,        false, FULLPRICE },
11          { "T2.3",        81L,        false, FULLPRICE },
12          { "T2.4",       120L,        false, FULLPRICE },
13          { "T2.5",       121L,        false,  DISCOUNT },
14          { "T2.6", Long.MAX_VALUE, false, DISCOUNT },
15          { "T2.7", Long.MIN_VALUE, false, ERROR },
16          { "T2.8",         0L,        false,     ERROR },
17          { "T3.1",       100L,        true,   DISCOUNT },
18          { "T3.2",       200L,        true,   DISCOUNT },
19          { "T4.1",        43L,        true,  FULLPRICE },
20      };
21
22      @DataProvider(name = "testset1")
23      public Object[][] getTestData() {
24          return testData1;
25      }
26
27      @Test(dataProvider = "testset1")
28      public void test_giveDiscount( String id, long bonusPoints,
                boolean goldCustomer, Status expected) {
29          assertEquals( OnlineSales.giveDiscount(bonusPoints,
                goldCustomer), expected );
```

[4] More sophisticated techniques for grouping tests together to allow subsets to be run will be explored in Chapter 11.

```
30      }
31
32  }
```

5.4.2   Test Results

The results of running the full set of tests (equivalence partition, BVA, decision tables, and statement coverage) against Fault 4 are shown in Figure 5.3.

```
PASSED: test_giveDiscount("T1.1", 40, true, FULLPRICE)
PASSED: test_giveDiscount("T1.2", 100, false, FULLPRICE)
PASSED: test_giveDiscount("T1.3", 200, false, DISCOUNT)
PASSED: test_giveDiscount("T1.4", -100, false, ERROR)
PASSED: test_giveDiscount("T2.1", 1, true, FULLPRICE)
PASSED: test_giveDiscount("T2.2", 80, false, FULLPRICE)
PASSED: test_giveDiscount("T2.3", 81, false, FULLPRICE)
PASSED: test_giveDiscount("T2.4", 120, false, FULLPRICE)
PASSED: test_giveDiscount("T2.5", 121, false, DISCOUNT)
PASSED: test_giveDiscount("T2.6", 9223372036854775807, false, DISCOUNT)
PASSED: test_giveDiscount("T2.7", -9223372036854775808, false, ERROR)
PASSED: test_giveDiscount("T2.8", 0, false, ERROR)
PASSED: test_giveDiscount("T3.1", 100, true, DISCOUNT)
PASSED: test_giveDiscount("T3.2", 200, true, DISCOUNT)
FAILED: test_giveDiscount("T4.1", 43, true, FULLPRICE)
java.lang.AssertionError: expected [FULLPRICE] but found [DISCOUNT]
===============================================
Command line suite
Total tests run: 15, Passes: 14, Failures: 1, Skips: 0
===============================================
```

Figure 5.3 Statement coverage Test results for `giveDiscount()` with Fault 4.

The statement coverage test T4.1 fails, indicating a fault in the code: Fault 4 has been found by this test. There is no value in running these tests against any other versions of the code, unless it has been verified that the extra test continues to provide 100% code coverage. The test data has been specifically developed to ensure statement coverage against the code version that contains Fault 4. The test coverage results are shown in Figure 5.4.

Element	Missed Instructions ↓	Cov.	Missed Branches	Cov.	Missed	Cxty	Missed	Lines	Missed	Methods
● OnlineSales()	▬	0%		n/a	1	1	1	1	1	1
● giveDiscount(long, boolean)	▬▬▬▬▬▬	100%	▬▬▬▬▬▬	100%	0	5	0	11	0	1
Total	3 of 32	90%	0 of 8	100%	1	6	1	12	1	2

JaCoCo Coverage Report > ⊞ example > ⊕ OnlineSales   ⚙ Sessions

OnlineSales

Figure 5.4 Statement coverage test coverage summary for `giveDiscount()` with Fault 4.

Full statement coverage has been achieved – there are no missed lines. There is no value in viewing the annotated source code once 100% coverage has been achieved.

5.5   Statement Coverage Testing in More Detail

5.5.1   Fault Model

The statement coverage fault model is where code that has not been executed in previous tests may contain a fault. These unexecuted statements tend to be associated with edge cases, or other unusual circumstances.

Statement coverage tests use carefully selected input values to ensure that every statement is executed. These tests attempt to find faults associated with individual lines in the source code.

5.5.2   Description

Tests are developed to cause all statements in the source code to be executed. The level of statement coverage achieved during testing is usually shown as a percentage – for example, 100% statement coverage means that every statement has been executed, 50% means that only half the statements have been covered.

Statement coverage is the *weakest form* of white-box testing.[5] However, 100% statement coverage will probably not cover all the logic of a program, or cause all the possible output values to be generated!

An additional benefit of statement coverage is that *unreachable* code is identified during the analysis stage (this code should be reviewed and probably deleted).

5.5.3   Analysis: Identifying Unexecuted Statements

Based on the coverage results from previous tests (usually black-box tests), the unexecuted statements can be easily identified.

For complex code, a control-flow graph (CFG) may be developed first to help with understanding the code flow at a more abstract level, but these are seldom required for statement coverage; CFGs are explained in Chapter 7. Statement coverage tests may also be developed before black-box tests, though this is not usual practice. In this case, CFGs are traditionally used to assist in developing the tests, though the experienced tester will probably not need to use them.

5.5.4   Test Coverage Items

Each statement in the source code is a TCI. Normally, a single line of source is regarded as being a statement. As in other forms of testing, using unique identifiers for the TCI makes the task of reviewing the test design easier.

5.5.5   Test Cases

Test data is selected to ensure that every statement, or node in the program, is executed. This selection requires the tester to review the code and select input parameter values that cause the required statements to be executed.

---

[5] All other forms of white-box structural testing ensure at least statement coverage.

Developing test cases to execute all the statements in the source code is challenging. The test data values are often based on reviewing already executed statements, and then identifying changes to the input parameters that will cause additional statements to execute. These data values can be identified during analysis, as shown in the example, or identified during development of the test cases.

Finally, using the specification, and never the source code, we can work out the expected results for each set of input values. It is worth repeating here that the expected results *must* come from the specification. It is all too easy to make the mistake of reading the expected results from the code – and the tester must be careful to avoid doing this.

5.6 Evaluation

Statement coverage has uncovered Fault 4 inserted into the method `giveDiscount()`.

5.6.1 Limitations

This chapter has already shown how statement coverage detects faults related to unexecuted statements, using Fault 4. Some benefits and limitations of statement coverage are now explored by inserting a new fault into the original code.

Fault 5

A new fault is now inserted on line 31 to demonstrate some limitations of testing with statement coverage. This fault is produced by modifying the if statement on line 31, incorrectly adding '`&& bonusPoints != 93`'. This creates an extra branch in the code, one which is not taken with the existing test data (as the value 93 is never used for `bonusPoints`). The result is that when `bonusPoints` is equal to 93, line 32 will not be executed. This is shown in Listing 5.3.

Listing 5.3 Fault 5.

```
22      public static Status giveDiscount(long bonusPoints, boolean
                goldCustomer)
23      {
24          Status rv = FULLPRICE;
25          long threshold = 120;
26
27          if (bonusPoints <= 0)
28              rv = ERROR;
29
30          else {
31              if (goldCustomer && bonusPoints != 93) // Fault 5
32                  threshold = 80;
33              if (bonusPoints > threshold)
34                  rv = DISCOUNT;
35          }
36
37          return rv;
38      }
```

Testing against Fault 5

The results of running the equivalence partition, BVA, decision tables, and statement coverage tests against this modification are shown in Figure 5.5. The fault is not found. This is to be expected – the inserted fault bears no relationship to the specification, and is unlikely to be found by any black-box test technique or statement coverage.[6] The tests provide full statement coverage,[7] as shown in Figure 5.6.

```
PASSED: test_giveDiscount("T1.1", 40, true, FULLPRICE)
PASSED: test_giveDiscount("T1.2", 100, false, FULLPRICE)
PASSED: test_giveDiscount("T1.3", 200, false, DISCOUNT)
PASSED: test_giveDiscount("T1.4", -100, false, ERROR)
PASSED: test_giveDiscount("T2.1", 1, true, FULLPRICE)
PASSED: test_giveDiscount("T2.2", 80, false, FULLPRICE)
PASSED: test_giveDiscount("T2.3", 81, false, FULLPRICE)
PASSED: test_giveDiscount("T2.4", 120, false, FULLPRICE)
PASSED: test_giveDiscount("T2.5", 121, false, DISCOUNT)
PASSED: test_giveDiscount("T2.6", 9223372036854775807, false, DISCOUNT)
PASSED: test_giveDiscount("T2.7", -9223372036854775808, false, ERROR)
PASSED: test_giveDiscount("T2.8", 0, false, ERROR)
PASSED: test_giveDiscount("T3.1", 100, true, DISCOUNT)
PASSED: test_giveDiscount("T3.2", 200, true, DISCOUNT)
PASSED: test_giveDiscount("T4.1", 43, true, FULLPRICE)
=================================================
Command line suite
Total tests run: 15, Passes: 15, Failures: 0, Skips: 0
=================================================
```

Figure 5.5 Statement coverage test results for `giveDiscount()` with Fault 5.

Element	Missed Instructions ▾	Cov.	Missed Branches	Cov.	Missed	Cxty	Missed	Lines	Missed	Methods
● OnlineSales()	▬	0%		n/a	1	1	1	1	1	1
● giveDiscount(long, boolean)	▬▬▬▬▬▬▬	100%	▬▬▬▬	87%	1	5	0	9	0	1
Total	3 of 30	90%	1 of 8	87%	2	6	1	10	1	2

Figure 5.6 Statement coverage test coverage summary for `giveDiscount()` with Fault 5.

There are no missed lines in the method `checkDiscount()`, so there is no value in examining the detailed source code report – all the lines will be marked as covered.

Demonstrating the Fault

The results of executing the code with Fault 5, using specially selected input values, are shown in Figure 5.7.

---

[6] This is referred to as an error of commission, which is discussed in more detail in Section 8.1.
[7] Test 4.1 is in fact now redundant – the code has been changed, and this test is no longer required to achieve full statement coverage.

```
$ check 93 true
FULLPRICE
```

Figure 5.7 Manual demonstration of Fault 6.

The wrong result is returned for the inputs (93,true). The correct result is DISCOUNT. We will need more sophisticated methods to find such faults, which are discussed in Chapter 6.

5.6.2 Strengths and Weaknesses

Strengths

• Statement coverage provides a minimum level of coverage by executing all the statements in the code at least once. There is a significant risk in releasing software before every statement has been executed at least once during testing – its behaviour has not been verified, and may well be faulty.

• Statement coverage can generally be achieved using only a small number of extra tests.

Weaknesses

• It can be difficult to determine the required input parameter values.

• It may be hard to test code that can only be executed in unusual or abnormal circumstances.

• It does not provide coverage for the *NULL else*. For example, in the code:

```
if (number < 3) number++;
```

statement coverage does not force a test case for number $\geq$ 3

• It is not demanding of compound decisions. For example, in the code:

```
if ( (a > 1) || (b == 0) ) x = x/a;
```

there are no test cases for each value of each individual Boolean condition in the decision,[8] or for the possible combinations of the Boolean conditions.

Statement coverage is generally used to supplement black-box testing – mainly because it is easy to measure the coverage automatically. If black-box testing does not result in the required coverage (normally 100%) then this white-box technique can be used to increase the coverage to the required level.

---

[8] A decision is a Boolean expression that is used to alter the flow of control in the code. These are used, for example, in if and while statements. Each Boolean sub-clause in a compound Boolean expression is referred to as a Boolean condition. In this example, (a > 1) and (b == 0) are Boolean conditions in the decision ((a > 1)||(b == 0)). Simple decisions have a single Boolean condition, as shown above, where (number < 3) is both a decision and also the single Boolean condition in that decision.

5.7   Key Points

- Statement coverage is used to augment black-box testing by ensuring that every statement is executed.
- Test coverage items are based on unexecuted statements.
- Input values for the test cases are selected by analysis of the decisions in the code (and therefore are dependent on the specific version of the code being tested).
- Statement coverage can be used in unit testing as shown, and can also be used when testing object-oriented software in exactly the same way. It can also be used in application testing, although for web applications, when the application is running on a remote server, setting up the server to produce coverage results and accessing those results can be challenging.

5.8   Notes for Experienced Testers

An experienced tester will perform black-box tests first and measure their coverage. Then, by reviewing the coverage results, additional tests can be developed to ensure full statement coverage. Working out the correct input values can be complex, and the experienced tester will often use the debugger to assist in doing this. One useful technique for complex decisions is to set a breakpoint at the line of code directly before the first unexecuted line, and then examine the value of the relevant variables. An experienced tester will probably develop the statement coverage test cases directly from the coverage results, without documenting the analysis or TCIs. Unlike in black-box testing, the test design work can be effectively reviewed by examining the coverage statistics generated by the test, without access to this documentation.

6 Branch Coverage

In this chapter, the next strongest form of white-box testing, branch coverage, is introduced.

6.1 Testing with Branch Coverage

This ensures that every branch in the code is taken during testing, or more formally, the coverage criteria during testing is *branch coverage*. Testing with branch coverage ensures that every branch is taken during tests, as well as verifying that the output is correct.

Definition: a *branch* is a transition from one line to another in the source code during execution. The lines may directly follow each other, or there may be a jump.

6.1.1 Branch Coverage Measurement

As for statement coverage, branch coverage can also be measured automatically for Java programs. The JaCoCo tool, as previously used for statement coverage, can also be used to measure branch coverage. Note that different tools may measure branches in different ways – in this chapter we use the JaCoCo branch report as the basis for testing.[1]

6.2 Example

Testing of the `OnlineSales.giveDiscount()` method with Fault 5, shown in Listing 6.1, is used in this chapter. As a reminder, the specification and code are shown again next.

To summarise the specification, `giveDiscount(bonusPoints, goldCustomer)` returns:

FULLPRICE if `bonusPoints` $\leq$ 120 and not a `goldCustomer`

---

[1] JaCoCo measures the outcome of each Boolean condition in a decision as a separate branch. Other tools may take a different approach, seen in many textbooks, of measuring just the outcomes of the decision itself as branches, and not of the individual Boolean conditions within the decision.

FULLPRICE if bonusPoints $\leq$ 80 and a goldCustomer

DISCOUNT if bonusPoints > 120

DISCOUNT if bonusPoints > 80 and a goldCustomer

ERROR if any inputs are invalid (bonusPoints < 1)

The source code with Fault 5 is repeated for easy reference in Listing 6.1.

Listing 6.1 Fault 5.

```
22    public static Status giveDiscount(long bonusPoints, boolean
          goldCustomer)
23    {
24       Status rv = FULLPRICE;
25       long threshold = 120;
26
27       if (bonusPoints <= 0)
28          rv = ERROR;
29
30       else {
31          if (goldCustomer && bonusPoints != 93) // Fault 5
32             threshold = 80;
33          if (bonusPoints > threshold)
34             rv = DISCOUNT;
35       }
36
37       return rv;
38    }
```

6.2.1   Analysis: Identifying Untaken Branches

For code that has already been tested with black-box and/or statement coverage, tests to develop full branch coverage can be developed by examining the branch coverage results of these tests.

For Fault 5, running the existing tests (equivalence partition, boundary value analysis (BVA), decision tables, statement coverage) with code coverage measurement enabled produces a coverage summary report, and highlighted source code. These are the same reports we saw in the previous chapter (Section 5.3.1) for statement coverage, except that now we will be examining different figures in the report. The coverage summary for these tests is shown in Figure 6.1.

JaCoCo Coverage Report > example > OnlineSales											Sessions
OnlineSales											
Element	Missed Instructions	Cov.	Missed Branches	Cov.	Missed	Cxty	Missed	Lines	Missed	Methods	
OnlineSales()		0%		n/a	1	1	1	1	1	1	
giveDiscount(long, boolean)		100%		87%	1	5	0	9	0	1	
Total	3 of 30	90%	1 of 8	87%	2	6	1	10	1	2	

Figure 6.1 Statement coverage test summary for giveDiscount() with Fault 5.

It is important to note that the statement coverage tests were developed to provide full statement coverage of giveDiscount() with Fault 4, and not with Fault 5. The tests are therefore not guaranteed to provide statement coverage for the version with Fault 5. However, in this example, we can see from the coverage summary that 100% statement coverage has been achieved (lines missed is 0).

Examining the missed branches reveals that we only have 87% coverage – this means that not all of the branches in the method have been taken. In order to identify which branches have not been taken, we now examine the source code coverage report (see Figure 6.2).

Figure 6.2 Statement coverage test details for giveDiscount() with Fault 5.

Line 31 is marked in medium grey (or yellow when viewed on the screen), indicating that it has not been fully executed. That means that some of the branches inside this line of source code have not been taken.

Hovering the cursor over the diamond on line 31 causes a detailed report of the branch coverage to appear in a popup box below the line. This is shown in Figure 6.3.

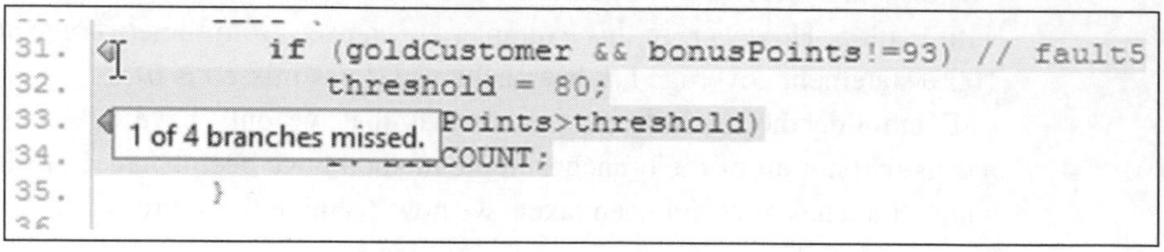

Figure 6.3 Branch coverage details.

The report that one of four branches has been missed indicates that the line contains four branches, and that one of these branches has not been taken. Recall that JaCoCo is typical of Java branch coverage tools in that it counts branches for the outcome of each Boolean condition[2] and not for the decision itself.

We can now examine the branch coverage report in more detail. There is one decision on line 31 – this is a compound decision:

- Decision 1: `goldCustomer && bonusPoints != 93`

There are two Boolean conditions in the decision on line 31:

- Condition 1: `goldCustomer`
- Condition 2: `bonusPoints != 93`

There are four branches in the code, two for each Boolean condition: one for the `true` outcome and one for the `false` outcome:

- Branch 1: `goldCustomer` is `false`
- Branch 2: `goldCustomer` is `true`
- Branch 3: `bonusPoints == 93`
- Branch 4: `bonusPoints != 93`

The first Boolean condition (`goldCustomer`) is evaluated first, and either branch 1 or branch 2 taken. If `goldCustomer` is true, then the second Boolean condition (`bonusPoints != 93`) is evaluated, and either branch 3 or branch 4 taken. Branch 4 is the only branch that results in line 32 being executed next. The other three branches all go to line 33.

A review of the test data shows that the value 93 has not been used in the tests, and therefore the untaken branch is the one identified as branch 3 in the list above. The requirement for this branch to be taken is that `goldCustomer` is true and `bonusPoints` is equal to 93.

These analysis results are summarised in Table 6.1, where the start and end line of each branch are shown, along with the constraints that must be met for that branch to

---

[2] The word condition has multiple meanings in software testing, so for clarity we use *test condition* to mean an IEEE test condition, and *Boolean condition* to refer to a sub-clause in a complex decision.

be taken. Only untaken branches need be considered – previous tests have covered all the other branches.

Table 6.1 Untaken branches in `giveDiscount()`.

Branch	Start line	End line	Condition
B1	31 (branch 3)	33	`goldCustomer && bonusPoints == 93`

6.2.2 Test Coverage Items

Each untaken branch in the code is a test coverage item (TCI), as shown in Table 6.2. As for statement coverage, there is little value in identifying which of the existing tests cause each of the other branches to be taken, and only the extra TCIs are identified.

Table 6.2 Extra branch coverage TCIs for `giveDiscount()`.

TCI	Branch	Test case
BC1	B1	To be completed

6.2.3 Test Cases

Test cases are developed to ensure that all the previously untaken branches are taken during execution of the branch coverage tests. Experience allows a minimum set of tests to be developed, but the emphasis is on ensuring full branch coverage.

The analysis has identified the conditions required for each untaken branch to be taken, and this assists in developing the test data as shown in Table 6.3.

In this example, as we have already identified, to execute the untaken branch the parameter `goldCustomer` must be true and the parameter `bonusPoints` must have the value 93. The expected results are determined from the specification. The input values (`93`, `true`) should produce `DISCOUNT`.

6.2.4 Verification of the Test Cases

As described previously, verification consists of two steps: first completing the TCIs table, and then reviewing your work.

Completing the TCIs Table

We can now complete the TCIs table, as shown in Table 6.4. The Test Case column is filled by referring to the TCI column in Table 6.3.

Table 6.3 Extra branch coverage test data for `giveDiscount()`.

ID	TCI	Inputs		Exp. results
		bonusPoints	goldCustomer	return value
T5.1	BC1	93	true	DISCOUNT

Table 6.4 Extra branch coverage test coverage items for `giveDiscount()`.

TCI	Branch	Test
BC1	B1	T5.1

Reviewing Your Work

In this example, we can see from Table 6.4 that every test case is covered, and from Table 6.3 that every branch coverage test covers a new branch coverage TCI. Comparing the test data for the equivalence partition, BVA, decision tables, statement coverage, and branch coverage tests (Tables 2.9, 3.3, 4.15, 5.3, and 6.3) we can see that there are no duplicate tests. This confirms that: (a) there are no missing tests, and (b) there are no unnecessary tests.

6.3   Test Implementation and Results

6.3.1   Implementation

The full test implementation, adding the branch coverage tests to the previously developed equivalence partition, BVA, decision tables, and statement coverage tests, is shown in Listing 6.2. This implementation represents the full set of tests required to effect branch coverage.[3]

Listing 6.2 `OnlineSalesTest` for branch coverage testing.

```
1  public class OnlineSalesTest {
2
3    private static Object[][] testData1 = new Object[][] {
4      // test, bonusPoints, goldCustomer, expected output
5      { "T1.1",    40L,     true,   FULLPRICE },
6      { "T1.2",   100L,    false,   FULLPRICE },
7      { "T1.3",   200L,    false,   DISCOUNT },
8      { "T1.4",  -100L,    false,      ERROR },
9      { "T2.1",     1L,     true,   FULLPRICE },
10     { "T2.2",    80L,    false,   FULLPRICE },
11     { "T2.3",    81L,    false,   FULLPRICE },
12     { "T2.4",   120L,    false,   FULLPRICE },
```

---

[3] Techniques for grouping individual tests into sets of tests/test suites, which can then be run independently, is discussed in Chapter 11.

```
13      { "T2.5",        121L,      false,   DISCOUNT },
14      { "T2.6", Long.MAX_VALUE, false, DISCOUNT },
15      { "T2.7", Long.MIN_VALUE, false, ERROR },
16      { "T2.8",         0L,       false,      ERROR },
17      { "T3.1",       100L,       true,    DISCOUNT },
18      { "T3.2",       200L,       true,    DISCOUNT },
19      { "T4.1",        43L,       true,    FULLPRICE },
20      { "T5.1",        93L,       true,    DISCOUNT }
21    };
22
23    @DataProvider(name = "testset1")
24    public Object[][] getTestData() {
25       return testData1;
26    }
27
28    @Test(dataProvider = "testset1")
29    public void test_giveDiscount( String id, long bonusPoints,
           boolean goldCustomer, Status expected) {
30       assertEquals( OnlineSales.giveDiscount(bonusPoints,
           goldCustomer), expected );
31    }
32
33 }
```

6.3.2 Test Results

The results of running the full set of tests (equivalence partition, BVA, decision tables, statement coverage, and branch coverage) against Fault 5 is shown in Figure 6.4.

```
PASSED: test_giveDiscount("T1.1", 40, true, FULLPRICE)
PASSED: test_giveDiscount("T1.2", 100, false, FULLPRICE)
PASSED: test_giveDiscount("T1.3", 200, false, DISCOUNT)
PASSED: test_giveDiscount("T1.4", -100, false, ERROR)
PASSED: test_giveDiscount("T2.1", 1, true, FULLPRICE)
PASSED: test_giveDiscount("T2.2", 80, false, FULLPRICE)
PASSED: test_giveDiscount("T2.3", 81, false, FULLPRICE)
PASSED: test_giveDiscount("T2.4", 120, false, FULLPRICE)
PASSED: test_giveDiscount("T2.5", 121, false, DISCOUNT)
PASSED: test_giveDiscount("T2.6", 9223372036854775807, false, DISCOUNT)
PASSED: test_giveDiscount("T2.7", -9223372036854775808, false, ERROR)
PASSED: test_giveDiscount("T2.8", 0, false, ERROR)
PASSED: test_giveDiscount("T3.1", 100, true, DISCOUNT)
PASSED: test_giveDiscount("T3.2", 200, true, DISCOUNT)
PASSED: test_giveDiscount("T4.1", 43, true, FULLPRICE)
FAILED: test_giveDiscount("T5.1", 93, true, DISCOUNT)
java.lang.AssertionError: expected [DISCOUNT] but found [FULLPRICE]
===============================================
Command line suite
Total tests run: 16, Passes: 15, Failures: 1, Skips: 0
===============================================
```

Figure 6.4 Branch coverage test results for giveDiscount() with Fault 5.

Test T5.1 fails, indicating that the fault in the code (Fault 5) has been found by the full branch coverage tests. The test coverage results are shown in Figure 6.5.

Figure 6.5 Branch coverage test coverage summary for giveDiscount() with Fault 5.

Full branch coverage has been achieved – there are no missed branches. The source code report identifies that all the branches have been taken, as shown in Figure 6.6,

Figure 6.6 Branch coverage test coverage details for giveDiscount() with Fault 5.

where all the fully executed lines are marked in light grey (green on the screen). In the following chapters we will not show the detailed source code coverage report when the summary report shows full coverage.

6.4 Branch Coverage in More Detail

6.4.1 Fault Model

The branch coverage fault model is where branches that have not been taken in previous tests (untaken branches) may contain a fault. As for statement coverage, these tend to be associated with edge cases or other unusual circumstances.

Branch coverage tests with input values carefully selected to ensure that every branch is taken during test execution. These tests attempt to find faults associated with individual branches in the source code.

6.4.2 Description

As with many forms of testing, there is more than one approach. In this book we use a tool to measure the branch coverage of the previously developed tests, and only develop new tests to complete the branch coverage. This is the approach most commonly used in practice.

However, there are alternative approaches:

- As we have seen, JaCoCo counts the outcome of each Boolean condition as a branch. The tester might select a different tool that counts the outcomes of each decision as branches instead. This would reduce the number of branches, which leads to slightly reduced test effectiveness. However, the tester must work with the tools that are available. See the discussion on decision coverage and condition coverage in Sections 8.3.2 and 8.3.3.
- The branches in the code may be identified from scratch without considering any of the previously written tests. This involves developing a control-flow graph[4] of the program, and then identifying all the edges in the graph as branches. In this approach, the decisions themselves (and not the Boolean expressions) are invariably used. Many books demonstrate this approach, but it is seldom used in practice for two reasons. First, it is very time-consuming to develop the control-flow graph for code of any significant length. Second, if the code is changed, either to fix a fault or add new features, the control-flow graph will have to be reviewed and possibly re-done, and the associated test implementation redeveloped. The rapid change of code in a modern, Agile development environment makes this approach less realistic than the approach shown in this book.

[4] Chapter 7 shows how to do this.

6.4.3   Goal

The goal of branch coverage is to make sure that every branch in the source code has been taken during testing. The ideal test completion criteria is 100% branch coverage.

Note that a branch is based on the evaluation of a Boolean expression, which can evaluate to `true` or `false`. A decision may be simple or compound. A simple decision contains a single Boolean expression, or *Boolean condition*, with no Boolean operators. A compound decision contains multiple Boolean conditions connected by Boolean operators. An example of each is shown in Snippet 6.1.

Snippet 6.1 Decisions and Boolean conditions

```
1    int f(int x, boolean special) {
2        int z = x;
3        if (x < 0)
4            z = -1;
5        else if ( x > 100 || (x > 50 && special) )
6            z = 100;
7        return z;
8    }
```

Line 3 contains a simple decision, with a single Boolean condition:

- $(x< 0)$

There are two associated branches:

- from line 3 to line 4 when x is less than 0;
- from line 3 to line 5 when x is not less than 0.

Line 5 contains a compound decision, with three Boolean conditions:

- $x > 100$
- $x > 50$
- special

There are six associated branches.

- the `true` outcome of $(x > 100)$: branch from line 5 to line 6 (short-circuit evaluation[5]);
- the `false` outcome of $(x > 100)$: branch to the next Boolean condition $(x > 50)$;
- the `true` outcome of $(x > 50)$: branch to the next Boolean condition (special);
- the `false` outcome of $(x > 50)$: branch from line 5 to line 7 (short-circuit evaluation);

---

[5] Short-circuit or lazy evaluation occurs when the evaluation of one Boolean condition means that subsequent Boolean conditions do not need to be evaluated – the result can be short-circuited.

- the `true` outcome of (`special`): branch from line 5 to line 6;
- The `false` outcome of (`special`): branch from line 5 to line 7.

6.4.4 Analysis: Identifying Untaken Branches

The results of the coverage tool are usually used to identify statements with untaken branches. Generally it is straightforward to do this by identifying any unexecuted lines, getting the count of untaken branches, and considering the test data.

6.4.5 Test Coverage Item

Each branch in the source code is a TCI.

6.4.6 Test Cases

Test cases are developed with test data selected to ensure that every branch is executed. The expected results *must* come from the specification. As for all white-box testing, it is very easy to make the mistake of reading this from the code, and the tester must be careful to avoid doing this.

6.5 Evaluation

Branch coverage has uncovered Fault 5 inserted into the method `giveDiscount ()`.

6.5.1 Limitations

Some benefits and limitations of branch coverage are now explored by making changes to *inject* faults into the original (correct) source code.

Fault 6

A new fault is inserted to demonstrate some limitations of branch coverage testing. The entire processing of the method is rewritten, as shown in lines 24–38 in Listing 6.3. This creates a path through the code that is not taken with any of the existing branch coverage test data.

Listing 6.3 Fault 6.

```
22    public static Status giveDiscount(long bonusPoints, boolean
              goldCustomer)
23    {
24        Status rv = ERROR;
25        long threshold = goldCustomer?80:120;
26        long thresholdJump = goldCustomer?20:30;
27
28        if (bonusPoints > 0) {
```

```
29              if (bonusPoints < thresholdJump)
30                  bonusPoints -= threshold;
31              if (bonusPoints > thresholdJump)
32                  bonusPoints -= threshold;
33              bonusPoints += 4 * (thresholdJump);
34              if (bonusPoints > threshold)
35                  rv = DISCOUNT;
36              else
37                  rv = FULLPRICE;
38          }
39
40      return rv;
41  }
```

BC Testing against Fault 6

The results of running the equivalence partition, BVA, decision tables, statement coverage, and branch coverage tests against this modification are shown in Figure 6.7.

```
PASSED: test_giveDiscount("T1.1", 40, true, FULLPRICE)
PASSED: test_giveDiscount("T1.2", 100, false, FULLPRICE)
PASSED: test_giveDiscount("T1.3", 200, false, DISCOUNT)
PASSED: test_giveDiscount("T1.4", -100, false, ERROR)
PASSED: test_giveDiscount("T2.1", 1, true, FULLPRICE)
PASSED: test_giveDiscount("T2.2", 80, false, FULLPRICE)
PASSED: test_giveDiscount("T2.3", 81, false, FULLPRICE)
PASSED: test_giveDiscount("T2.4", 120, false, FULLPRICE)
PASSED: test_giveDiscount("T2.5", 121, false, DISCOUNT)
PASSED: test_giveDiscount("T2.6", 9223372036854775807, false, DISCOUNT)
PASSED: test_giveDiscount("T2.7", -9223372036854775808, false, ERROR)
PASSED: test_giveDiscount("T2.8", 0, false, ERROR)
PASSED: test_giveDiscount("T3.1", 100, true, DISCOUNT)
PASSED: test_giveDiscount("T3.2", 200, true, DISCOUNT)
PASSED: test_giveDiscount("T4.1", 43, true, FULLPRICE)
PASSED: test_giveDiscount("T5.1", 93, true, DISCOUNT)
=================================================
Command line suite
Total tests run: 16, Passes: 16, Failures: 0, Skips: 0
=================================================
```

Figure 6.7 Branch coverage test results for `giveDiscount()` with Fault 6.

All the tests have passed – the fault has not been found. This is to be expected as (a) the inserted fault bears no relationship to the specification and is unlikely to be found by any black-box test technique, and (b) the fault is not revealed by achieving either statement coverage or branch coverage of the code.

The tests provide full statement and branch coverage, as shown in Figure 6.8. Tests T4.1 and T5.1 (see Figure 6.7) are in fact redundant for this version of the code – the code has been changed, and these tests are no longer required to achieve statement or branch coverage.

Element	Missed Instructions ▾	Cov. ⬦	Missed Branches ⬦	Cov. ⬦	Missed ⬦	Cxty ⬦	Missed ⬦	Lines ⬦	Missed ⬦	Methods ⬦
● OnlineSales()	▬	0%		n/a	1	1	1	1	1	1
● giveDiscount(long, boolean)	▬▬▬▬▬▬	100%	▬▬▬▬▬▬▬	100%	0	5	0	9	0	1
Total	3 of 30	90%	0 of 8	100%	1	6	1	10	1	2

Figure 6.8 Branch coverage test coverage summary for `giveDiscount()` with Fault 6.

Demonstrating the Fault

The results of executing the code with Fault 6, using specially selected input values, are shown in Figure 6.9. Note that the wrong result is returned for both the inputs (20, `true`) and (30, `false`). The correct result is `FULLPRICE` in both cases.

```
$ check 20 true
DISCOUNT
$ check 30 false
DISCOUNT
```

Figure 6.9 Manual demonstration of Fault 6.

6.5.2 Strengths and Weaknesses

Branch coverage ensures that each output path from each Boolean condition (each decision at source level) is taken at least once during testing. Note that 100% branch coverage guarantees 100% statement coverage – but the test data is harder to generate. Branch coverage is a stronger form of testing than statement coverage, but it still does not exercise either all the reasons for taking each branch, or combinations of different branches taken.

Strengths

- It resolves the *NULL else* problem – branch coverage testing makes sure that both the `true` and `false` outcomes are covered in testing.

Weaknesses

- It can be difficult to determine the required input parameter values.
- If the tool only counts decisions as branches, or if a control-flow graph has been manually developed, then it is undemanding of compound decisions. In these cases it does not explore all the different reasons (i.e. the Boolean conditions) for the decision evaluating as `true` or `false`.

Branch coverage, like statement coverage, is usually used as a supplementary measure of black-box testing – mainly because it is easy to measure automatically.

If black-box testing does not result in the required coverage – normally 100% – then this white-box technique can be used to increase the coverage to the required level.

6.6   Key Points

- Branch coverage is used to augment black-box and statement coverage testing, by ensuring that every branch is taken.
- Test cases are based on untaken branches.
- Input values for the test data are selected by analysis of the decisions/Boolean conditions in the code.

6.7   Notes for Experienced Testers

The experienced tester will use the type of branch coverage as measured by the tools they use (at the decision level or at the Boolean condition level). Analysis of the code to determine the values needed to cause each branch to execute will usually be done in the tester's mind. Perhaps a comment will also be added to the test code to identify branches that cannot be taken. As discussed previously, if an audit trail is not maintained by the tester, then the design process cannot be easily reviewed.

In advanced testing, exception coverage can be regarded as a form of branch coverage. Each exception raised and caught is regarded as a branch.

As with all white-box testing, tests that achieve full branch coverage will often become outdated by changes to the code. The experienced tester may, however, leave these tests in the code as extra tests.

Developing tests to achieve full branch coverage is practically impossible in code of any significant size. The experienced tester will focus these tests just on the critical code.

7   All Paths Coverage

This chapter introduces all paths coverage testing, which is the strongest form of white-box testing based on the program structure.[1] All the paths, from entry to exit of a block of code (usually a method, the test item), are executed during testing.

Developing all paths tests is complex and time-consuming. In practice it is seldom used and would only be considered for critical software. However, as the strongest form of testing based on program structure, it is of theoretical importance, and is an important element in the body of knowledge for software testing.

In statement and branch testing, control-flow graphs (CFGs) are seldom used in practice. Tests can be more efficiently developed to supplement black-box tests, as shown in the previous chapters, using automated tools to measure the coverage. However, in all paths testing, CFGs are essential. This chapter provides an understanding of how to develop and use them.

7.1   Testing with All Paths Coverage

A path is a sequence of the statements executed during a single run of a block of code. All paths coverage refers to execution of all the paths that start on the first statement and end on the last statement of the block of code, also referred to as an *end-to-end path*. The paths are usually identified at the source-code level.

In order to identify these paths, a graph is produced and provides a simplified representation of the code. This is referred to as CFG. Once the CFG has been developed, then all the end-to-end paths are identified and test data developed to cause these paths to be executed. Identifying the paths directly from the source code takes experience, and is usually only achievable for smaller sections of code.

Definition: an end-to-end path is a single flow of execution from the start to the end of a section of code. This path may include multiple executions of any loops on the path.

---

[1] If all paths coverage has been achieved, then coverage has also been achieved for all other forms, including statement and branch coverage. Both are discussed in previous chapters.

7.2   Example

The source code for `giveDiscount` with Fault 6, which was not found by the previous test techniques, is repeated for reference in Listing 7.1.

Listing 7.1 Fault 6.

```
22    public static Status giveDiscount(long bonusPoints, boolean
             goldCustomer)
23    {
24        Status rv = ERROR;
25        long threshold = goldCustomer?80:120;
26        long thresholdJump = goldCustomer?20:30;
27
28        if (bonusPoints > 0) {
29            if (bonusPoints < thresholdJump)
30                bonusPoints -= threshold;
31            if (bonusPoints > thresholdJump)
32                bonusPoints -= threshold;
33            bonusPoints += 4 * (thresholdJump);
34            if (bonusPoints > threshold)
35                rv = DISCOUNT;
36            else
37                rv = FULLPRICE;
38        }
39
40        return rv;
41    }
```

The method contains paths through the code not taken by the tests to date. One of these paths is faulty, and it takes a systematic approach to identify and test every path.

7.2.1   Code Analysis

Unlike for statement and branch testing, no tools exist to identify path coverage in anything but the simplest of examples. Thus, we will develop an abstract representation of the program in the form of a graph and use that to identify the end-to-end paths.

Control Flow Graphs

A CFG is a directed graph showing the flow of control through a segment of code. These are mainly used to represent code at the source-code level. Each node in the graph represents one or more indivisible statements in the source code. Each edge represents a jump or branch in the flow of control. A node with two exits represents a block of code terminating in a decision, with `true` and `false` exits (such as an *if* statement).

The CFG is language-independent, and provides a simplified model of the source code. This allows sequential blocks of code, branches, and paths to be easily identified.

Development of the CFG

The CFG is developed systematically, starting at the beginning of the code and working down until all the code has been incorporated into the CFG. Where possible, to maintain consistency, `true` branches are placed on the right and `false` branches on the left. The steps in the development of the CFG for this example are shown below:

1. The CFG starts with the entry point (line 22). From here, the code always executes to line 28. Lines 22–28 form a block of indivisible statements,[2] so this is represented by a single node, labelled (22..28) (Figure 7.1). It is recommended that you label the nodes with the line numbers they contain – it is much more informative than just numbering the nodes 1, 2, 3, etc. Remember that each node must represent an indivisible block of code (containing no branches).

Figure 7.1 CFG stage 0.

2. On line 28, if the decision (`bonusPoints > 0`) is `true`, then control branches to line 29. If not, the control branches to line 38. This is shown in Figure 7.2. A quick inspection of the code shows that there are no jumps between lines 38 and 41, so this node is labelled 38..41. The expression `bonusPoints > 0` shows the expression that must be `true` to take the right-hand branch.

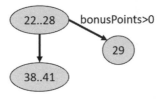

Figure 7.2 CFG stage 1.

3. On line 29, if the decision (`bonusPoints < thresholdJump`) is `true`, then control branches to line 30. Otherwise, control branches to line 31. After line 30, control always goes to line 31 (Figure 7.3).

---

[2] At the source-code level, the ternary conditional operator ('? :'), often referred to as the question-mark-colon operator, is regarded as a single line of code.

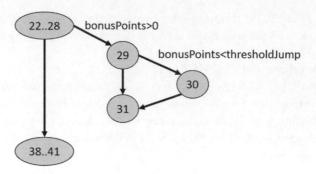

Figure 7.3 CFG stage 2.

4.   On line 31, if the decision (bonusPoints > thresholdJump) is true, then control branches to line 32. Otherwise control branches to line 33, this first line in node 33..34. After line 32, control always goes to line 33 (Figure 7.4).

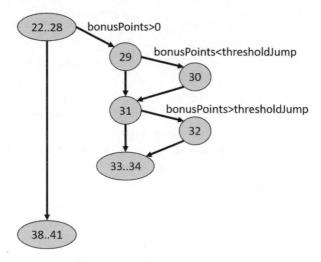

Figure 7.4 CFG stage 3.

5.   On line 34, if the decision (bonusPoints>threshold) is true, then control branches to line 35. Otherwise, control branches to line 36 (Figure 7.5).
6.   After line 37, control always passes to line 38. This is also the case for line 35 (Figure 7.6). This completes the CFG.

Identifying the Candidate Paths
By tracing all the start-to-end paths through the CFG, the candidate paths can be identified. These are candidate paths: not of them are logically possible to take. A systematic approach must be taken to avoid missing paths. Working through

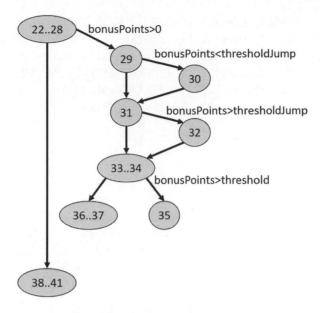

Figure 7.5 CFG stage 4.

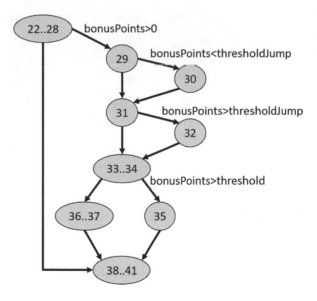

Figure 7.6 CFG for giveDiscount() with Fault 6.

the CFG, starting at the top and taking the left-hand branches first, identifies the following paths:

1.   Path 1, nodes (22..28)–(38..41)
2.   Path 2, nodes (22..28)–(29)–(31)–(33..34)–(36..37)–(38..41)
3.   Path 3, nodes (22..28)–(29)–(31)–(33..34)–(35)–(38..41)

4. Path 4, nodes (22..28)–(29)–(31)–(32)–(33..34)–(36..37)–(38..41)
5. Path 5, nodes (22..28)–(29)–(31)–(32)–(33..34)–(35)–(38..41)
6. Path 6, nodes (22..28)–(29)–(30)–(31)–(33..34)–(36..37)–(38..41)
7. Path 7, nodes (22..28)–(29)–(30)–(31)–(33..34)–(35)–(38..41)
8. Path 8, nodes (22..28)–(29)–(30)–(31)–(32)–(33..34)–(36..37)–(38..41)
9. Path 9, nodes (22..28)–(29)–(30)–(31)–(32)–(33..34)–(35)–(38..41)

These are summarised in Figure 7.7.

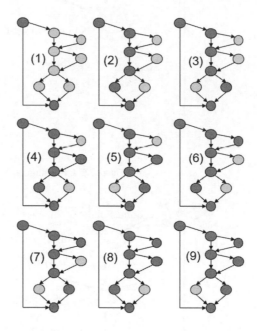

Figure 7.7 End-to-end paths through the CFG.

Identifying the Possible Paths

Not all the paths are logically possible. The possible paths are identified by mentally executing each path in the final CFG (Figure 7.6), following the code at the same time, and working out whether there is any possible input data that follows the path, starting using existing test data. The results of this are shown below (the approach is explained in more detail in Section 7.4.5):

1. Path 1, nodes (22..28)–(38..41)
   covered by `bonusPoints = -100`, and `goldCustomer = false` (T1.4)
2. Path 2, nodes (22..28)–(29)–(31)–(33..34)–(36..37)–(38..41)
   not possible
3. Path 3, nodes (22..28)–(29)–(31)–(33..34)–(35)–(38..41)
   covered by `20, true` or `30, false`

4.   Path 4, nodes (22..28)–(29)–(31)–(32)–(33..34)–(36..37)–(38..41) covered by `1, true` (T2.1)
5.   Path 5, nodes (22..28)–(29)–(31)–(32)–(33..34)–(35)–(38..41) covered by `40, true` (T1.1)
6.   Path 6, nodes (22..28)–(29)–(30)–(31)–(33..34)–(36..37)–(38..41) not possible
7.   Path 7, nodes (22..28)–(29)–(30)–(31)–(33..34)–(35)–(38..41) not possible
8.   Path 8, nodes (22..28)–(29)–(30)–(31)–(32)–(33..34)–(36..37)–(38..41) not possible
9.   Path 9, nodes (22..28)–(29)–(30)–(31)–(32)–(33..34)–(35)–(38..41) not possible

Results of the Analysis

This analysis of the CFG has produced three results:

1. the possible end-to-end paths;
2. where available, existing test data that causes a path to be taken; and
3. where no previous test causes a path to be taken, criteria or values for the new test data.

These results are summarised in Table 7.1.

Table 7.1 Paths and data for `giveDiscount()` with Fault 6.

Path	Input values	Existing test
1	(−100,false)	T1.4
3	(20,true) or (30,false)	New test required
4	(1,true)	T2.1
5	(40,true)	T1.1

7.2.2 Test Coverage Items

The analysis has been done for the version of `giveDiscount()` with Fault 6. Each uncovered path shown in Table 7.1 is a test coverage item (TCI), as shown in Table 7.2.

Table 7.2 All path TCIs for `giveDiscount()` with Fault 6.

TCI	Path	Test case
AP1	Path 3	To be completed

7.2.3 Test Cases

Each path must be tested in a separate test case. The analysis (see Table 7.1) provides criteria for the necessary input data values for each. The data values for the expected results are derived from the specification: the input (20, true) produces the output FULLPRICE.

Table 7.3 All paths test cases for giveDiscount()/Fault 6.

ID	Test cases covered	Inputs		Exp. results
		bonusPoints	goldCustomer	return value
T6.1	AP1	20	true	FULLPRICE

7.2.4   Verification of the Test Cases

Completing the Test Coverage Items Table

Using the data from Table 7.3, the test coverage items table is completed, as shown in Table 7.4.

Table 7.4 Completed all paths TCI table.

TCI	Path	Test case
AP1	Path 4	T6.1

Reviewing Your Work

In this example, we can see from Table 7.4 that the single TCI is covered. Table 7.3 shows the new test case T6.1 required to cover this TCI.

7.3   Test Implementation and Results

7.3.1   Implementation

The full test implementation, including the previously developed equivalence partition, boundary value analysis (BVA), statement coverage, and branch coverage tests, which are necessary to provide full all paths cover, is shown in Listing 7.2.

Listing 7.2 OnlineSalesTest for all paths testing.

```
1   public class OnlineSalesTest {
2
3       private static Object[][] testData1 = new Object[][] {
4           // test, bonusPoints, goldCustomer, expected output
5           { "T1.1",      40L,       true,  FULLPRICE },
6           { "T1.2",     100L,      false,  FULLPRICE },
7           { "T1.3",     200L,      false,   DISCOUNT },
8           { "T1.4",    -100L,      false,      ERROR },
9           { "T2.1",       1L,       true,  FULLPRICE },
10          { "T2.2",      80L,      false,  FULLPRICE },
11          { "T2.3",      81L,      false,  FULLPRICE },
12          { "T2.4",     120L,      false,  FULLPRICE },
```

```
13      { "T2.5",      121L,      false,  DISCOUNT },
14      { "T2.6", Long.MAX_VALUE, false, DISCOUNT },
15      { "T2.7", Long.MIN_VALUE, false, ERROR },
16      { "T2.8",       0L,       false,    ERROR },
17      { "T3.1",      100L,      true,   DISCOUNT },
18      { "T3.2",      200L,      true,   DISCOUNT },
19      { "T4.1",       43L,      true,   FULLPRICE },
20      { "T5.1",       93L,      true,   DISCOUNT },
21      { "T6.1",       20L,      true,   FULLPRICE },
22  };
23
24  @DataProvider(name = "testset1")
25  public Object[][] getTestData() {
26      return testData1;
27  }
28
29  @Test(dataProvider = "testset1")
30  public void test_giveDiscount( String id, long bonusPoints,
          boolean goldCustomer, Status expected) {
31      assertEquals( OnlineSales.giveDiscount(bonusPoints,
          goldCustomer), expected );
32  }
33
34 }
```

7.3.2   Test Results

The results of running the full set of tests (equivalence partition, BVA, decision tables, statement coverage, branch coverage, all paths) against the implementation of giveDiscount() with Fault 6 is shown in Figure 7.8.

```
PASSED: test_giveDiscount("T1.1", 40, true, FULLPRICE)
PASSED: test_giveDiscount("T1.2", 100, false, FULLPRICE)
PASSED: test_giveDiscount("T1.3", 200, false, DISCOUNT)
PASSED: test_giveDiscount("T1.4", -100, false, ERROR)
PASSED: test_giveDiscount("T2.1", 1, true, FULLPRICE)
PASSED: test_giveDiscount("T2.2", 80, false, FULLPRICE)
PASSED: test_giveDiscount("T2.3", 81, false, FULLPRICE)
PASSED: test_giveDiscount("T2.4", 120, false, FULLPRICE)
PASSED: test_giveDiscount("T2.5", 121, false, DISCOUNT)
PASSED: test_giveDiscount("T2.6", 9223372036854775807, false, DISCOUNT)
PASSED: test_giveDiscount("T2.7", -9223372036854775808, false, ERROR)
PASSED: test_giveDiscount("T2.8", 0, false, ERROR)
PASSED: test_giveDiscount("T3.1", 100, true, DISCOUNT)
PASSED: test_giveDiscount("T3.2", 200, true, DISCOUNT)
PASSED: test_giveDiscount("T4.1", 43, true, FULLPRICE)
PASSED: test_giveDiscount("T5.1", 93, true, DISCOUNT)
FAILED: test_giveDiscount("T6.1", 20, true, FULLPRICE)
java.lang.AssertionError: expected [FULLPRICE] but found [DISCOUNT]
===============================================
Command line suite
Total tests run: 17, Passes: 16, Failures: 1, Skips: 0
===============================================
```

Figure 7.8 All paths test results for giveDiscount() with Fault 6.

The fault is found by the new test: T6.1. Note that the previous white-box tests (T4.1, T5.1) have been invalidated by changing the code – there is no guarantee that the statement coverage and branch coverage tests developed for Fault 5 provide full coverage for Fault 6. However, the coverage tool confirms that full statement coverage and branch coverage have still been achieved by these tests. Interestingly, tests T4.1 and T5.1 are redundant, as the equivalence partition, BVA, and decision tables tests also happen to achieve full statement coverage and branch coverage for the version of the code with Fault 6.

Test Results against Correct Implementation

The results of running the full set of tests against the correct implementation (see Figure 2.4) of `giveDiscount()` are shown in Figure 7.9. All the tests have passed. The coverage results are shown in Figure 7.10.

```
PASSED: test_giveDiscount("T1.1", 40, true, FULLPRICE)
PASSED: test_giveDiscount("T1.2", 100, false, FULLPRICE)
PASSED: test_giveDiscount("T1.3", 200, false, DISCOUNT)
PASSED: test_giveDiscount("T1.4", -100, false, ERROR)
PASSED: test_giveDiscount("T2.1", 1, true, FULLPRICE)
PASSED: test_giveDiscount("T2.2", 80, false, FULLPRICE)
PASSED: test_giveDiscount("T2.3", 81, false, FULLPRICE)
PASSED: test_giveDiscount("T2.4", 120, false, FULLPRICE)
PASSED: test_giveDiscount("T2.5", 121, false, DISCOUNT)
PASSED: test_giveDiscount("T2.6", 9223372036854775807, false, DISCOUNT)
PASSED: test_giveDiscount("T2.7", -9223372036854775808, false, ERROR)
PASSED: test_giveDiscount("T2.8", 0, false, ERROR)
PASSED: test_giveDiscount("T3.1", 100, true, DISCOUNT)
PASSED: test_giveDiscount("T3.2", 200, true, DISCOUNT)
PASSED: test_giveDiscount("T4.1", 43, true, FULLPRICE)
PASSED: test_giveDiscount("T5.1", 93, true, DISCOUNT)
PASSED: test_giveDiscount("T6.1", 20, true, FULLPRICE)
=================================================
Command line suite
Total tests run: 17, Passes: 17, Failures: 0, Skips: 0
=================================================
```

Figure 7.9 All paths test results for `giveDiscount()`.

Element	Missed Instructions	Cov.	Missed Branches	Cov.	Missed	Cxty	Missed	Lines	Missed	Methods
OnlineSales()		0%		n/a	1	1	1	1	1	1
giveDiscount(long, boolean)		100%		100%	0	4	0	9	0	1
Total	3 of 26	88%	0 of 6	100%	1	5	1	10	1	2

Figure 7.10 All paths test coverage summary for `giveDiscount()`.

These confirm that full statement coverage and branch coverage have been achieved. A manual analysis would be required to confirm that the four possible end-to-end paths have also been executed, providing 100% all paths coverage.[3]

7.4   All Paths Coverage Testing in More Detail

7.4.1   Fault Model

The all paths fault model is where a particular sequence of operations, reflected by a particular path through the code, does not produce the correct result. These faults are often associated with complex or deeply nested code structures, where the wrong functionality is executed for a specific situation.

By testing every end-to-end path at least once, all paths testing attempts to find these faults.

7.4.2   Description

All paths testing causes every possible path from entry to exit of the program to be taken during test execution. By inspection of the code, input data is selected to cause execution of every path. Expected results are derived from the specification.

7.4.3   Analysis: Developing Control-Flow Graphs

A CFG is a directed graph, used to model a block of code. The nodes represent lines of code, and the edges represent branches between these lines. They are an essential tool in identifying end-to-end paths in a block of code. They display the fundamental structure of the code, allowing paths to be identified independently from the details contained within the code.

Control-flow graphs for the basic programming constructs of sequences, selection (if), selection (if–then–else), and iteration (while and do-while) are shown in Figure 7.11–7.17.[4]

Sequence

In Figure 7.11 the code in lines 1–7 is always executed as a sequence, as there are no branches, so this sequence of code is represented as a single node. The node is referenced by its identifier (1..7).

There is no standard convention for including braces '{' and '}' and other non-executable source code notation, except to be consistent. The benefit of always including the braces is that it is much easier to review CFGs and ensure that no lines have been left out.

---

[3] This might be achieved by tracing the execution of the method giveDiscount () using the debugger.
[4] Most textbooks recommend numbering the nodes sequentially and placing the line numbers outside the node. This makes using the CFGs more difficult, requiring frequent references between different diagrams. In this book, we use the line number(s) as the node identifier.

```
1 int f()
2 {
3       int x,y;
4       x = 10;
5       y = x+3;
6       return y;
7 }
```

(1..7)

Figure 7.11 CFG for sequence.

Selection/If–Then

```
1 int f(int a)
2 {
3       int x=0;
4       if (a>10)
5           x=a;
6       return x;
7 }
```

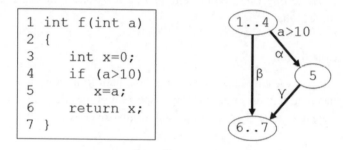

Figure 7.12 CFG for selection (if–then).

In Figure 7.12, considering the flow of execution in the code, lines 1–4 are executed as a sequence. If the decision on line 4 is `true`, then line 5 is executed next. After line 5, lines 6 and then 7 execute. If the decision on line 4 is `false`, then lines 6 and then 7 execute.

Considering the CFG, node (1..4) executes first. If the decision (a > 10) at the end of node (1..4) is `true`, then control moves to node (5), and then to node (6..7). If the decision at the end of node (1..4) is `false`, then control moves to node (6..7).

This demonstrates how each node in the CFG represents a sequence of one or more lines of code, and how the edges in the CFG reflect the decisions and subsequent branches in the code. Be consistent: always keep the `false` branch on the left and the `true` branch on the right.

If the decisions are included next to the `true` branch, then the CFGs can be used for subsequent analysis without the need to refer back to the source code.

The edges may be annotated, using different symbols to prevent any confusion with either the node identifiers or the decisions. Here, the Greek characters α, β, and γ are used. The edges are not used for any of the techniques included in this book, and will be omitted from future CFG diagrams.

The edge β from node (1..4) to node (6..7) is referred to as a *null-else* statement. This branch is taken if the decision is `false`, but contains no executable code (hence null).

Selection/If–Then–Else

```
1 int f(int a)
2 {
3      int x=0;
4      if (a>10)
5           x=a;
6      else
7           x=-a;
8      return x;
9 }
```

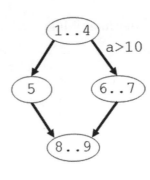

Figure 7.13 CFG for selection (if–then–else).

In Figure 7.13, the code in lines 1–4 is always executed as a sequence, represented by node (1..4). If the decision (a > 10) in node (1..4) evaluates to true, then node (5) is executed, and control moves to node (8..9). If the decision in node (1..4) evaluates to false, then node (6..7) is executed, and control moves to node (8..9).

Selection/Switch

In Figure 7.14, a previous block of code ending on line 1 is executed as a sequence, node (1). Depending on the value of *a*, control then jumps to either node (2..4), node (5..7), or node (8..10). The lines in node (2..4) execute as a sequence, and control moves to node (11). The lines in node (5..7) execute as a sequence, and control moves

```
   . . .
1 switch (a) {
2      case 0:
3           b=33;
4           break
5      case 1:
6           b=-44;
7           break;
8      default:
9           ok=false;
10          break;
11 }
   . . .
```

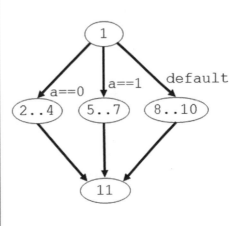

Figure 7.14 CFG for selection (switch).

to node (11). The lines in node (8..10) execute as a sequence, and control moves to node (11).

Iteration/While

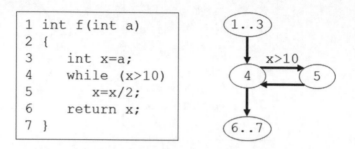

```
1 int f(int a)
2 {
3     int x=a;
4     while (x>10)
5         x=x/2;
6     return x;
7 }
```

Figure 7.15 CFG for iteration (while).

In Figure 7.15, the code in lines 1–3 is always executed as a sequence – node (1..3). The *while* statement must be in its own node as the decision is evaluated every time through the loop; compare this with the *if* statement in node (1..4) in Figure 7.12.

If the decision (x > 10) in node (4) evaluates to true, then node (5) is executed, and then control returns to node (4), where the decision is re-evaluated. If the decision in node (4) evaluates to false, on the first or any subsequent iteration, then the loop exits, and control jumps to node (6..7).

Iteration/Do-While

```
1 int f(int a)
2 {
3     int x=a;
4     do {
5         x=x/2;
6     } while (x>10);
7     return x;
8 }
```

Figure 7.16 CFG for iteration (do-while).

In Figure 7.16, the code in lines 1–3 is always executed as a sequence, node (1..3). The body of the do-while loop is then executed, node (4..5). If the decision (x > 10) in node (6) evaluates to true, then control jumps back to node (4..5). If the decision in node (6) evaluates to false, then control jumps to node (7..8).

Note the difference in structure from the previous example. The decision is evaluated after each execution of the loop, not before.

Iteration/For

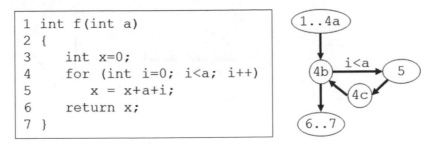

```
1 int f(int a)
2 {
3     int x=0;
4     for (int i=0; i<a; i++)
5         x = x+a+i;
6     return x;
7 }
```

Figure 7.17 CFG for iteration (for).

In Figure 7.17, line 4 contains three separate parts, and must be divided into three sub-lines as follows:

4a   int i = 0;
4b   i<a
4c   i++

The code in lines 1–3, followed by the first part of the for-loop (line 4a), is always executed as a sequence, node (1..4a). The decision (i < a) in the for-loop, in node (4b), is then evaluated. If true, then the body of the for-loop, on node (5), is then executed, followed by the for-loop increment in node (4c). Control then returns to re-evaluating the decision in node (4a). When the decision in node (4b) evaluates to false, then node (6) is executed next.

Multiple Statements on One Line

Real code often has lines that contain multiple statements. As in the for-loop example, these are handled by breaking down the line into sub-lines. Two examples are shown below.

```
1 int f()
2 {
3   int x=10; int y=x+3; return y;
4 }
```
(1..4)

Figure 7.18 Sequence with multiple statements on one line.

In Figure 7.18, the code on lines 1–4 are always executed as a sequence. This means that the multiple statements on line 3 can be ignored from a CFG viewpoint, as shown in the CFG which represents this sequence as a single node (1..4).

In Figure 7.19, the code on line 4 contains two statements that do not form an indivisible sequence, and must be divided into two sub-lines as follows:

4a   if (a > 10)
4b   x = a;

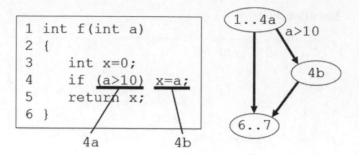

Figure 7.19 Selection with multiple statements on one line.

Lines 1–4a are executed as a sequence, node (1..4a). Then, if the decision (a > 10) on line 4a/node (4a) is `true`, line 4b/node (4b) is executed, followed by lines 6 and 7, node (6..7). Then, if the decision on line 4a/node (4a) is `false`, control passes directly to lines 6 and 7, node (6..7).

7.4.4   Analysis: Identifying End-to-End Paths

Instead of considering a program as being constructed from the individual statements (shown connected by branches in a CFG), a program can also be considered as being constructed from a number of paths from start to finish.

The only complexity is in handling loops: a path that makes i iterations through a loop is considered to be distinct from a path that makes $i + 1$ iterations through the loop, even if the same nodes in the CFG are visited in both iterations. Most programs, therefore, have a very large number of paths.

It is easier to base the paths on the CFG than the original source code: each path is represented by a sequence of the nodes visited. Consider the source code for a method `condIsNeg(int x, boolean flag)` which returns `true` iff[5] x is negative and the flag is `true`. The code is shown in Listing 7.3.

Listing 7.3 Source code for `condIsNeg()`.

```
1  boolean condIsNeg(int x, boolean flag) {
2      boolean rv = false;
3      if (flag && (x < 0))
4          rv = true;
5      return rv;
6  }
```

The paths for `boolean condIsNeg(int,boolean)` are shown in Figure 7.20.

---

[5] If and only if.

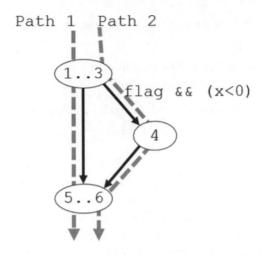

Figure 7.20 Paths for `condIsNeg()`.

The paths for `boolean condIsNeg(int,boolean)` can be documented by listing the nodes executed for each path as follows:

> Path 1: Nodes: (1..3)→(5..6)
> Path 2: Nodes: (1..3)→(4)→(5..6)

Loops and Paths

Loops introduce an extra level of complexity. Consider the simple loop shown in Figure 7.21.

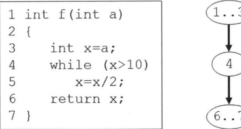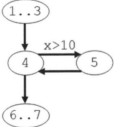

```
1 int f(int a)
2 {
3     int x=a;
4     while (x>10)
5         x=x/2;
6     return x;
7 }
```

Figure 7.21 Paths with iterations.

There are a very large number of possible end-to-end paths through this code:

1.   Nodes: (1..3)→(4)→(6..7)
2.   Nodes: (1..3)→(4)→(5)→(4)→(6..7)
3.   Nodes: (1..3)→(4)→(5)→(4)→(5)→(4)→(6..7)
4.   . . .

To reduce the large number of different paths where loops are involved, equivalence classes of paths are selected. For the purposes of testing, two paths are considered equivalent if they differ only in the number of loop iterations. This gives two classes of loops:

- ones with 0 iterations; and
- ones with n iterations ($n > 0$).

The number of start-to-finish paths, and the nodes on each path, can be calculated using the technique of *basis paths*.

Basis Paths

The flow of control through a CFG can be represented by a regular expression. The expression is then evaluated to give the number of end-to-end paths. Loops can be executed an indefinite number of times: this is resolved by treating them as code segments that can be executed exactly zero or one times.

There are three operators defined for the regular expression:

- . *concatenation* – this represents a sequence of nodes in the graph;
- + *selection* – this represents a decision in the graph (e.g. the if statement);
- ()* *iteration* – this represents a repetition in the graph (e.g. the while statement).

Consider the following example:

```
1    i = 0;
2    while (i < list.length) {
3        if (list[i] == target)
4            match++;
5        else
6            mismatch++;
7        i++;
8    }
```

This is represented by the CFG in Figure 7.22.

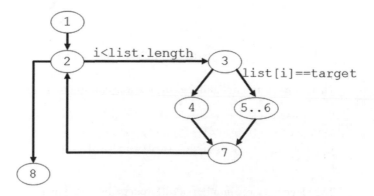

Figure 7.22 CFG for basis paths example.

This CFG can be represented by the following regular expression, where the numbers are the nodes shown in Figure 7.22, using the operators described before:

$$1 \cdot 2 \cdot (3 \cdot (4 + (5..6)) \cdot 7 \cdot 2)^* \cdot 8$$

The loops are simplified by replacing $(expression)^*$ with $(expression + 0)$, representing the two equivalence paths, one with a single iteration through the loop *expression*, and one with no iterations, where 0 represents the *null* statement. This gives:

$$1 \cdot 2 \cdot ((3 \cdot (4 + (5..6)) \cdot 7 \cdot 2) + 0) \cdot 8$$

This can be described as node 1 followed by 2 followed by either 3 followed by either 4 or 5..6 followed by 7 followed by 2, or null, followed by 8. Expanding this, where the + symbol represents alternatives, gives the following paths:

    Alternative 1. 1–2–8
    Alternative 2. 1–2–3–4–7–2–8
    Alternative 3. 1–2–3–(5..6)–7–2–8

By replacing each of the node numbers (and nulls) by the value 1, and then evaluating the expression as a mathematical formula (using + for addition and · for multiplication), the number of paths can be calculated as follows:

$$paths = 1 \cdot 1 \cdot ((1 \cdot (1 + 1) \cdot 1 \cdot 1) + 1) \cdot 1 = 3$$

In practice the paths can often be identified by hand without using this technique.

Note: for *null-else* statements, where there is an *if* with no *else*, the expression $(n + 0)$ is used. The node n represents the `true` decision, and the node 0 represents the *null* else decision.

7.4.5   The Possible Paths in Fault 6

The possible paths are identified by mentally executing each path in the final CFG (Figure 7.6), following the code in parallel to understand the processing, and identifying the input data constraints at each decision point required to follow the selected path.

If conflicting constraints are found, then that path is impossible. Otherwise, input data can be selected that matches the constraints. If possible, data values, and combinations of values from previous tests are used (refer to Listing 3.1), so that duplicate tests can be easily identified and eliminated.

- **Path 1**
  Nodes: (22..28)→(38..41): these must be in the correct sequence

    –   Branch (22..29)→(38..41): requires (`bonusPoints > 0`) to be `false`

Therefore, bonusPoints must be zero or negative.

Test T1.4 meets this condition with the input values (-100, false)

- **Path 2**

  Nodes: (22..28)→(29)→(31)→(33..34)→(36..37)→(38..41)

  - Branch (22..29)→(29): requires (bonusPoints > 0)
  - Branch (29)→(31): requires (bonusPoints < thresholdJump) to be false
  - Branch (31)→(33..34): requires (bonusPoints > thresholdJump) to be false
  - Branch (33..34)→(36..37): requires (bonusPoints > threshold) to be false

The input bonusPoints must be greater than or equal to zero on entry. At node (29) it must be greater than or equal to thresholdJump (20 or 30, depending on goldCustomer).

At node (31) it must be less than or equal to thresholdJump. This implies that bonusPoints must be equal to thresholdJump.

On node (33) the value is increased by 4 * thresholdJump, that is by 80 or 120.

So if the inputs are goldCustomer is true and bonusPoints equals 20, then on node (34) bonusPoints is modified to 100, which is greater than the threshold (80).

If the inputs are goldCustomer is false and bonusPoints equals 30, then on node (34) bonusPoints is modified to 150, which is greater than the threshold (120).

In both cases, the decision at node (34) will be true, but the required value for this path is false. Thus, the path is impossible.

- **Path 3** Nodes: (22..28)→(29)→(31)→(33..34)→(35)→(38..41)

  - Branch (22..29)→(29): requires (bonusPoints > 0)
  - Branch (29)→(31): requires (bonusPoints < thresholdJump) to be false
  - Branch (31)→(33..34): requires (bonusPoints > thresholdJump) to be false
  - Branch (33..34)→(35): requires (bonusPoints > threshold)

The input bonusPoints must be greater than or equal to zero on entry. At node (29) it must be greater than or equal to thresholdJump (20 or 30, depending on goldCustomer).

At node (31) it must be less than or equal to thresholdJump. This implies that bonusPoints must be equal to thresholdJump.

On node (33) the value is increased by 4 * thresholdJump, that is by 80 or 120.

So if the inputs are goldCustomer is true and bonusPoints equals 20, then on node (34) bonusPoints is modified to 100, which is greater than the threshold (80).

If the inputs are `goldCustomer` is `false` and `bonusPoints` equals 30, then on node (34) `bonusPoints` is modified to 150, which is greater than the threshold (120).

In both cases, the decision at node (34) will be `true` as required. None of the existsing tests have either 20 or 30 as input values for `bonusPoints`, so a new test is required. The input data may be either (`20`, `true`) or (`30`, `false`).

- **Path 4** Nodes: (22..28)→(29)→(31)→(32)→(33..34)→(36..37)→(38..41)

    – Branch (22..28)→(29): requires (`bonusPoints > 0`)
    – Branch (29)→(31): requires (`bonusPoints < thresholdJump`) to be `false`
    – Branch (31)→(32): requires (`bonusPoints > thresholdJump`) – note that node (32) modifies `bonusPoints`
    – Branch (33..34)→(36..37): requires (`modified bonusPoints > threshold`) to be `false`

The input `bonusPoints` must be greater than or equal to zero on entry. At node (29) it must be greater than or equal to `thresholdJump` (20 or 30, depending on `goldCustomer`).

At node (31), `bonusPoints` must be greater than `thresholdJump` (20 or 30).

Therefore, `bonusPoints` must be greater than zero, greater than or equal to `thresholdJump` (20 or 30) at node (29), and greater than `thresholdJump` at node (31).

At node (32), the value of `bonusPoints` is reduced by `thresholdJump`, and at node (33..34) this value is increased by 4 `*` `thresholdJump`, that is by 80 or 120.

So if the inputs are `goldCustomer` is `true` and `bonusPoints` is greater than 20, then on node (30) `bonusPoints` is reduced by 20, and at (33..34) `bonusPoints` is increased by 80, giving an overall change of +60 to the value. The value must be less than or equal to 80 here, so the minimum value of `bonusPoints` is 1, and the maximum is 20.

If the inputs are `goldCustomer` is `false` and `bonusPoints` equals 30, then on node (30) `bonusPoints` is reduced by 30, and at (33..34) `bonusPoints` is increased by 120, giving an overall change of +90 to the value. The value must be less than or equal to 120 here, so the minimum value of `bonusPoints` is 1, and the maximum is 30.

Test T2.1 matches these constraints, with the input values (`1`, `true`).

- **Path 5** Nodes: (22..28)→(29)→(31)→(32)→(33..34)→(35)→(38..41)

    – Branch (22..28)→(29): requires (`bonusPoints > 0`)
    – Branch (29)→(31): requires (`bonusPoints > thresholdJump`) to be `false`
    – Branch (31)→(32): requires (`bonusPoints < thresholdJump`) – note that node (32) modifies `bonusPoints`
    – Branch (32)→(33..34) is always taken

- Branch (33..34)→(35): requires (modified bonusPoints > threshold)

The input bonusPoints must be greater than or equal to zero on entry. At node (29) it must be greater than or equal to thresholdJump (20 or 30, depending on goldCustomer).

At node (31), bonusPoints must be greater than thresholdJump (20 or 30).

Therefore, bonusPoints must be greater than zero, greater than or equal to thresholdJump (20 or 30) at node (29), and greater than threshold Jump at node (31).

At node (32), the value of bonusPoints is reduced by thresholdJump, and at node (33..34) this value is increased by 4 * thresholdJump, that is by 80 or 120.

So if the inputs are goldCustomer is true and bonusPoints is greater than 20, then on node (30), bonusPoints is reduced by 20, and at (34) bonusPoints is increased by 80, giving an overall change of +60 to the value at node (35). The value must be greater than 80 here, so the minimum value of bonusPoints is 21 and the maximum is large (Long.MAX_VALUE − 60 to be exact).

If the inputs are goldCustomer is false and bonusPoints equals 30, then on node (30) bonusPoints is reduced by 30, and at (34) bonusPoints is increased by 120, giving an overall change of +90 to the value at node (35). The value must be greater 120 here, so the minimum value of bonusPoints is 31, and the maximum again large (Long.MAX_VALUE − 90).

Test T1.1 matches these constraints with the input values (40, true).

- **Path 6** Nodes: (22..28)→(29)→(30)→(31)→(33..34)→(36..37)→(38..41)

  - Branch (22..28)→(29): requires (bonusPoints >0)
  - Branch (29)→(30): requires (bonusPoints < thresholdJump) – note that node (30) modifies bonusPoints
  - Branch (31)→(33..34): requires (modified bonusPoints > thresholdJump) to be false
  - Branch (33..34)→(36..37): requires (modified bonusPoints > threshold) to be false

The input bonusPoints must be greater than or equal to zero on entry. At node (29) it must be less than thresholdJump (20 or 30, depending on goldCustomer).

At node (31), bonusPoints must be less than or equal to threshold Jump (20 or 30).

Therefore, bonusPoints must be greater than zero, less than threshold Jump (20 or 30) at node (29), and less than or equal to thresholdJump at node (31).

At node (30), the value of bonusPoints is reduced by thresholdJump, and at node (33..34) this value is increased by 4 * thresholdJump, that is by 80 or 120.

So if the inputs are goldCustomer is true and bonusPoints less than 20, then on node (30), bonusPoints is reduced by 20, and at (34) bonusPoints is increased by 80, giving an overall change of +60 to the value at node (35). The value must be greater than 80 here, but the maximum value it can have is 59, so this is impossible.

So if the inputs are goldCustomer is false and bonusPoints less than 30, then on node (30), bonusPoints is reduced by 30, and at (34) bonusPoints increased by 120, giving an overall change of +90 to the value at node (35). The value must be greater than 120 here, but the maximum value it can have is 119, so this is also impossible.

- **Path 7** Nodes: (22..28)→(29)→(30)→(31)→(33..34)→(35)→(38..41)

  – Branch (22..28)→(29): requires (bonusPoints > 0)
  – Branch (29)→(30): requires (bonusPoints < thresholdJump) – note that node (30) modifies bonusPoints
  – Branch (31)→(33..34): requires (modified bonusPoints > thresholdJump) to be false
  – Branch (33..34)→(35): requires (modified bonusPoints > threshold)

For any value of bonusPoints, if it is less than thresholdJump (20 or 30) at node (29), then it will always be less than threshold (80 or 120) at node (33..34), so this path is impossible.

- **Path 8** Nodes: (22..28)→(29)→(30)→(31)→(32)→(33..34)→(36..37)→(38..41)

  – Branch (22..28)→(29): requires (bonusPoints > 0)
  – Branch (29)→(30): requires (bonusPoints < thresholdJump) – note that node (30) modifies bonusPoints
  – Branch (31)→(32): requires (bonusPoints > thresholdJump) – note that node (32) modifies bonusPoints
  – Branch (33..34)→(36..37): requires (modified bonusPoints > threshold) to be false

For any value of bonusPoints, it is not possible to have bonusPoints less than thresholdJump at node 30, followed by the modified (reduced) value of bonusPoints greater than thresholdJump at node 31. So this path is impossible.

- **Path 9** Nodes: (22..28)→(29)→(30)→(31)→(32)→(33..34)→(35)→(38..41)

  – Branch (22..28)→(29): requires (bonusPoints > 0)
  – Branch (29)→(30): requires (bonusPoints < thresholdJump) – note that node (30) modifies bonusPoints

–   Branch (31)→(32): requires (bonusPoints > thresholdJump) – note that node (32) modifies bonusPoints

–   Branch (33..34)→(35): requires (modified bonusPoints > threshold)

As for Path 8, for any value of bonusPoints, it is not possible to have bonusPoints less than thresholdJump at node 30, followed by the modified (reduced) value of bonusPoints greater than thresholdJump at node 31. So this path is impossible.

7.4.6   Test Coverage Items

Each unique path from start to finish is a TCI. Remember that the standard technique is for each loop to be in two different paths: one with zero times through the loop, and one with at least one time through the loop.

Each TCI should be given a unique identifier (for example: AP1 for path 1). It is useful, in order to ensure that no paths are missed, to list the edges in the CFG covered by each path.

7.4.7   Test Cases

Data values are selected to ensure that every path is followed. This selection requires the tester to review the code carefully, and select input parameter values that cause these paths to be executed.

The expected results *must* come from the specification. It is very easy to make the mistake of reading the output from the code and using this as the expected results – the tester must be careful to avoid doing this.

Hint: it is usually easier to begin with the simplest path from entry to exit, and by reading the source code work out the required input values required to cause it to be executed. Then examine the source code and see what changes to the inputs are required to cause similar paths to be executed. There should be one test per path.

7.5   Evaluation

Achieving full all paths coverage can be a very tedious exercise. Note that even though every path has been executed, every reason for taking every decision has not.

7.5.1   Limitations

The source code shown in Listing 7.4 contains three types of fault not found (except by chance) by the standard black-box and white-box unit test techniques. The basic algorithm is quite different to that used previously: it uses a lookup table, and searches for a matching entry to determine the return value.

Listing 7.4 Faults 7, 8, and 9.

```
23    public static Status giveDiscount(long bonusPoints, boolean
          goldCustomer)
24    {
25
26        Object[][] lut = new Object[][] {
27            { Long.MIN_VALUE,              0L,   null, ERROR },
28            {               1L,            80L,  true, FULLPRICE },
29            {              81L, Long.MAX_VALUE, true, DISCOUNT },
30            {               1L,           120L, false, FULLPRICE },
31            {             121L, Long.MAX_VALUE, false, DISCOUNT },
32            {            1024L,          1024L, true, FULLPRICE
              },//Fault 7
33        };
34
35        Status rv = ERROR;
36
37        bonusPoints & = 0xFFFFFFFFFFFFFEFFL; // Fault 8
38
39        for (Object[] row:lut)
40            if ( (bonusPoints >= (Long)row[0]) &&
41                 (bonusPoints <= (Long)row[1]) &&
42                 (((Boolean)row[2] == null)||((Boolean)row[2] ==
                     goldCustomer)))
43                rv = (Status)row[3];
44
45        bonusPoints = 1/(bonusPoints - 55); // Fault 9
46
47        return rv;
48    }
```

It is much more difficult to insert faults that can evade all paths testing, and the code has been completely rewritten to achieve these. The inserted faults are explained as follows:

- Fault 7: lines 26–33 contain a faulty lookup table. Line 31 will cause a failure for the input value 1024.

  The performance of many algorithms can be improved by the use of lookup tables, but the risk is that the tables are incorrect.

- Fault 8: line 37 shows a faulty bitwise manipulation. Note that the constant 0xFFFFFFFFFFFFFEFFL is a long hexadecimal value, with an E where there should be an F three hex digits from the end. This mistake results in a single bit being 0. This will cause a failure for the input value 256, as clearing this bit will change the value to zero. There is no reason to do a bit manipulation in this code, but networking and graphics code are examples where this may be required.

- Fault 9: line 45 shows a divide by zero fault. This will cause an (unhandled) Java exception to be raised for the input value 55. As it is unhandled, it will cause the program to crash, and by default Java produces a stack dump. Dead code like this, which manipulates local variables that are never used again, can sometimes be identified and removed by the compiler – but in this case the code executes and causes a crash with the input value 55.

Division is frequently used in algorithms, and if divide-by-zero exceptions are not handled correctly they will cause software failures.

The results of running the all paths tests against these faults in shown in Figure 7.23.

```
PASSED: test_giveDiscount("T1.1", 40, true, FULLPRICE)
PASSED: test_giveDiscount("T1.2", 100, false, FULLPRICE)
PASSED: test_giveDiscount("T1.3", 200, false, DISCOUNT)
PASSED: test_giveDiscount("T1.4", -100, false, ERROR)
PASSED: test_giveDiscount("T2.1", 1, true, FULLPRICE)
PASSED: test_giveDiscount("T2.2", 80, false, FULLPRICE)
PASSED: test_giveDiscount("T2.3", 81, false, FULLPRICE)
PASSED: test_giveDiscount("T2.4", 120, false, FULLPRICE)
PASSED: test_giveDiscount("T2.5", 121, false, DISCOUNT)
PASSED: test_giveDiscount("T2.6", 9223372036854775807, false, DISCOUNT)
PASSED: test_giveDiscount("T2.7", -9223372036854775808, false, ERROR)
PASSED: test_giveDiscount("T2.8", 0, false, ERROR)
PASSED: test_giveDiscount("T3.1", 100, true, DISCOUNT)
PASSED: test_giveDiscount("T3.2", 200, true, DISCOUNT)
PASSED: test_giveDiscount("T4.1", 43, true, FULLPRICE)
PASSED: test_giveDiscount("T5.1", 93, true, DISCOUNT)
PASSED: test_giveDiscount("T6.1", 20, true, FULLPRICE)
=================================================
Command line suite
Total tests run: 17, Passes: 17, Failures: 0, Skips: 0
=================================================
```

Figure 7.23 All paths test results for `giveDiscount()` with Faults 7, 8, and 9.

The tests all pass – they do not find any of these faults, even though all paths is regarded as the *strongest* form of white-box testing (based on the program structure).[6]

Demonstrating the Faults

The results of executing the code with Faults 7, 8, and 9, using carefully selected input values for `bonusPoints`(256, 1024, and 55), are shown in Figure 7.24.

Note that the wrong result is returned for all the inputs.

- The input (256, true) should return DISCOUNT.
- The input (1024, true) should also return DISCOUNT.
- The input (55, true) should return FULLPRICE, and not raise an exception

This demonstrates an interesting issue: given a set of test data, which is not exhaustive, it is usually possible to design a fault for the code that is not found by that data.

---

[6] Suggested reading for other forms of white-box testing is provided in Chapter 14.

```
$ check 256 true
ERROR
$ check 1024 true
FULLPRICE
$ check 55 true
Exception in thread "main" java.lang.ArithmeticException: / by zero
        at example.OnlineSales.giveDiscount(OnlineSales.java:45)
        at example.Check.check(Check.java:21)
        at example.Check.main(Check.java:16)
```

Figure 7.24 Manual demonstration of Faults 7, 8, and 9.

7.5.2 Strengths and Weaknesses

All paths testing matches the flow of control through a program, but can be difficult to realise for complex programs, in particular as each path has to be carefully analysed to determine if it is executable, and if so to develop the criteria that cause its execution.

Strengths

- All paths testing covers all possible paths, which may have not been exercised using other methods.
- All paths testing is guaranteed to achieve statement coverage and branch coverage.

Weaknesses

- Developing the CFG and identifying all the paths in complex code can be difficult and time-consuming.
- When code contains loops, decisions must be made as to how to limit their execution. This is necessary to limit the number of paths to a reasonable number, but as a result weakens the testing.
- All paths does not explicitly evaluate the Boolean conditions in each decision (the individual Boolean sub-expressions that make up a compound Boolean expression).
- It does not explore faults related to incorrect data processing (e.g. bitwise manipulation or arithmetic errors).
- It does not explore non-code faults (for example, faults in a lookup table).

7.6 Key Points

- All paths testing is used to augment black-box and white-box testing, by ensuring that every end-to-end path is executed. It is the strongest form of testing based on a program's structure.[7]

---

[7] There are other forms of path testing than end-to-end paths, which are weaker, but may be easier to design tests for. However, all paths testing is the strongest form of path testing: it is a superset of all the other forms of path testing.

- Every unexecuted end-to-end path in the software is a TCI.
- Input values for the test data are selected by analysis of the paths and decisions in the code.

7.7   Notes for the Experienced Tester

Identifying all the possible paths is a complex task, even for an experienced tester. For simple code it is unlikely that there will be any unexecuted paths once black-box and white-box testing has been completed. For complex code, especially with loops, a thorough analysis will probably be required, and peer review is almost essential to ensure that no paths have been omitted. Exploratory programming and the debugger are often used to try to find data values that will follow a particular exit from a node.

An experienced tester will often be able to develop the CFG without detailing all the steps as shown for the example in this chapter. They will also probably be able to identify the conditions required for each path without laboriously stepping through the code. However, even for the experienced tester, developing all paths tests is a time-consuming and difficult task.

8 Black-Box and White-Box Testing

Dynamic testing confirms the correct operation of a program, which is referred to as the *test item*, by executing it. As shown in Figure 8.1, the test process can be modelled as the comparison of the outputs of a real system with those of an ideal system. The ideal system represents the specification. The real system represents the software being tested.

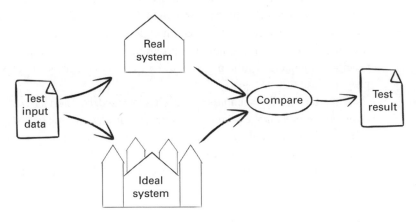

Figure 8.1 Software testing procedure.

Test conditions are developed, according to the test design technique selected, which guides the selection of suitable test input data. The test input data is then used as an input to the ideal system in order to determine the correct output (referred to as the expected results). The test input data is provided as inputs to the real system. The real system executes, and the actual results are collected and compared with the expected results. If they are identical, or equivalent, then the test result is a pass. Otherwise the test result is a fail. As we have seen in the previous chapters, the test is usually executed by an automated test tool.

The test data is derived from the set of test conditions, each of which has been chosen to validate particular features or aspects of the system. The result of the test is a pass or fail. However, for a test to be useful it does not have to produce a pass result. Even a failed test gives us new knowledge about the system: it tells us for which inputs the software is not working as specified.

8.1   Comparison of Black-Box and White-Box Testing

Black-box testing (also referred to as specification-based or functional testing) is based entirely on the program specification, and uses no knowledge of the inner workings of the program code. Black-box testing aims to verify that the program meets the specified requirements, without any knowledge of the program implementation.

The principles of black-box and white-box testing can be applied to testing at different stages of development: from *unit testing* as the code is progressively developed, to *application testing* for each release of the overall system.

Black-box testing techniques are characterised by how a subset of the possible combinations of input values has been selected. For example, *boundary value analysis* (BVA) means to select all the possible boundary values for every input and output parameter.

Key point: black-box test cases and test data are derived solely from the functional specifications.

White-box testing (also referred to as implementation-based or structural testing) uses the *implementation* of the software to derive tests. The tests are designed to exercise a particular aspect of the program code, such as the statements or the decisions it contains. By examining how the program works, and selecting test data to cause specific components of the program to be executed, the tests can expose errors in the program structure or logic.

White-box testing techniques are characterised by their *coverage criteria*. This refers to the percentage of the components that have been exercised by the test. For example, 100% *statement coverage* means that all the lines of source code in a program have been executed at least once during the test.

Key point: white-box test cases are derived from the code; the test data is derived from both the code and the functional specifications.

Table 8.1 compares some of the key characteristics of black-box and white-box testing.

Table 8.1 Comparison of black-box and white-box testing.

Black-box testing	White-box testing
Tests are only dependent on the specification.	Tests are dependent on both the implementation and the specification.
Tests can be reused if the code is updated, which may be to fix a fault or add new features.	Tests are generally invalidated by any changes to the code, and cannot be reused.
Tests can be developed before the code is written as they only require the specification.	Tests can only be developed after the code is written as they require both the specification and the executable code.
Tests do not ensure that all of the code has been executed. They may miss *errors of commission* (see Section 8.1.3).	Tests do not ensure that the code fully implements the specification. They miss *errors of omission*.
Few tools provide automated coverage measurement of any black-box tests.	Many tools provide automated coverage measurement of white-box tests.

8.1.1 Black-Box Testing

Black-box testing can be expressed in a number of different ways:

- testing against the specification;
- using test coverage criteria based on the specification;
- developing test cases derived from the specification; and
- *exercising* the specification.

They all reflect the idea of testing the function of the software using the specification as a source of test cases.

Regarding software as a mapping from input values to output values, the purpose of black-box testing is to ensure that every value in the input domain maps to the correct value in the output domain (Figure 8.2). This is ideally achieved by exercising all the mappings in the specification. As discussed in Section 1.6, exhaustive testing is seldom feasible, and so a subset of possible inputs must be selected to cover key mappings between the input and output domains.

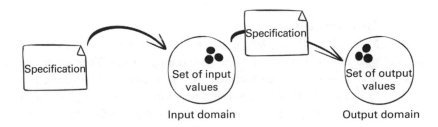

Figure 8.2 Specification model of testing.

Measurement
It is difficult to automatically measure the degree of coverage of the specification that black-box testing has achieved. Correct implementation of black-box tests therefore relies heavily on the quality of the tester's work.

8.1.2 White-Box Testing

Likewise, white-box testing can be expressed in a number of different ways:

- testing against the implementation;
- using test coverage criteria based on the implementation;
- developing test cases derived from the implementation; and
- *exercising* the implementation.

They all reflect the idea of testing the correct operation of the software using the structure of the implementation as a source of test cases.

Regarding software as a set of components that create output values from input values, the purpose of white-box testing is to ensure that executing the components (e.g.

statements, branches, etc.) always results in the *correct* output values (Figure 8.3). The specification is still needed to ensure that the output values are correct.

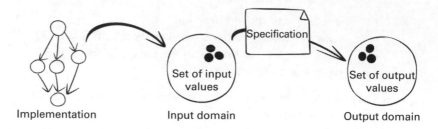

Figure 8.3 Implementation model of testing.

This testing is ideally achieved by exercising all the components (including combinations and sequences of components) in the implementation. As discussed already, exhaustive testing is seldom feasible, and so a subset of possible inputs must be selected to exercise key sets of components.

Measurement

Many programming languages and test environments provide tools that can measure what was executed in the code during testing. They do this by recording which instructions have been executed. This is referred to as *instrumenting* the code. Using these recordings, tools can calculate simple coverage figures, such as percentage of lines executed, or percentage of branches taken during the tests. We have seen some examples of this in Chapters 5 and 6. Achieving 100% coverage of these simple criteria does not necessarily indicate complete testing – there may be complex end-to-end paths, as discussed in Chapter 7. However, achieving less than 100% coverage clearly indicates that there is untested code or untested branches.

These measurement tools are aften used to determine the coverage provided by black-box testing. Following this, white-box testing can then be used to augment the black-box testing and improve the test coverage.

It can be argued that setting any goal less than 100% coverage does not assure quality. However, a lot of effort may be expended to achieve this. The same effort might be better spent using a different test approach (for example: static testing instead of dynamic testing). Using coverage-based white-box techniques, such as statement testing or branch testing, a typical goal is to attain 80–90% coverage or more before releasing.[1]

However, these recommendations are not absolute and safety-critical software may require more testing. One strategy that usually increases coverage quickly is to first attain a base level coverage throughout the entire test program before striving for higher coverage in critical code.

---

[1] R.B. Grady, *Practical Software Metrics for Project Management and Process Improvement.* Prentice-Hall, 1992. O. Vinter and P. Poulsen. Experience-driven software process improvement. In *Proc. Conf. Software Process Improvement* (SPI 96). International Software Consulting Network, 1996.

8.1.3 Errors of *Omission* and *Commission*

Both black-box and white-box testing approaches have weaknesses:

- White-box testing does not typically find faults relating to missing functionality (referred to as *errors of omission*): there is no implementation for these as a basis to develop tests.
- Black-box testing does not typically find faults relating to extra functionality (referred to as *errors of commission*): there is no specification for these as a basis from which to develop tests.

Consider the example `boolean isZero(int x)`, that should return `true` if x is `zero` and `false` otherwise. Example source code is given in Snippet 8.1.

Snippet 8.1 Errors of omission and commission

```
1    public static boolean isZero(int x)
2    {
3        if ((x + 1) / 15 > 56) return true;
4        return false;
5    }
```

This snippet contains two errors:

- **Error of omission**: there is no functionality in the code to return true when x is equal to 0. This is required by the specification.
- **Error of commission**: there is extra functionality in the code, on line 3, which returns true when the expression $(x + 1)/15 > 56$ evaluates to `true`. This is not in the specification.

This is a simple example, and it is easy to see that the code is not correct with respect to the specification. In longer or more complex code, it is generally much more difficult to identify these faults. In this case, what appears to be a single mistake by the developer has led to both types of error: changing the decision in line 3 to (x==0) would fix both faults. Often errors of omission lead to matching errors of commission, and vice-versa.

Error handling is often a source of omission faults in complex code, where incorrect input data is not identified correctly. Misunderstanding the specification is often a source of faults of commission, where extra input conditions are identified by the programmer that were not in the specification.

Another way of looking at this is from the coverage viewpoint:

- **Black-box** testing provides for coverage of the *specification*, but not full coverage of the *implementation*. That is, there may be code in the implementation that incorrectly produces results not stated in the specification.

- **White-box** testing provides for coverage of the *implementation*, but not of the *specification*. That is, there may be behaviour stated in the specification for which there is no code in the implementation.

It is for these reasons that black-box testing is done first, to make sure the code is complete. This is then augmented by white-box testing, to make sure the code does not add anything extra.

8.1.4   Usage

Black-box and white-box testing techniques are generally used in succession to max-imise coverage. The degree of coverage is usually based on the quality requirements of the test item. For example, software that decides whether to sound an alarm for a hospital patient will have higher quality requirements than software that recommends movies to watch. Based on these quality requirements, the tester can decide whether to stop testing early, as discussed in Section 1.8.

Black-box testing is used initially to verify that the software satisfies the specification:

- Use equivalence partitions to verify the basic operation of the software by ensuring that one representative of each partition is executed (see Chapter 2).
- If the specification contains boundary values, use BVA to verify correct opera-tion at the edges (see Chapter 3).
- If the specification states different processing for different combinations of inputs, use decision tables to verify correct behaviour for each combination (see Chapter 4).

These black-box test techniques can be further augmented:

- If the specification contains state-based behaviour, or different behaviour for different sequences of inputs, then use state-based/sequential testing to verify this behaviour (see Section 8.2.7 in this chapter).
- If there are reasons to suspect that there are faults in the code, perhaps based on past experience, then use error guessing/expert opinion to try to expose them (see Section 14.3.3).
- If the typical usage of the software is known, or to achieve a large number of tests, use random test data to verify the correct operation under these usage patterns (see Chapter 12).

We measure the statement and branch coverage for each of these black-box tests. If the required coverage has not been achieved, we can add white-box techniques to further enhance the quality of the testing:

- Use statement coverage to ensure that 100% of the statements have been exe-cuted. Investigate the uncovered statements and identify test coverage items (TCIs) and test cases specifically for these (see Chapter 5).

- Use branch coverage to ensure that 100% of the branches have been taken. Investigate the branches that were missed and develop TCIs and test cases specifically for these (see Chapter 6).

These white-box test techniques can be further augmented:

- If the code contains complex end-to-end paths, then use all paths testing to ensure coverage of these (see Chapter 7).
- If the code contains complex data usage patterns, then use DU pair testing to ensure coverage of these (see Section 8.3.1).
- If the code contains complex decisions, then use CC/DCC/MCC/MCDC testing to ensure coverage of these (see Sections 8.3.2–8.3.6).

In all cases, the decision to proceed with further tests is a judgement call and a *cost–benefit* trade-off: balancing the extra time and work required to do the extra tests justified against the extra confidence they will provide in the software quality. We discussed this in detail in Chapter 1.

Some factors to consider when deciding what test techniques to use, and when to use them in the development process:

- Black-box tests can be written before, or in parallel with, the code (as they are based on the specifications).
- It normally serves no purpose to execute white-box tests before black-box tests.
- White-box testing can *never* be used as a substitute for black-box testing (see Section 8.1.3 for details).
- White-box tests must be reviewed, and probably changed, every time the code is modified.

8.2   Black-Box Testing: Additional Matters

In this section we address some special cases that may arise during black-box testing.

8.2.1   Strings and Arrays

Strings and arrays are more complex to handle: they contain a large number of data values, and may have no specific length limit. There is no standard approach for handling these. We therefore provide some guidelines on applying black-box techniques to these data structures.[2] First, we consider error cases, and then normal cases.

Error Cases
Generally there are a number of categories of error cases:

- a null reference;
- a string or array of length 0;

---

[2] They have no impact on white-box testing.

- a string or array which is too long by exceeding its specified maximum length (e.g. 13 digits for a modern ISBN number);[3]
- invalid data, such as a String being specified to only include *printable* characters; an integer array may be specified to contain only positive values; and
- invalid relationships, such as a string being specified to only contain characters in alphabetical order; an integer array may be specified to be in descending order.

Normal Cases

Normal cases are more difficult to categorise. Rather than selecting just one value from each equivalence partition, a number of different values may be selected.

For boundary values, both the length of the data structure and of the data it contains should be considered.

For combinations, a number of tests may be generated from each, again selecting a number of values to represent each cause rather than just one.

The complexity of the data selected will depend on the complexity of the specification. It may be useful to select one data set that includes the same value in each location in the string or array, if this is allowed. For strings representing contact information (such as names, addresses, or phone numbers), one might use a telephone directory to discover very short, very long, and a number of typical values. For arrays representing ints, such as a list of numbers to be subject to statistical tests, one might select a few small data sets and one large data set with known characteristics. And as always, it is important to ensure that the output cases are all covered – these often provide additional guidance on selecting input values.

8.2.2   Discontinuous Input Partitions

Sometimes the specification will state the same processing for different ranges of values (a discontinuous partition), or different processing for the same range of values (overlapping partitions). These two situations are discussed below.

Consider the example `boolean isZero(int x)`. There is one input partition with the single value 0, and a second input partition with all the values except 0, as shown in Figure 8.4.

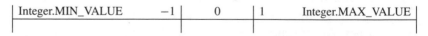

| Integer.MIN_VALUE | −1 | 0 | 1 | Integer.MAX_VALUE |

Figure 8.4 Value line for discontinuous partitions.

---

[3] For example, the maximum array length in Java is 2^{31}, but whether this can be allocated depends on various system configuration parameters.

The best way to handle discontinuous ranges for input parameters is to separate out the contiguous ranges of values. So, in this example, x should be treated as having the following three equivalence partitions:

x.EP 1   `Integer.MIN_VALUE..−1`
x.EP 2   `0`
x.EP 3   `1..Integer.MAX_VALUE`

and the associated boundary values:

x.BVA 1   `Integer.MIN_VALUE`
x.BVA 2   `−1`
x.BVA 3   `0`
x.BVA 4   `1`
x.BVA 5   `Integer.MAX_VALUE`

The reasoning behind this is that the values −1 and +1 are special: they are immediate predecessors and successors to the value 0, which is treated differently. The software must correctly identify these as boundary values. They are values that are likely to be associated with faults in the software.

8.2.3   Overlapping Output Partitions

Consider a different example with overlapping ranges for the return value. The method `int tax(int x, boolean fixed)` calculates the tax payable on an amount specified by the parameter x. The tax may be either a fixed amount with the value 56, or a variable amount calculated at 1% (or `x/100`). The return value is one of the following:

*   −1 indicating an error, if *amount* < 0;
*   56, if fixed is `true` (fixed tax); and
*   `x/100`, which is 1% of the amount if fixed is `false` (variable tax).

Considering the non-error case, the variable tax can therefore have a value from 0 to Integer.MAX_VALUE/100, and the fixed tax can only have a single value, 56. This gives the return value two partitions with overlapping values:

1.   A partition containing all the values from 0 to Integer.MAX_VALUE/100.
2.   The value 56, which is in a single-valued partition of its own.

The value lines for these partitions are shown in Figure 8.5. The overlap is indicated by the dashed lines in Partition 1.

There is a third error partition not shown in the figure, with the single value −1. The values from Integer.MIN_VALUE to −2, and above Integer.MAX_VALUE/100, are not possible return values so need not be considered – there are no inputs that should cause any of these values to be returned.

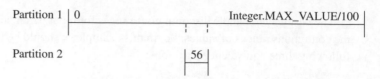

Figure 8.5 Value line for overlapping partitions.

The best way to handle these overlapping ranges for outputs is to ignore the overlap, and treat each range of values separately. So, in this example, x should be treated as having the equivalence partitions:

x.EP 1   0..Integer.MAX_VALUE/100
x.EP 2   56
x.EP 3   −1

and the boundary values:

x.BVA 1   0 (from EP2)
x.BVA 2   Integer.MAX_VALUE/100(from EP2)
x.BVA 3   56 (from EP3)
x.BVA 4   −1

The reasoning behind this is that the values 55 and 57 are not special: they are not values at the boundary of a partition, and are not likely to be associated with faults in the software. However, 56 is a special value as it is produced by special processing – in this example by two different types of processing.

In summary, the guidelines for treating overlapping partitions are as follows:

- divide overlapping input ranges into separate partitions; and
- treat overlapping output ranges by using as few partitions as possible.

8.2.4   In-band Error Reporting

A special case exists where errors are reported *in-band*; that is, via the same mechanism as used for normal processing, and sometimes even using the same values. Typical examples are the Boolean value false, and the integer value −1. The same value can be used both to indicate that some requirement is not met and also to indicate errors. The alternative, raising an exception, is much easier to test for – but the tester must be able to test both types of error reporting. An example is shown below.

Consider an enhanced version of the method inRange(int x, int low, int high), where true is returned if the inputs are valid and x is within the range of values from low to high. False is returned either if the inputs are invalid (i.e. low greater than high), or if x is not in the range.

In this example, there are three equivalence partitions for the Boolean return value:

1.   true, representing that x is in range;
2.   false, representing that x is not in range;
3.   false, representing that the inputs are invalid.

This leads to two non-error cases and one error case, for the return value. Test data for the input error case (`low < high`) will also cover the output error case (`return value == false`). Test data for the input non-error cases will also cover the output non-error cases (`return value == true`) and (`return value == false`).

A similar approach would be taken for integers or other in-band error reporting mechanisms.

As part of *design for testability*, improved error handling can be provided by *out-of-band* reporting. In Java, this might be achieved by throwing an exception. However, a tester must be prepared to test code that uses either approach.

8.2.5 Handling Relative Values

Another problem related to input (and output) parameters, is that not all partitions are defined by absolute values. Some partitions may be defined as relative to another input, or by a relationship between inputs.

Consider the method `int largest(int x, int y)`. There are three different cases to consider for x:

1.   x is less than y: `x < y`
2.   x is equal to y: `x == y`
3.   x is greater than y: `x > y`

First we will consider the input x. The approach is to treat y as though it had a fixed value. Working along the value line for x, starting at `Integer.MIN_VALUE`, the processing is identical until we reach the value y. So the first partition contains the values from `Integer.MIN_VALUE` up to the value `y - 1`, for any value of y.

If y has the value `Integer.MIN_VALUE`, then we treat this as an empty partition. And if y has the value `Integer.MIN_VALUE+1`, then we treat this as a single-valued partition.

The next partition has the single value y. When we move to y + 1 then the processing changes, as now x is greater than y.

Finally, working along the value line from y + 1 we reach `Integer.MAX_VALUE` with the same processing.

The value lines for the partitions for input x are shown in Figure 8.6 – these are relative partitions, as they are relative to the value of y.

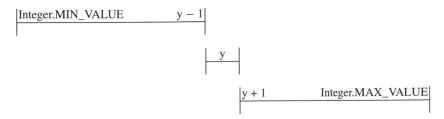

Figure 8.6 Relative partitions for x.

There are three corresponding cases for y, where we treat x as though it had a fixed value:

1.   `y < x`
2.   `y == x`
3.   `y > x`

In summary, for relative partitions, treat x as a constant when considering y, and y as a constant when considering x. This gives the following partitions for x:

*   `Integer.MIN_VALUE..y − 1`
*   `y`
*   `y + 1..Integer.MAX_VALUE`

And the following partitions for y:

*   `Integer.MIN_VALUE..x − 1`
*   `x`
*   `x + 1..Integer.MAX_VALUE`

The boundary values for x are:

*   `Integer.MIN_VALUE`
*   `y − 1`
*   `y`
*   `y + 1`
*   `Integer.MAX_VALUE`

with the boundary values for y being as follows:

*   `Integer.MIN_VALUE`
*   `x − 1`
*   `x`
*   `x + 1`
*   `Integer.MAX_VALUE`

These partitions are subject to the interpretation discussed before for empty partitions and single-valued partitions.

8.2.6   Classic Triangle Problem

A classic testing problem[4] is to classify a triangle as equilateral, isosceles, scalene, or invalid based on the lengths of its sides. Let us consider the equivalence partitions for this problem, using the method:

```
string classify(int x, int y, int z)
```

The parameters x, y, and z are the lengths of the three sides.

---

[4] See G.J. Myers. *The Art of Software Testing*. Wiley, 2004.

Clearly negative numbers are invalid, and we will consider 0 as invalid as well. We will also consider the data invalid if the points are co-linear (on the same straight line), or if the sum of the shortest two sides is less than the longest side (leaving a gap) – see Figure 8.7.

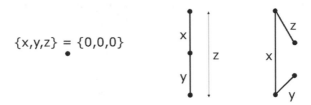

Figure 8.7 Invalid triangles.

Using the principles of overlapping partitions we have considered, this gives the following partitions for x:

```
x.EP 1   Integer.MIN_VALUE..0
x.EP 2   1..y − 1
x.EP 3   y
x.EP 4   y + 1..y + z-1
x.EP 5   1..z − 1
x.EP 6   z
x.EP 7   z + 1..y + z − 1
x.EP 8   y + z..Integer.MAX_VALUE
```

and similar partitions for y and z.

8.2.7 Testing Sequences of Inputs/State-Based Testing

Many software systems are state-based – their behaviour is based not only on the current inputs, but also on their current state (essentially defined by the history of previous inputs). When the system reaches a particular state, this is based on the sequence of inputs to date.

A simple example would be software for a touch-controlled lamp. When it is off, a touch toggles the lamp to on; when it is on, a touch toggles the lamp to off. The system has two states, ON and OFF. Which state the system is in is based on how many times it has been toggled, and the behaviour of a toggle depends on which state the system is in.

The fault model of state-based testing is to find faults in the software associated with these different states. Typically this will mean that the software fails to reach a particular state correctly, or that when the software is in that state, it fails to function correctly.

State behaviour can be defined using a state diagram.[5] This shows all the states, the transitions between the states, the input events that cause these transitions, and the actions to be taken on each state transition. Figure 8.8 shows the state diagram for the touch-controlled lamp. The boxes represent states. The arrows represent transitions between the states. The initial arrow to the OFF state indicates that the system starts in that state. And the label `toggle()` indicates an event, or method call, that should cause the transition to take place.[6] For simplicity, no actions are shown here.

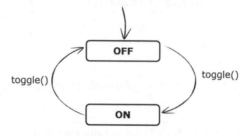

Figure 8.8 State diagram for lamp.

State-based testing raises the events that should cause the software to transition between different states by calling the methods on the state diagram. The tests can check that the correct state transitions have taken place, and that the correct actions have occurred.

Well-established test design strategies for selecting test coverage criteria for state-based testing are:

* piecewise (test some transitions);
* all transitions (test every transition at least once);
* all round-trip paths (test all paths starting and ending at the same state);
* M-length signatures (often it is impossible to directly access the state in order to verify that a transition has taken place correctly. In this case sequences of events which produce a unique set of outputs are used to verify that the software is in the expected state. These are called signatures. The outputs will be return values either from the methods which cause state transitions, or from other methods, not on the state diagram, which do not. This strategy tests all signatures of up to M transitions, for some value of M. The disadvantage of using signatures is that they change the state that the software is in, and the test must take this into account);
* all n-event transition sequences (test all sequences of transitions for a particular value of n); and
* exhaustive testing (testing all possible sequences of transitions).

---

[5] A state table may also be used, providing the same information but in tabular form.
[6] Exactly how this happens is not part of the state diagram. In this case, a hardware sensor would detect that the lamp has been touched, and software would then call the `toggle()` method.

Each transition is specified by the following:

- A starting state.
- An event (usually a function or method call) that causes the transition.
- A guard (this is a Boolean expression that must be true for the transition to occur. These allow the state diagram to be reduced in size by allowing the same event to cause different transitions from a state under different conditions).
- Actions that should occur as a result of the transition. Generally, for software, these are expressed as values that should change (e.g. a counter). They may also state other methods which should be called: (e.g. `turnBulbOn()` and `turnBulbOff()`).
- The ending state that the software should be in after the transition.

Transitions are tested as follows:

- Verify that the software is in the required starting state for the test.
- Set values, if required, to ensure that the transition guard is true.
- Raise the event (call a function or method) that should cause the transition.
- Check that the software is now in the expected ending state for the test.
- Check that any required actions have occurred.

State-based testing applies to all software that maintains state between calls. This is particularly important for object-oriented software, as all the attributes represent states (see Chapter 9).

8.2.8   Floating Point Numbers

All the examples in this book are based on integer numbers: floating point is significantly more difficult to handle. Floating point in Java (and most languages) uses the IEEE 754 representation – this is also supported by most modern hardware. Unlike integers, there is a sign bit, and also the values do not wrap around. Floating point is best regarded as an approximation: if a small value is added to a large value it may have no impact, and the difference between two large values may be returned as 0.0 even if they are not equal. Many fractions and decimals (such as 1/3 or 0.1) cannot be represented exactly in floating point. For example, the Java statement `System.out.printf("%19.17f",0.1f)` produces the output 0.10000000149011612 when executed, and not 0.10000000000000000 as you might expect!

The following list discusses a few problems that the software tester may experience with floating point, and suggests remedies for these.

- **Comparing to a constant.** Comparing a returned floating point return value with a constant floating point value is likely to fail. Instead, it needs to be compared to a range of values, representing the minimum and maximum allowable values. For example, if the answer must be correct to six decimal places, then the allowable limits would be the expected value ± 0.0000005. If the software is not specified with an accuracy margin, then strictly speaking it cannot be tested. TestNG supports ranges for floating point assertions.

- **Boundary values.** Given a value between 0.0 and 1.0, what are the boundary values of the partition below 0.0 and the partition above 1.0? For the partition below, is it −0.1, −0.0001, or −0.0000000001? And for the partition above is it 1.01, 1.0001, or 1.0000000001? If the programming language or libraries support it, then you can use these features to find floating point numbers just below and just above a value. For example, in Java, the methods `Java.lang.Math.nextUp()` and `.nextAfter()` can be used to do this.
- **Handling cumulative errors.** Because not every number can be exactly represented, and values can get lost when subtracting or adding a very small number from/to a very large one, errors tend to accumulate in software that uses floating point. In order to handle this, the maximum allowable error needs to be specified for such software, and then, as for comparing to a constant, this provides the upper and lower bounds on a correct output.
- **Input and output conversion.** It is easy to make a mistake when reading or writing floating point numbers. For example, the visible format of the number may change depending on its value (0.000001 vs 1.0000E-6). It is therefore important to understand where these changes take place, and to test software input and output with very large and very small floating point numbers to make sure they are handled correctly.
- **Special values.** Floating point has a number of special values: NaN (not a number), positive infinity, and negative infinity. These are usually error values, and should be included as extra input partitions.

The software tester using floating point is advised to read one of the standard works on writing code that uses floating point.

8.2.9   Numeric Processing

The examples in the book focus on logic processing, which does not produce a calculated result. This section considers numeric processing, which returns the result of a numeric calculation. For equivalence partition and BVA testing, the input partitions should be handled the same way, but the output partitions may require a bit more analysis.

Consider the method `int add10(int x)`, which adds 10 to the input value if it is between 0 and 90, and raises an `IllegalArgumentException` otherwise.

The input partitions for x are easy to identify, as shown in Figure 8.9.

| Integer.MIN_VALUE | −1 | 0 | 90 | 91 | Integer.MAX_VALUE |

Figure 8.9 Value line for x.

The output partitions for the return value of add10() are derived using the same logic as used in Chapter 2, but they require some calculations on the behalf of the tester, as shown in Figure 8.10.

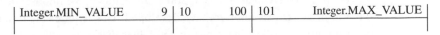

| Integer.MIN_VALUE   9 | 10   100 | 101   Integer.MAX_VALUE |

Figure 8.10 Value line for add10().

There is an additional output from the method, the IllegalArgumentException, which is discussed further in Section 11.8.

The value line allows the following to be identified for the return value:

- The range [Integer..MIN_VALUE..9] is not possible – there is no input value that produces an output in this range.
- The value 10 is produced as an output from the smallest valid value for x of 0.
- The value 100 is produced as an output from the largest valid value for x of 90.
- The range [101..Integer.MAX_VALUE] is not possible – there is no input value that produces an output in this range.

In this example, the equivalence partitions and boundary values are:

- Input   x:[Integer.MIN_VALUE..-1][0..90][101..Integer. MAX_VALUE]
- Output return value: [10..100]
- Output exception: [IllegalArgumentException]

The return values may produce overlapping partitions, as discussed in Section 8.2.3. Floating point return values can also require significant analysis – see Section 8.2.8. In some cases it may not be possible to identify all of the output partition boundaries.

8.3   White-Box Testing: Some More Techniques

The techniques discussed here are less generally used than the fundamental techniques of statement and branch coverage. This is essentially due to the lack of standardised tools to measure their coverage. But, as with other white-box techniques, the tests are invalidated every time a change is made, and so they are generally reserved for use on software that has passed all its previous tests, and that has a requirement for a particularly high level of quality (such as in the aerospace or medical devices industries).

8.3.1   Dataflow Coverage/Definition–Use Pairs

Unlike the control-flow path techniques considered so far, the principle in definition–use (DU) pair testing is to use dataflow as a coverage metric. Each path between the writing of a value to a variable (*definition*) and its subsequent reading (*use*) is executed during testing. The motivation is to verify the correctness of a program with all the possible flows of data through the program. The fault model is that the flow of data is not handled correctly.

Every possible DU pair is a TCI. Some DU pairs will be impossible to execute and do not form TCIs. Test cases are then developed. This requires the tester to review the code carefully and select input parameter values that cause DU paths to be followed. As for other forms of white-box testing, each test case is likely to cover a number of TCIs. The expected results are derived from the specification. It is easy to make the mistake of reading the expected results directly from the code.

DU pair testing provides comprehensive testing of the dataflow in a program, but generating the test data is a time-consuming exercise.

Strengths

- This is a strong form of testing.
- It generates test data in the pattern that data is manipulated in the program rather than following abstract branches.

Weaknesses

- The number of test cases can be very large, up to $\sum_{i=1}^{N} d_i \cdot u_i$, where d_i is the number of definitions for variable i, u_i is the number of uses, and N is the number of variables (this includes arguments, local variables, and class attributes).
- With object references, or pointer variables in a language such as C, it can be difficult to determine which variable is being referenced.
- With arrays it is difficult to determine which element in the array is being referenced (the solution often used is to treat the entire array as a single variable).

8.3.2   Condition Coverage

So far, we have considered the use of control-flow path and dataflow paths as coverage criteria.

For white-box testing, another recognised coverage criteria is the Boolean conditions that cause each decision to be evaluated as true or false. A complex decision is formed from multiple Boolean conditions. Condition coverage (often abbreviated to CC) extends decision coverage by ensuring that, for complex decisions, each Boolean condition within the decision is tested for its true or false values. Note: for this technique, it is not required that the decision itself take on true or false values. The fault model for condition coverage is that some Boolean conditions are not handled correctly.

The goal of condition coverage is for every Boolean condition in every decision to take on the values true and false. Even though in practice some languages may not in fact evaluate later conditions if earlier ones determine the value of the decision (short-circuit evaluation), this is ignored in condition coverage. Each condition in each decision in the source code has two test coverage items – for true and false outcomes.

Test cases are developed, with input data selected to ensure that every Boolean condition in every decision takes on the values true and false. This selection requires the tester to review the complex decisions and the Boolean conditions in the code, and to select input parameter values that cause the necessary outcomes from each Boolean condition. The expected results come from the specification.

Comment

Some languages, such as Java, support left-to-right evaluation and short-circuit evaluation. This means that subsequent conditions in a decision may not actually be evaluated, depending on the results of previous ones.

For example, in the decision $(a \ || \ (b \ \&\& \ c))$:

- If a is true, then neither b nor c is evaluated – the expression must evaluate to true.
- If a is false, and b is false, then c is not evaluated – the expression must evaluate to false.

The standard definitions of condition coverage and decision condition coverage do not take this into consideration, but the tester may decide to do so.

Strengths

- Condition coverage focuses on Boolean condition outcomes.

Weaknesses

- It can be difficult to determine the required input parameter values.
- It does not always achieve decision coverage.

8.3.3 Decision Coverage

In decision coverage (often abbreviated to DC), every decision is evaluated to true and false. This is equivalent to branch coverage if a coverage measurement tool is used that identifies decisions as branches (or if a control-flow graph has been used).

8.3.4 Decision Condition Coverage

In decision condition coverage (often abbreviated to DCC), tests are generated that both cause every decision to be taken at least once (decision coverage), and also every Boolean condition to be true and false at least once (condition coverage).

Each decision has two TCIs (for true and false outcomes), and every Boolean condition in each decision has two TCIs (for true and false outcomes). Test data is selected for the test cases to ensure that every decision takes on the value true and false, and that every Boolean condition in every decision takes on the value true and false. This selection requires the tester to review the complex decisions and the Boolean conditions in the code, and select input parameter values that cause the necessary outcomes from each decision and Boolean condition. Even though in practice some languages may not in fact evaluate later Boolean conditions if earlier ones determine the value of the decision, this is ignored.

Strengths

- The decision condition coverage provides stronger coverage that just condition coverage or decision coverage.

Weaknesses

- Even though every decision is tested, and every Boolean condition is tested, not every possible *combination* of Boolean conditions is tested.
- It can be difficult to determine the required input parameter values.

Decision condition coverage is equivalent to branch coverage if a coverage measurement tool is used that identifies Boolean conditions as branches.

8.3.5   Multiple Condition Coverage

In multiple condition coverage (often abbreviated to MCC), tests are generated to cause every possible combination of Boolean conditions for every decision to be tested. The goal is to achieve 100% coverage of every combination of Boolean conditions (which will also achieve 100% coverage of every decision). Even though in practice some languages may not evaluate later Boolean conditions if earlier ones determine the value of the decision, this is ignored. A *truth table* is the best way to identify all the possible combinations of values. The fault model is that some combinations of Boolean conditions are not handled correctly.

Each combination is a TCI. Each decision with n Boolean conditions has 2^n test coverage (assuming the Boolean conditions are independent) – one for each combination of Boolean conditions. Test cases are developed with test data selected to ensure that every combination of Boolean conditions in every decision is covered. This selection requires the tester to review the complex decisions and the Boolean conditions in the code, and select input parameter values that cause the necessary combinations. The expected results come from the specification.

Comment

Not all combinations of Boolean conditions are always possible. Even though multiple condition testing covers every possible combination of Boolean conditions in each decision, it does not cause every possible combination of decisions in the program to be taken.

Strengths

- Multiple condition coverage tests all possible combinations of Boolean conditions in every decision.

Weaknesses

- It can be expensive: n Boolean conditions in a decision give 2^n TCIs.
- It can be difficult to determine the required input parameter values.

8.3.6 Modified Condition/Decision Coverage

The previous technique of multiple condition coverage can generate a very large number of tests. This can be reduced by only considering those combinations of Boolean conditions that cause a discernible effect on the output of the software. The test conditions for modified condition/decision coverage[7] (often abbreviated to MC/DC) are based on decision condition coverage, with additional conditions to verify the independent effect of each Boolean condition on the output.

Each decision has two TCIs (for true and false outcomes) and every Boolean condition in each decision has two TCIs (for true and false outcomes). In addition, TCIs must be created that show the effect on the output of changing each of the Boolean conditions independently.

Consider the method `func(a,b)` shown in Snippet 8.2. Test cases must be created to show the independent effect of changing the value of the Boolean conditions `(a > 10)` and of `(b == 0)` on the returned value.

Snippet 8.2 Example of complex decisions for MC/DC

```
1    int func(int a, int b) {
2        int x = 100;
3        if ( (a > 10) || (b == 0) ) then x = x/a;
4        return x;
5    }
```

The tester must review the complex decisions and Boolean conditions in the code, and select input parameter values for the test data to ensure that:

- every decision takes on the value true and false;
- every Boolean condition in every decision takes on the value true and false;
- the effect on the output value of changing the value of every Boolean conditions is shown.

For example, using the method `func(int a, int b)` as defined above:

- The input data `(a = 50, b = 1)` should result in the output value 2.
- Adding the input data `(a = 5, b = 1)` should result in the output value 100. This shows the independent effect of changing the Boolean condition `(a > 10)`.

---

[7] K.J. Hayhurst, D.S. Veerhusen, J.J. Chilsenski, and L.K. Rierson. A practical tutorial on modified condition/decision coverage. Technical report. NASA, 2001.

- And adding the input data (a = 5,b = 0) should result in the output value 20. This shows the independent effect of changing the Boolean condition (b == 0).

Strengths

- Modified condition/decision coverage provides stronger coverage that condition decision coverage, but without the large number of tests produced by multiple condition coverage. MCC will produce 2^n tests, for n Boolean conditions; MCDC will produce in the order of n tests (with a minimum of $n + 1$).
- This technique has been reported as being very successful in code where complex decisions are made (for example, in the aerospace industry), and in particular where decisions with very large numbers of Boolean conditions are used.
- Event-based software is likely to require complex decisions, and thus the technique may be of applicability to GUI and web-based software.

Weaknesses

- It is not as thorough as MCC.

8.3.7   Test Ranking

Not all testing techniques can be directly compared to each other in terms of their effectiveness, but a number of the white-box techniques can.

The standard comparison ranks the techniques as shown in Figure 8.11. The techniques labelled nearer the top of the figure are described as being *stronger* than those lower down. This means that they guarantee to provide at least the same level of coverage as the techniques lower down. However, the stronger techniques invariably take more time and effort to implement. The stronger techniques are said to *subsume* the weaker ones, as they provide at least the same level of coverage. The *stronger* arrow represents the subsumes relationship.

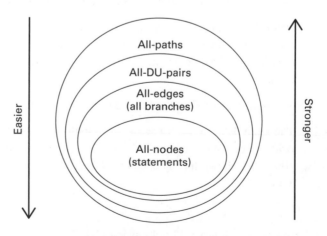

Figure 8.11 Coverage criteria ranking.

8.4   Repair-Based Testing

Following the discovery of faults at any stage in the software development process, the faults are prioritised and repaired. Following this repair, additional tests are often developed to thoroughly verify that the fault has been correctly repaired. These are often a combination of black-box tests and white-box tests.

There are three different levels of such tests that can be developed: specific, generic, and abstracted.

8.4.1   Specific Repair Test

The specific repair test verifies that the software now operates correctly for the specific data inputs that caused the failure. This will often consist of a white-box test that ensures that executing the new/modified code provides the correct output.

8.4.2   Generic Repair Test

To ensure that the repair works for other data values, and not just those that caused the failure, the conditions that caused the failure should be analysed, and black-box tests developed that exercise these conditions. The generic repair test verifies that the repair works for these different data values.

8.4.3   Abstracted Repair Test

In order to broaden the value of finding a fault, it is useful to abstract the fault as far as possible. Then additional black-box tests can be developed that attempt to find other places in the code where the same mistake may have been made by the programmer, leading to similar faults. If the fault has a characteristic signature (often caused by cut-and-paste operations), then this can be searched for in the code.

8.4.4   Example

Consider a program that at some point has to search a list of data for a particular entry. The data is kept in a linked list, and due to a mistake by the programmer the code never finds the penultimate entries in the list (i.e. entries that are second-from-last). This fault eventually causes a failure, which is reported by a customer. The fault is then located by replicating the customer's conditions and debugging the code. Subsequently the fault is repaired by rewriting a line of code in the method that handles traversing the list.

To verify the repair, a white-box unit test is developed that exercises the new line of code. This verifies that the method now produces the correct result for the data that previously caused a failure. A black-box unit test is then developed that ensures that, for different sets of data, the second-last entry can be found in this list. A system test may be developed to verify that the entire system now behaves correctly in situations when the second-last entry is important.

Finally, additional unit tests or system tests are developed that check that, for any other lists or collections of data in the program, the second-to-last entry is located correctly.

8.4.5   Using Repair-Based Tests

These additional tests are run immediately after the repair to verify it. They can also be added to the standard tests for the method, to ensure that the fault is not repeated – and that a developer does not by mistake revert to a previous version of the code.

Prior to release of a software product, the risk of repaired faults having been re-introduced can be reduced by re-running all the repair-based tests separately.

9   Testing Object-Oriented Software

The black-box and white-box unit test techniques described in Chapters 2–7 have been applied to a single static method. This allows key concepts of the test design techniques to be introduced without the additional complexities introduced by classes and objects. The same techniques can be applied to testing the instance methods[1] of a class – this is unit testing where the unit is a class.

9.1   Testing in Class Context

In general, methods interact with each other and cannot be tested independently: they need to be tested in the context of their class hierarchy. Methods interact with other methods via class attributes. Testing in class context refers to testing methods not individually, but in the wider context of their class.

Typically, setter methods must be called first to initialise any attributes used by the method being tested. Then the method itself is called, passing required inputs as parameters. The method return value must be verified, and then any changes the method has made to the attributes must be verified by calling getter methods. Thus the interaction of a number of methods must be tested, not the operation of a single method. Whether setters and getters is good object-oriented (OO) design is an open question, but the software tester needs to know how to access the attributes.

In this chapter, the essential topic of designing tests for class context is addressed. The test data may be derived using any of the previously covered black-box or white-box techniques. The topic is introduced through an example, followed up by a more detailed description of OO testing in Section 9.4.

9.2   Example

The class `SpaceOrder` supports processing orders to book space in a warehouse. The key method is `acceptOrder()`, which decides whether an order for space can be accepted or not. In general, all orders must fall within a specified minimum and

---

[1] Methods which are not static.

maximum amount of space. However, for special customers, orders for space less than the minimum will also be accepted.

We demonstrate the technique using equivalence partition testing. Tests for other black-box and white-box techniques would be developed in exactly the same way, but then the specific data values produced by these other black-box and white-box techniques would be used instead.

A UML[2] class diagram is used to define the attributes and methods in the class (Figure 9.1).

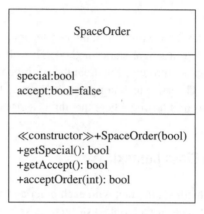

Figure 9.1 SpaceOrder class diagram.

It is assumed that the reader is familiar with the UML notation, but as a reminder the class diagram is interpreted as follows:

- The upper box specifies the class name: SpaceOrder.
- The middle box specifies the attributes:
    - special is a Boolean;
    - accept is a Boolean, initialised to false.

- The lower box specifies the methods:
    - the public constructor SpaceOrder() accepts a single Boolean parameter;
    - the public method getSpecial() has no parameters and returns a Boolean value;
    - the public method getAccept() has no parameters and returns a Boolean value;
    - the public method acceptOrder() accepts a single integer parameter and returns a Boolean value.

The source code is provided for reference in Listing 9.1.

---

[2] Useful examples can be found in M. Fowler. *UML Distilled*. Addison-Wesley, 2018. See www.omg.org/spec/UML for the formal definition.

Listing 9.1 SpaceOrder class.

```
1  public class SpaceOrder {
2
3    protected boolean special;
4    protected boolean accept = false;
5
6    public SpaceOrder(boolean isSpecial) {
7      special = isSpecial;
8    }
9
10   public boolean getSpecial() {
11     return this.special;
12   }
13
14   public boolean acceptOrder(int space) {
15     boolean status = true;
16     this.accept = false;
17     if (space <= 0)
18       status = false;
19     else if (space <= 1024 && (space >= 16 || this.special))
20       this.accept = true;
21     return status;
22   }
23
24   public boolean getAccept() {
25     return this.accept;
26   }
27
28 }
```

Definitions for the methods are as follows:

- **void example.SpaceOrder(boolean isSpecial)**
  Constructor
  Parameters:
  > isSpecial – specifies whether this SpaceOrder should be special or not

- **boolean example.SpaceOrder.getSpecial()**
  Returns:
  > the value of special

- **boolean example.SpaceOrder.acceptOrder(int space)**
  Determine whether a warehouse space order can be accepted.

  If valid input data, set accept true if order can be accepted, and false if not.

  If invalid input data (value of space), set accept false.

  An order can be accepted as follows. For all orders, the space must not be greater than the maximum space of 1024 m^2. For a standard order, the space must be at least the minimum space of 16m^2 (a special order has no lower limit).

> **Parameters:**
>> space – space in m^2 requested in the order (must be greater than 0)
>
> **Returns:**
>> true if valid input data, and the attribute accept has been set (to either true or false). Otherwise false

- `boolean example.SpaceOrder.getAccept()`
> **Returns:**
>> the value of `accept` (whether the `SpaceOrder` has been accepted or not)

9.2.1   Analysis

During unit testing in the previous chapters, there was a single static method to test (the method `giveDiscount()` – see Chapters 2–7). In contrast, a class may contain many methods, and a decision must be made which should be tested.

9.2.2   Deciding on Which Methods to Test

From a software testing viewpoint, there are five categories of method. For the class `SpaceOrder`, we now consider each category:

1.   **Static methods** – none in this example.
2.   **Constructors** – include this constructor in the test to ensure that the attributes are correctly initialised:

   - `SpaceOrder(boolean)`

3.   **Accessor methods** (getters and setters) – the general rule is to only test these if they are manually written or contain more than a single assignment (setter) or return statement (getter). However, in this example the class is small and the getters and setters can easily be verified through a code review.[3] Therefore we will not test these:

   - `getAccept()`
   - `getSpecial()`

4.   **Methods with no class interaction** (do not read or write any of the class attributes) – none (if present, these can be tested individually using non-OO approaches, as shown in Chapters 2–7).
5.   **Methods with class interaction** (read and/or write the class attributes) – we will test all of these:

   - `acceptOrder(int)`

---

[3] There is a small risk associated with this approach, as even a single assignment or return statement can have a fault.

9.2.3   Selecting a Test Technique

We must now decide which test technique to use to select test data. For simplicity, we will demonstrate equivalence partition testing in this example. Exactly the same approach would be used for boundary value analysis (BVA) and decision table testing. The approach is also similar for statement coverage and branch coverage testing.

Only the results of the analysis are shown, not all the intermediate results. Refer to Chapter 2 for details of deriving the natural ranges, value lines, and equivalence partitions.

Constructors and Initialisation

First we identify the attribute values set by the constructor(s) and class initialisation. The class has a single constructor defined, which sets the value for `special`. Table 9.1 lists the attribute values set by the class initialisation and constructors. The UML class diagram specifies that the `accept` attribute is initialised to `false`.

Table 9.1 Constructors and initialisation.

Constructor	Attribute	Value
`SpaceOrder(x:bool)`	`special`	`true` or `false` (as passed to the constructor)
	`accept`	`false` (specified in the class diagram)

Accessor Methods

We have decided not to test the getter and setter methods. However, some of the attributes can only be accessed via their setters and getters, so it is important to identify these for each attribute. Table 9.2 lists the getter and setter methods.

The method `acceptOrder()` reads and writes to attributes (`special` and `accept`) but is not regarded as a *pure* getter or a setter method, as it does other processing.

Table 9.2 Accessors.

Attribute	Getters	Setters
`special`	`getSpecial()`	–
`accept`	`getAccept()`	–

Other Methods

There are no methods with no class interaction, and there is a single method with class interaction. Table 9.3 details this single method, listing the attributes read and written.

Equivalence Partitions

Using the technique shown in Chapter 2, equivalence partition tests are developed for the inputs and outputs for each method. The full working of each step will not be shown, just the results of each – refer to Chapter 2 for details.

Table 9.3 Other methods.

Method	Read	Written
acceptOrder(int)	special	accept

Both the inputs to, and the outputs from, a method may be explicit or implicit:

- Explicit inputs are parameters passed to the method.
- Implicit inputs are attributes read by the method.
- An explicit output is the return value from a method, or an exception raised.
- Implicit outputs are attributes written by the method.

In order to achieve full equivalence partition coverage, all of these must be included. The only parameter with *interesting* value lines (that require analysis) is the input parameter space passed to acceptOrder(), as shown in Figure 9.2. All the other parameters are Boolean and do not require further analysis to identify their equivalence partitions.

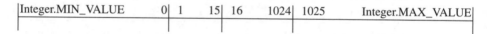

| Integer.MIN_VALUE | 0 | 1 | 15 | 16 | 1024 | 1025 | Integer.MAX_VALUE |

Figure 9.2 Value Line for space.

The equivalence partitions for the inputs and outputs of all the methods being tested are identified in Table 9.4.

Table 9.4 OO equivalence partitions for SpaceOrder.

Method	Name	Equivalence partition
SpaceOrder()	isSpecial	true
		false
	special	true
		false
	accept	false
acceptOrder()	space	(*) Integer.MIN_VALUE..0
		1..15
		16..1024
		1025..Integer.MAX_VALUE
	special	true
		false
	accept	true
		false
	return value	true
		false

As in previous chapters, the asterisk (*) indicates an input error partition. Where there is only a single method with a particular name, then just the method name can be used,[4] as shown here. If an attribute is both an input and an output for a method, then the input and output equivalence partitions must be separately listed – however, this is not needed here.

9.2.4 Test Coverage Items

Every equivalence partition for every parameter for every method is a test coverage item (TCI), as shown in Table 9.5. The input error coverage items are identified by '*'.

Table 9.5 OO equivalence partition TCI for `SpaceOrder`.

TCI	Method	Name	Equivalence partition	Test case
EP1	SpaceOrder()	isSpecial	true	
EP2			false	
EP3		special	true	
EP4			false	
EP5		accept	false	
EP6*	acceptOrder()	space	Integer.MIN_VALUE..0	
EP7			1..15	
EP8			16..1024	To Be Completed Later
EP9			1025..Integer.MAX_VALUE	
EP10		special	true	
EP11			false	
EP12		accept	true	
EP13			false	
EP14		return value	true	
EP15			false	

9.2.5 Test Cases

The values selected for each equivalence partition are shown in Table 9.6.

Table 9.6 Selected OO equivalence partition data values.

Method	Name	Equivalence Partition	Value
acceptOrder()	space	Integer.MIN_VALUE..0	−5000
		1..15	7
		16..1024	504
		1025..Integer.MAX_VALUE	5000

The test cases can now be developed. The significant difference in developing OO test cases is that, unlike in Chapters 2–7, where a single method is called, multiple

[4] If multiple methods have the same name, then the full method signatures, including the parameter list, are required to uniquely specify each method.

methods must be called for OO testing – and they must be called in the correct order for the test to work.[5]

In the test cases table (Table 9.7), the required sequence of method calls is shown for test case T1. Each call includes the test data consisting of the input parameters and the expected return values. It is normal practice to develop test cases for the constructor(s) first, then for any accessor methods being tested, and finally for the other methods. Showing the TCIs opposite the relevant method call makes reviewing the test cases easier.

Table 9.7 Equivalence partition test case T1.

ID	TCI covered	Inputs	Expected return value
T1	EP1	`new SpaceOrder(true)`	
	EP3	`getSpecial()`	`true`
	EP5	`getAccept()`	`false`

The test case shown for T1 is developed as follows:

- Line 1 calls the constructor, which generates an instance of class `SpaceOrder`, providing the value `true` (EP1) as an input. The constructor has no return value.
- Line 2 calls `getSpecial()`. This returns the value of the attribute `special`. This should have been set to `true` by the constructor if it is working correctly (which is EP3), so the expected return value is `true`.
- Line 3 calls `getAccept()`. This returns the value of the attribute `accept`. According to the specification, its default value at initialisation is `false`, so this is the return value that is expected (EP5).

The other test cases are now developed in a similar manner. The full set of test cases is shown in Table 9.8. As in Chapters 2–7, it is best to approach this systematically, trying to cover the test coverage items in order while trying to avoid unnecessary duplication, and covering the error TCI last.

Counting the maximum number of TCIs for each method being tested gives an indication of the minimum number of test cases expected: the constructor has a maximum of two (for `isSpecial`), and `acceptOrder()` has a maximum of four (for `space`), so a minimum of six test cases is expected.

9.2.6   Verification of the Test Cases

As for the previous black-box and white-box test techniques, the verification consists of two steps: first completing the test cases table, and then reviewing your work.

---

[5] Not all books show this level of detail in designing OO tests, but we recommend this as good practice. Otherwise, when implementing the tests, the tester has to redo the analysis to work out the methods and the ordering required.

Table 9.8 Equivalence test cases.

ID	Test cases covered	Inputs	Expected results return value
T1	EP1 EP3 EP5	new SpaceOrder(true) getSpecial() getAccept()	true false
T2	EP2 EP4	new SpaceOrder(false) getSpecial()	false
T3	[EP1] EP7,10,14 EP12	new SpaceOrder(true) acceptOrder(7) getAccept()	true true
T4	[EP2] EP8,11,[14] [EP12]	new SpaceOrder(false) acceptOrder(504) getAccept()	true true
T5	[EP2] EP9,[10,14] EP13	new SpaceOrder(false) acceptOrder(5000) getAccept()	true false
T6	[EP2] EP6*,15 [EP13]	new SpaceOrder(false) acceptOrder(-5000) getAccept()	false false

Completing the TCI Table

The Test Case column in the TCIs table can now be completed (Table 9.9). This is done by reading the TCIs for each test case in Table 9.8.

Table 9.9 Completed TCI table for SpaceOrder.

TCI	Method	Name	Equivalence partition	Test case
EP1	SpaceOrder()	isSpecial	true	T1
EP2			false	T2
EP3		special	true	T1
EP4			false	T2
EP5		accept	false	T1
EP6*	acceptOrder()	space	Integer.MIN_VALUE..0	T6
EP7			1..15	T3
EP8			16..1024	T4
EP9			1025..Integer.MAX_VALUE	T5
EP10		special	true	T3
EP11			false	T4
EP12		accept	true	T3
EP13			false	T5
EP14		return value	true	T3
EP15			false	T6

Reviewing Your Work

As in previous chapters, the purpose of the review is to ensure that there are no uncovered TCIs and no unnecessary (duplicate) test cases.

In this example, we can see from Table 9.9 that every test coverage item is covered, and from Table 9.8 that each test case covers additional TCIs (no duplication).

9.3   Test Implementation and Results

9.3.1   Test Implementation

The test implementation for equivalence partition testing *in class context* for the methods in class `SpaceOrder` is shown in Listing 9.2.

Listing 9.2 `SpaceOrder` equivalence partition test implementation.

```
1  public class SpaceOrderTest {
2
3          @DataProvider(name = "constructorData")
4          public Object[][] getConstructorData() {
5              return new Object[][] {
6                      //          TID  isSpecial, e_special,
                                        e_accept
7                      {"SpaceOrderTest T1", true,  true,  false},
8                      {"SpaceOrderTest T2", false, false, false},
9              };
10         }
11
12         @Test(dataProvider = "constructorData")
13         public void testConstructor(String tid, boolean
                   isSpecial, boolean expectedSpecial, boolean
                   expectedAccept) {
14             SpaceOrder o = new SpaceOrder(isSpecial);
15             assertEquals( o.getSpecial(), expectedSpecial );
16             assertEquals( o.getAccept(), expectedAccept );
17         }
18
19         @DataProvider(name = "acceptOrderData")
20         public Object[][] getAcceptOrderData() {
21             return new Object[][] {
22                     //              TID  special, space, e_rv
                                            e_accept
23                     { "SpaceOrderTest T3", true, 7, true,
                               true},
24                     { "SpaceOrderTest T4", false, 504, true,
                               true},
25                     { "SpaceOrderTest T5", false, 5000, true,
                               false},
26                     { "SpaceOrderTest T6", false, -5000, false,
                               false},
27             };
28         }
29
```

```
30        @Test(dataProvider = "acceptOrderData", dependsOnMethods
              = {"testConstructor"})
31        public void testAcceptOrder(String tid, boolean special,
32                    int sqm, boolean expectedReturn, boolean
                        expectedAccept) {
33            SpaceOrder o = new SpaceOrder(special);
34            assertEquals( o.acceptOrder(sqm), expectedReturn );
35            assertEquals( o.getAccept(), expectedAccept );
36        }
37
38 }
```

Note the following points in the test code:

- The method testConstructor, on lines 12–17, uses parameterised data to implement test cases T1 and T2. The data is provided by the data provider named constructorData defined on lines 3–10.
- The method testAcceptOrder(), on lines 30–36, uses parameterised data to implement test cases T3 to T6. The data is provided by the data provider named acceptOrderData defined on lines 19–28. Making this test method depend on the method testConstructor forces the constructor tests to run first.[6]
- The test code only makes a single call to the method under test, matching the test cases. This makes reviewing the test code easier and also makes debugging easier if a test fails.

9.3.2   Test Results

Running these tests against the class SpaceOrder produces the results shown in Figure 9.3. All the tests have passed.

```
PASSED: testConstructor("SpaceOrderTest T1", true, true, false)
PASSED: testConstructor("SpaceOrderTest T2", false, false, false)
PASSED: testAcceptOrder("SpaceOrderTest T3", true, 7, true, true)
PASSED: testAcceptOrder("SpaceOrderTest T4", false, 504, true, true)
PASSED: testAcceptOrder("SpaceOrderTest T5", false, 5000, true, false)
PASSED: testAcceptOrder("SpaceOrderTest T6", false, -5000, false, false
    )

===============================================
Command line suite
Total tests run: 6, Passes: 6, Failures: 0, Skips: 0
===============================================
```

Figure 9.3 Equivalence partition test results for class SpaceOrder.

---

[6] This feature is described in Chapter 11.

9.4   A More Detailed Look at Testing Object-Oriented Software

In this section we will first examine OO programming and the environment in which OO software runs. There follows a description of the fault models for OO testing, and some more discussion on the activities shown in the test example in Section 9.2. Finally, a number of other OO test techniques are summarised.

9.4.1   Object-Oriented Programming

Object-orientation can be defined as programming with classes, inheritance, and messages.[7] *Classes* provide a wrapper to encapsulate data (attributes) and associated code (methods). *Inheritance* provides a mechanism for code reuse, especially useful for implementing common features. *Messages* (or method calls) provide the interface to an object.

Classes are the foundation of OO programming, and contain a collection of attributes and methods. The attributes are usually hidden from external access, and can only be accessed via methods: this is referred to as data encapsulation. Classes have relationships with other classes: they can inherit attributes and methods from other classes, and can invoke methods on objects of other classes.

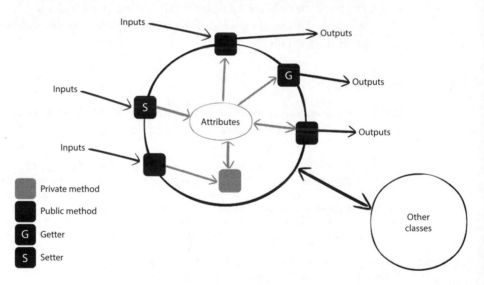

Figure 9.4 Object-oriented execution model.

Figure 9.4 summarises the environment in which methods execute. The inputs labelled are the explicit inputs or parameters passed in the method call, and the outputs are the explicit outputs or values returned by the method call. Public methods

---

[7] R. Binder. *Testing Object Oriented Systems: Models, Patterns, and Tools.* Addison-Wesley, 2010.

are placed on the class boundary: they are accessible from outside the class. Private methods and private attributes are hidden inside the class[8] – they are not accessible from outside the class, and cannot be accessed or used by the tester. The important features of the diagram are:

- Methods whose single function is to set the value of an attribute are referred to as *setters* – marked with an **S**.
- Methods whose single function is to get an attribute value are referred to as *getters* – marked with a **G**.
- For test purposes, methods that do *any* processing are not regarded as getters or setters, and are unlabelled in the diagram. These other methods may be passed input parameters, may read attributes as inputs, do processing, call other methods both public and private, write attributes as outputs, return a value as an output, or raise an exception as an output. Public methods may be called by the tester. Private methods may only be called from within the class.
- Classes may have relationships with other classes: these may be inheritance relationships, where one class reuses all the code of another class (the *is-a* relationship, also referred to as generalisation/specialisation); and aggregation relationships, where one class contains a collection of other classes (the *has-a* relationship).

9.4.2 Testing Object-Oriented Software

Object-oriented testing, is a large and complex area[9] – see Section 14.3 for suggested additional readings in the topic.

This chapter covers the essential test technique that underlies all OO testing: testing in class context. This is used to test code in a class where the data is protected from outside access and methods interact with each other through attributes.

9.4.3 Fault Models

The features of object orientation are intended to improve code quality and support code reuse. But the concepts are complex and introduce their own *fault models* in addition to those associated with software more generally:

Classes: objects retain the values of their attributes (referred to more formally as their *state*) between method calls. In many cases, the order in which these methods are called is important for correct operation. Generally, the code that ensures this ordering is distributed over many methods. This provides many opportunities for what are referred to as *state control* faults, where an object does not behave correctly in a particular state (see Section 8.2.7).

---

[8] It is unusual to use public attributes in Java.
[9] Binder, *Testing Object Oriented Systems* is probably the most thorough reference book.

Inheritance: inheritance leads to a *binding* between objects and different classes and interfaces.[10] Dynamic binding occurs at runtime, where a decision is made by the Java VM as to which overridden method to use. Complex inheritance structures, or a poor understanding of inheritance in Java, may provide many opportunities for faults due to unanticipated bindings or misinterpretation of correct usage.

Messages: programming mistakes when making calls, where the wrong parameters are passed or the correct parameters are passed but mixed up are a leading cause of faults in procedural languages. Object-oriented programs typically have many short methods, and therefore provide an increased risk of these *interface* faults.[11]

9.4.4   Testing in Class Context

The methods in a class must be tested in the context of the other methods defined in the class. This is an essential element of all tests for OO software, as all methods execute in class context. The early chapters examine conventional models of testing using static methods, which accept all their inputs as arguments to the method, and return the result.

A conventional unit test has the structure shown in Snippet 9.1.

Snippet 9.1 A conventional test

```
1    actual_result = Classname.method( p1, p2, p3 );
2    check_equals( actual_result, expected_results );
```

The operation of the test is straightforward:

- On line 1, the method being tested is called with the test input data values – here p1, p2, and p3 are used as examples. The return value is stored in a temporary variable: `actual_result`.

- Subsequently, on line 2, the *actual results* returned by the method call are compared with the *expected results* as specified for the test. If they are the same, then the test passes. Otherwise the test fails.

In practice, this is more usually coded in a single line, as shown in Snippet 9.2.

Snippet 9.2 A conventional test on one line

```
1    check_equals( Classname.method( p1, p2, p3 ),
                expected_results );
```

---

[10] This refers to a Java Interface, or an abstract class in more general terms.
[11] Interface here means an API, or the definition of the parameters to a method call, and *not* a Java Interface.

To test software in an OO environment, an object (an instance of the class being tested) must be created first. When a method is called, some or all of the inputs and outputs for the method may be attributes rather than explicitly passed parameters and return values. In this example, other methods need to be called beforehand to set some of the input values (setters) and afterwards to fetch some of the output values (getters).

The structure of a typical OO unit test is shown in Snippet 9.3. This test structure is referred to as *testing in class context*. Note how this contrasts with a conventional test as shown in Snippet 9.1.

Snippet 9.3 Testing in class context

```
1    object = new Classname( p1 );
2    object.setParameter2( p2 );
3    actual_status = object.method_under_test( p3 );
4    check_equals( actual_status, expected_status );
5    actual_result = object.get_result();
6    check_equals( actual_result, expected_results );
```

The variables p1, p2, and p3 are the same as the parameters passed directly to the method in the conventional test. The actual results are the same as in the conventional test. But the operation of this test is more complex, and has interesting subtleties:

- On line 1, an object is created by calling the constructor with the value p1. The value is stored in a private attribute `paramP1` (not shown in the snippet).
- On line 2, the value p2 is set. Again, this value is stored internally, in attribute `paramP2`.
- On line 3, the method being tested is called with the value p3. The method `method_under_test()` uses the attributes `paramP1` and `paramP2` as inputs, along with the parameter p3. It returns a Boolean value to indicate whether the method succeeded. The result of the method is stored in a private attribute, `theResult`. The returned status is stored in the variable `actual_status`.
- On line 4, the actual status is compared with the expected status. If they are the same, then the test continues. Otherwise the test fails.
- On line 5, the attribute `theResult` is retrieved using the getter method `get_result()` – these are the actual results.
- On line 6, the actual results are compared with the expected results. If they are the same, then the test passes. Otherwise the test fails.

This demonstrates the various additional mechanisms that OO test code uses for inputs and outputs in class context. All the conventional black-box and white-box techniques described in this book can be applied to testing methods in class context: equivalence partitions, boundary values, decision tables, random tests, statement coverage, branch coverage, and all paths coverage. The test conditions will be essentially the same; the key differences are in the analysis, the test cases, and the test implementations, which all need to take the class context issues into account.

9.4.5   Analysis for OO Testing

There are three parts to the analysis. The first is deciding which methods will be tested. The second is analysing the class and its interface. The third is, as for conventional unit testing, analysing the test specifications (and possibly the code) by applying the test design technique(s) selected in order to identify the TCIs.

9.4.6   Test Coverage Items

The TCIs are identified for the test design technique(s) selected using the results of the analysis.

9.4.7   Test Cases

Not only the data values to be used, but the sequence of method calls, must be decided on. This can be left until the implementation phase, but it is important at implementation time to know which method is to be called (as different methods may have the same parameter name for different purposes), and the sequence may have an impact on the data values.

As shown for the worked example in Section 9.2.2, test cases should be developed for the following:

1.   Static methods – these are not dependent on the constructor. Usually they are independent, but if they interact through static attributes then they should be considered *in class context* along with the other methods.
2.   The constructor(s) – including the default constructor. Note that the constructor is called after the other object initialisation has taken place.
3.   Simple methods that do not use the class attributes.
4.   Accessor methods (getters and setters) – if they are to be tested.
5.   The other methods, which do use the class attributes.

It is recommended to limit each test case to one primary method call being tested, though this may require a number of supporting method calls, as we have seen. This makes reviewing the test cases for correct ordering and completeness much easier.[12]

It is not always necessary to use separate tests for each input error case (unlike in equivalence partition testing), as long as the input error values are inputs to different methods and do not cause error hiding.

---

[12] When the test code is being implemented, multiple test cases can be condensed into a single test method if required for improved performance.

9.4.8   Test Implementation

There are two categories of OO test methods: those that can run in any order, and those that require other methods to be run first. In the example shown, the test methods create a new instance of the class for each test, and thus can run in any order (see Chapter 11 for how test priority or test dependencies can be used to enforce a particular ordering). If one test case relies on another one to be run first, then they must either both be included in the same test in the required order, or test dependencies must be used.

Once the test cases have been defined, test implementation is usually very straight-forward.

9.4.9   Overview of Advanced OO Testing

There are a large number of OO testing techniques, and the following sections sum-marise a number of these. Additional reading on these techniques is recommended for the OO tester, and further readings are presented in Section 14.3.

The form of testing demonstrated in the example at the start of this chapter can be termed *conventional testing in class context*. Matching the fault models, there are two other forms of OO testing that are summarised in this section: inheritance testing and state-based testing. Inheritance testing is primarily a test automation issue – running tests designed for one class against a different class (a subclass). This issue is addressed in Chapter 11. State-based testing verifies the behaviour of sequences of inputs, usually specified using the UML state diagram.

9.4.10   Inheritance Testing

This form of testing specifically addresses the inheritance fault model. The purpose of inheritance testing is to verify that the classes within an inheritance hierarchy behave correctly. A simple form of inheritance testing verifies that inherited super-class methods continue to work correctly in the context of the subclass. This can be extended to ensure that all the methods in an entire inheritance tree continue to operate correctly.

The Liskov Substitution Principle

However, not all subclasses are designed to fully support their superclass behaviour. Such subclasses are referred to as not being *Liskov substitutable*.[13] For inheritance testing:

- If a subclass is fully substitutable, then whatever functionality its superclass has, the subclass also supports. It may of course also have additional features. To verify inheritance, the superclass tests are executed against each subclass. This verifies that the subclasses work in *superclass context*.

---

[13] See B.H. Liskov and J.M. Wing. A behavioral notion of subtyping. *ACM Transactions on Programming Languages and Systems*, Vol. 16, No. 6, 1994.

- If a subclass is not fully substitutable, then only a subset (and maybe none) of the superclass tests can be reused in the subclass inheritance test. Analysis must be performed to select the applicable tests. This analysis is made more difficult as the standard UML class diagram does not specify whether a subclass is fully substitutable or not.
- In both cases, additional tests must be written to verify the subclass.

Once the tests to be run have been selected, inheritance testing is primarily a test automation question – see Section 11.9 for an example.

9.4.11   State-Based Testing

This form of testing specifically addresses the class encapsulation/state fault model. The purpose of state-based testing is to verify that a class behaves correctly with regards to its state specification (e.g. UML state machine diagram). A state diagram contains states and transitions between those states. State-based testing verifies that the software transitions correctly between the states. There are three simple test strategies:

- all transitions – every transition is verified at least once;
- all end-to-end paths – every path from the start state to the end state is verified at least once. If there is no end state, which is common in software state diagrams, then every paths from the state to every terminal state[14] can be used; and
- all circuits – every path that starts and ends in the same state is verified.

Each transition is specified by an event that causes the transition, and an accompanying action which should occur (an *event–activity pair*). The correct operation of a transition is verified by:

- checking that the software is in the correct start state (this may have already been done by the verification of the previous transition);
- raising the event (i.e. call the method specified with the correct parameter values);
- checking that the specified activity has taken place correctly;
- checking that the software is in the correct end state.

It is not always possible to fully check that an object is in the correct state, or that the correct activity has taken place.[15] In this case a partial check can be done.

A state diagram for `SpaceOrder` is shown in Figure 9.5.

There are two states and three transitions explicitly specified in the diagram. There are also four transitions that are implied by the diagram, but not explicitly stated. These implicitly specified transitions are method calls not shown on the state diagram – they should cause a transition back to the same state, and have no associated action. In this example, the effect of calling `getSpecial()` and `getAccept()` in each of the

---

[14] A terminal state is one with no transitions to another state.
[15] This is a design for testability (DFT) issue – a class with state-based behaviour is easier to test if the designer takes testability into account.

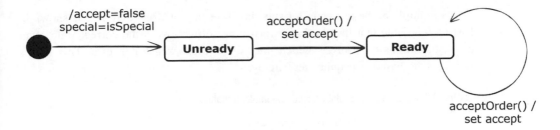

Figure 9.5 State diagram for `SpaceOrder`.

two states in not shown, and so the implicit requirement is that they cause no effect. The full set of transitions to be tested, with added numbering for later reference, is shown in Table 9.10.

The importance of the state diagram is that calling `getAccept()` in the unready state does not produce a valid result, as `acceptOrder()` has not been called.

Table 9.10 Transitions for `SpaceOrder`

Number	Start state	Event	End state
1	Start	Constructor	Unready
2	Unready	`getSpecial()`	Unready
3	Unready	`getAccept()`	Unready
4	Unready	`acceptOrder()`	Ready
5	Ready	`getSpecial()`	Ready
6	Ready	`getAccept()`	Ready
7	Ready	`acceptOrder()`	Ready

Using the all-transitions strategy results in seven TCIs, one for each transition. When verifying that the state transitions have taken place correctly:

- You cannot fully verify that the software is in the unready state: the best partial check is that `getAccept()` returns `false`, and `getSpecial()` returns the provided value of `isSpecial`.
- You can verify that the software is in the ready state if `acceptOrder()` has set `accept` to `true` by calling `getAccept()`, which should return `true`, and `getSpecial()`, which should return the provided value of `isSpecial`.
- You cannot verify that the software is in the ready state if `acceptOrder()` has set `accept` to `false`.

Therefore, the transition from unready to ready should be checked by setting values for `special` and `space` that should set `accept` to `true`. This allows both the unready and ready states to be uniquely identified (if the software is working correctly). The transition from ready to ready by calling `acceptOrder()` can only be (partially) verified by using a value for `space` that causes `accept` to be set to `false`.

An example of the test code for state-based testing of SpaceOrder is shown in Listing 9.3. Note that the checks to verify the software is in the correct state often cause transitions themselves, which must also be checked for in turn. This makes writing state-based tests quite challenging.

Listing 9.3 SpaceOrder state-based test implementation.

```
1  public class SpaceOrderStateTest {
2
3    @Test
4    public void allTransitionsTest() {
5      // transition 1
6      SpaceOrder o = new SpaceOrder(false);
7      // check activity and state for t1
8      assertFalse(o.getSpecial());
9      assertFalse(o.getAccept());
10     // check activity and state for t2 and t3
11     assertFalse(o.getSpecial());
12     assertFalse(o.getAccept());
13     // transition 4
14     o.acceptOrder(1000);
15     // check activity and state for t4
16     assertFalse(o.getSpecial());
17     assertTrue(o.getAccept());
18     // check activity and state for t5 and t6
19     assertFalse(o.getSpecial());
20     assertTrue(o.getAccept());
21     // transition 7
22     o.acceptOrder(2000);
23     // check activity and state for t7
24     assertFalse(o.getSpecial());
25     assertFalse(o.getAccept());
26   }
27
28 }
```

The order in which transitions are tested is important. It would be possible to put each transition test into a separate test method and use dependencies to force them to execute in the correct order (this is discussed in Section 11.9.2). The other approach, shown in Listing 9.3, is to test all the transitions in a single method. This is simpler to implement, but has the disadvantage that it is more difficult to debug a failed test, as the test covers multiple transitions.

The results of running these tests against SpaceOrder are shown in Figure 9.6. All the tests have passed, showing as far as is possible that each transition in the state

```
PASSED: allTransitionsTest
===================================================
Command line suite
Total tests run: 1, Passes: 1, Failures: 0, Skips: 0
===================================================
```

Figure 9.6 All transition state test results for SpaceOrder.

diagram works. The test effectiveness is limited by being unable to access the object state. A tester can only test what is possible.

9.4.12   UML-Based Testing

The UML (Unified Modelling Language) is the main analysis and design tool for OO software. There are a large number of diagrams in UML 2.5.[16] Each of these is a potential source of information and test coverage items for the tester. Method testing in class context and inheritance testing make use of the class diagrams. State-based testing makes use of the state machine diagrams, but all of the other diagrams can also be used to generate tests.

Each item on each diagram has a meaning, and therefore represents a testable property of the software system. For example, the *relationships* between classes and any associated *multiplicities* are useful sources of tests in the class diagram, and the interaction between classes and methods are useful sources of tests in the sequence diagram, activity diagram, and interaction overview diagram.

9.4.13   Built-In Testing

Encapsulation can make testing difficult, especially when trying to access the class attributes in order to verify the actual results match the expected results. There are a number of solutions to this, such as using Java reflection to access private attributes at runtime.[17] Another solution, which is available in many languages, is the use of assertions for *built-in testing* or BIT. The tests are referred to as built-in as the test assertions are built into the code, rather than being located in an external test class.

This can be very effective for ensuring that assumptions that the programmer has made are in fact true when required in the code. They can also be effective in verifying that *class invariants* are maintained by every method, by asserting them at the end of every method.[18] In Java, assertions can be turned on at runtime, so that during testing they are enabled, and in deployment they are disabled.

However, they are less effective in replacing the usual unit tests, as often they need to refer to not only the current value of the method variables (attributes, parameters, and local variables) but also the original values just when the method started execution. Having the code keep copies of these values for testing can be very inefficient in terms of memory space and execution time. It also increases the effort required to code each method, and increases the chances of making a mistake.

An example of BIT is shown in Listing 9.4, where an extra attribute `acceptedSpace` has been added to the class.

---

[16] There are both official and unofficial diagrams – see www.uml-diagrams.org for details.

[17] Java Reflection can be used to examine classes at runtime – see *The Reflection API tutorial* at https://docs.oracle.com/javase/tutorial/reflect/index.html for further information.

[18] Class invariants are constraints on the class attributes that must always hold – they are often used for safety-critical software, as discussed in Section 14.3.9. For example, in a tunnel management system, the number of trains in the tunnel might be constrained to always be less than two.

Listing 9.4 SpaceOrder with BIT.

```
1   public class SpaceOrder {
2
3     boolean special;
4     boolean accept = false;
5     int acceptedSpace = 0; // must always be in [0..1024]
6
7     public SpaceOrder(boolean isSpecial) {
8       special = isSpecial;
9       assert acceptedSpace >= 0 && acceptedSpace <= 1024;
10    }
11
12    public boolean getSpecial() {
13      return special;
14    }
15
16    public boolean acceptOrder(int space) {
17      assert acceptedSpace >= 0 && acceptedSpace <= 1024;
18      boolean status = true;
19      acceptedSpace = 0;
20      accept = false;
21      if (space <= 0) {
22        status = false;
23      }
24      else if (space <= 1024 && (space >= 16 || special)) {
25        accept = true;
26        acceptedSpace = space;
27      }
28      // Check correct result here?
29      assert acceptedSpace >= 0 && acceptedSpace <= 1024;
30      return status;
31    }
32
33    public boolean getAccept() {
34      return accept;
35    }
36
37  }
```

It is straightforward to verify the safety conditions via the Java assert statement. These are placed at the end of the constructor on line 9, and at the start and end of acceptOrder() on lines 17 and 29. To avoid code duplication, a method to check the safety conditions could be implemented, and called on these lines instead.

However, an assertion to verify that the method acceptOrder() has worked correctly cannot always be so easily implemented. Line 29 checks that acceptedSpace is valid, but it does not check that either the attribute accept or the return value is correct. This would require access to the values of the special attribute and the space parameter when the method was entered – but these may have been changed during the method. In this case they have not been modified, but a different algorithm or a fault in the code could have modified either of these. As the values at the end of the method cannot be relied on to represent the values at the start of the method, copies need to be made at the start of the method. In this simple code, copies could be easily kept, but this would introduce the possibility of further faults. And also, in general, complete copies of any referenced objects would be required: this is a non-trivial problem and often unrealistic to implement.[19] For example, if an array of counters is passed as an input, then a copy of the entire array would need to be made, including copies of every counter in the array.

The results of running the equivalence partition tests against `SpaceOrder` with built-in tests are shown in Figure 9.7. All the tests pass – not only are the correct values returned and verified in the tests in `SpaceOrderTest`, but also all the assertions checked in the BITs have succeeded.

```
PASSED: testConstructor("SpaceOrderTest T1", true, true, false)
PASSED: testConstructor("SpaceOrderTest T2", false, false, false)
PASSED: testAcceptOrder("SpaceOrderTest T3", true, 7, true, true)
PASSED: testAcceptOrder("SpaceOrderTest T4", false, 504, true, true)
PASSED: testAcceptOrder("SpaceOrderTest T5", false, 5000, true, false)
PASSED: testAcceptOrder("SpaceOrderTest T6", false, -5000, false, false
    )
===============================================
Command line suite
Total tests run: 6, Passes: 6, Failures: 0, Skips: 0
===============================================
```

Figure 9.7 Equivalence partition and BIT test results for class `SpaceOrder`.

9.5 Evaluation

The tests developed for conventional testing in class context are evaluated in this section by introducing a number of different faults and examining the test results.

9.5.1 Limitations

Three types of fault are demonstrated:

- a simple typo fault that you would expect to find with equivalence partition testing;
- a more complex, state-based fault; and
- a more complex, inheritance-based fault (in a new subclass).

9.5.2 Simple Typo Fault

Listing 9.5 shows a simple fault in class `SpaceOrder`, where a typo leads to a basic processing fault on line 19 (1024 has been entered by mistake as 10240).

---

[19] Java provides no support for taking such copies – just copying an object reference is not sufficient, as the object attributes may be changed by the method being tested.

Listing 9.5 SpaceOrder with simple typo fault.

```
1   public class SpaceOrder {
2
3     protected boolean special;
4     protected boolean accept = false;
5
6     public SpaceOrder(boolean isSpecial) {
7       special = isSpecial;
8     }
9
10    public boolean getSpecial() {
11      return this.special;
12    }
13
14    public boolean acceptOrder(int space) {
15      boolean status = true;
16      this.accept = false;
17      if (space <= 0)
18        status = false;
19      else if (space <= 10240 && (space >= 16 || this.special))
              // typo fault
20        this.accept = true;
21      return status;
22    }
23
24    public boolean getAccept() {
25      return this.accept;
26    }
27
28  }
```

The results of running the SpaceOrder equivalence partition tests are shown in Figure 9.8. The simple fault has been detected – as for any equivalence partition test, there is no guarantee that any particular fault will be found.

```
PASSED: testConstructor("SpaceOrderTest T1", true, true, false)
PASSED: testConstructor("SpaceOrderTest T2", false, false, false)
PASSED: testAcceptOrder("SpaceOrderTest T3", true, 7, true, true)
PASSED: testAcceptOrder("SpaceOrderTest T4", false, 504, true, true)
PASSED: testAcceptOrder("SpaceOrderTest T6", false, -5000, false, false
    )
FAILED: testAcceptOrder("SpaceOrderTest T5", false, 5000, true, false)
java.lang.AssertionError: expected [false] but found [true]
        at example.SpaceOrderTest.testAcceptOrder(SpaceOrderTest.java
          :40)
================================================
Command line suite
Total tests run: 6, Passes: 5, Failures: 1, Skips: 0
================================================
```

Figure 9.8 SpaceOrder equivalence partition test results for typo fault.

9.5.3 State-Based Fault

Listing 9.6 shows a more subtle fault in class `SpaceOrder`.

Listing 9.6 `SpaceOrder` with state fault.

```
1  public class SpaceOrder {
2
3      boolean special;
4      boolean accept = false;
5      boolean locked = false;
6
7      public SpaceOrder(boolean isSpecial) {
8          special = isSpecial;
9      }
10
11     public boolean getSpecial() {
12         return this.special;
13     }
14
15     public boolean acceptOrder(int space) {
16         if (locked)
17             return false;
18         boolean status = true;
19         this.accept = false;
20         if (space <= 0)
21             status = false;
22         else if (space <= 1024 && (space >= 16 || this.special))
23             this.accept = true;
24         return status;
25     }
26
27     public boolean getAccept() {
28         locked = true;
29         return this.accept;
30     }
31
32  }
```

Support for a new attribute locked has been incorrectly added to the class. This prevents `acceptOrder()` from working correctly if it is called more than once – the first time it is called it corrupts the object. In essence, this introduces a new state, locked, which is not in the state diagram, and `acceptOrder()` does not work in this state. See lines 5, 16, 17, and 28.

The results of running the equivalence partition tests in class context against this fault are shown in Figure 9.9. Note that the fault has not been detected. A more systematic exploration of state-based behaviour is required to reliably detect such faults, as discussed in Section 9.4.11.

Demonstrating the Fault

The results of running the state-based tests (from Section 9.4.11) against the faulty implementation of `SpaceOrder` are shown in Figure 9.10. The fault has been found.

```
PASSED: testConstructor("SpaceOrderTest T1", true, true, false)
PASSED: testConstructor("SpaceOrderTest T2", false, false, false)
PASSED: testAcceptOrder("SpaceOrderTest T3", true, 7, true, true)
PASSED: testAcceptOrder("SpaceOrderTest T4", false, 504, true, true)
PASSED: testAcceptOrder("SpaceOrderTest T5", false, 5000, true, false)
PASSED: testAcceptOrder("SpaceOrderTest T6", false, -5000, false, false
        )
===============================================
Command line suite
Total tests run: 6, Passes: 6, Failures: 0, Skips: 0
===============================================
```

Figure 9.9 Equivalence partition test results for state fault.

This systematic testing of the transitions is more likely to find state-based faults than conventional testing in class context.

```
FAILED: allTransitionsTest
java.lang.AssertionError: expected [true] but found [false]
        at example.SpaceOrderStateTest.allTransitionsTest(
            SpaceOrderStateTest.java:22)
===============================================
Command line suite
Total tests run: 1, Passes: 0, Failures: 1, Skips: 0
===============================================
```

Figure 9.10 State test results for state fault.

9.5.4 Inheritance Fault

Listing 9.7 shows a simple fault in class TrackableSpaceOrder, which inherits from SpaceOrder.

Listing 9.7 TrackableSpaceOrder with inheritance fault.

```
1  public class TrackableSpaceOrder extends SpaceOrder {
2
3     private long code = 0;
4
5     public TrackableSpaceOrder(boolean isSpecial) {
6             super(isSpecial);
7         }
8
9     public void setTrackCode(int newValue) {
10        code = newValue;
11     }
12
13    public int getTrackCode() {
14        return (int)code;
15     }
```

```
16
17      @Override
18         public boolean acceptOrder(int space) {
19         return true;
20      }
21
22  }
```

The method `acceptOrder()` has been overridden on lines 17–20. The implementation on line 19 is incomplete. This is often seen where an empty or *skeleton* method is coded initially, and the developer has forgotten to complete it.

The results of running the equivalence partition tests for `SpaceOrder` against an instance of class `TrackableSpaceOrder` are shown in Figure 9.11. How to do this is discussed in Section 11.9.

```
PASSED: testAcceptOrder("SpaceOrderTest T5", false, 5000, true, false)
FAILED: testAcceptOrder("SpaceOrderTest T3", true, 7, true, true)
java.lang.AssertionError: expected [true] but found [false]
        at example.TrackableSpaceOrderInhTest.testAcceptOrder(
            TrackableSpaceOrderInhTest.java:26)

FAILED: testAcceptOrder("SpaceOrderTest T4", false, 504, true, true)
java.lang.AssertionError: expected [true] but found [false]
        at example.TrackableSpaceOrderInhTest.testAcceptOrder(
            TrackableSpaceOrderInhTest.java:26)

FAILED: testAcceptOrder("SpaceOrderTest T6", false, -5000, false, false
        )
java.lang.AssertionError: expected [false] but found [true]
        at example.TrackableSpaceOrderInhTest.testAcceptOrder(
            TrackableSpaceOrderInhTest.java:25)
=================================================
Command line suite
Total tests run: 4, Passes: 1, Failures: 3, Skips: 0
=================================================
```

Figure 9.11 Equivalence partition test results for inheritance fault.

Three of the `SpaceOrder` tests have failed when run against a `TrackableSpaceOrder` instance.

Note that tests T1 and T2 cannot be used as they call the constructor in `SpaceOrder`, which is not a normal method of the class.

9.5.5   Strengths and Weaknesses

The limitations of conventional testing in state context are related both to the weaknesses of the underlying test technique (equivalence partition, BVA, decision tables, statement coverage, branch coverage, all paths, etc.) and to the additional complications introduced by testing in class context.

The conventional tests may find state-based and inheritance faults, but they are more likely to be found by systematic testing against those fault models.

9.6   Key Points

- Methods need to be tested *in class context*, using setter and getter methods to assist in the tests.
- All black-box and white-box test techniques can be used to perform conventional testing in class context.
- Object-oriented programs have special features that require testing: two key ones are state-based behaviour and inheritance.
- As the test code does not have access to private attributes, built-in testing can be a useful technique. It is particularly useful for verifying state invariants.
- There are many other aspects of testing OO programs not shown here: every UML diagram is a specification, and therefore a potential source of test cases and test data.

9.7   Notes for Experienced Testers

The experienced tester can often do all the test design work in their mind, and code the tests directly from the class specifications, especially for a small class. This includes:

- selecting the methods to test (in particular, whether to test the getters and setters);
- for conventional testing in class context, deciding on the test design technique (for example: one or more of equivalence partition, BVA, decision tables, statement coverage, branch coverage, all paths);
- identifying the test coverage items based on the test design technique;
- designing the test cases;
- writing the test code.

Especially in an agile development environment, an experienced tester may use the user stories and acceptance criteria as the basis of OO tests. This is relatively straightforward when the model that the classes implement matches the user problem domain closely. In this case particular user actions can be easily matched to method calls, and the sequence of interactions listed in an acceptance criteria for a user story can be easily mapped to a sequence of method calls.

The experienced tester will also probably code tests directly from the state diagram or inheritance tree, having made sure that the tests are designed to allow inheritance testing.

10 Application Testing

In this chapter we present the essential elements of testing a user application based on the example of a web application. The testing of desktop and mobile applications is very similar – the key difference is the test automation tools, a topic we discuss in Chapter 11.

Application testing has additional complexities in comparison to unit testing. The key differences are: how to locate the inputs on the screen, how to locate the outputs on the screen, and how to automate the tests running over the user interface.

10.1 Testing Web Applications with User Stories

Many different elements of an application's specification can be used as the *test basis* for application testing. Modern, Agile development processes focus on the user requirements expressed in the form of user stories. Larger systems may contain a number of stories which can be grouped into collections called *epics*.

Definition: a *user story* is a way for a *stakeholder* to state their requirements.

User stories usually take the form:

As a <role>, I want <to do something> so that I can <achieve a goal>.

A stakeholder may be an end-user, the sponsor of the project, a representative from sales or marketing, etc. The role refers to the part that the stakeholder is playing for that story.

Each user story is detailed with *acceptance criteria* (also called *confirmations*) which the stakeholders will use to verify that the system has been designed and implemented correctly. These acceptance criteria provide the basis for test cases for automated tests for the stories.

As in previous chapters, we will first consider a small example, and then discuss some of the underlying principles and issues in more detail.

10.2 Example

A fuel depot wants a web-based system to enable the dispatcher to determine whether a load of fuel to be received at the depot will fit in a single tank. Low-volatility fuels can fill a tank completely. High-volatility fuels require expansion space to be left for safety reasons. The tank capacity is 1200 litres without the expansion space, and 800 litres with it. All loads are considered to the nearest litre (decimal points in the fuel loads are not to be supported).

Following conversations with the user, the following story has been developed:

Story S1: *As a fuel depot dispatcher, I want to check if a fuel load fits in a tank so I can decide whether to accept it or not.*

The following detailed acceptance criteria have been agreed with the customer:

S1A1   Check a low-volatility fuel load that fits in a tank.
S1A2   Check a high-volatility fuel load that fits in a tank.
S1A3   Check a low-volatility fuel load that does not fit in a tank.
S1A4   Check a high-volatility fuel load that does not fit in a tank.
S1A5   List tank capacities.
S1A6   Exit when done (this is a general requirement of all software used in the depot company).
S1A7   Identify a user input data error – this criterion was suggested to the customer by the development team, based on their experience on web application design.

This means we have one user story with seven acceptance criteria.

10.2.1   Analysis

To develop the tests, we need to identify:

1. the different screens that the application presents;
2. the user interface elements on each screen we need to interact with; and
3. how input and output data is represented on the screen.

Trial Runs

The user interface can be most easily investigated by using *trial runs* of the software to determine how each story is achieved. An example of this follows for the Fuel Checker application described above. Each screen in the trial is shown in Figures 10.1–10.4, along with a brief explanation.

- Figure 10.1(a): at startup, the Enter Data screen is displayed.
- Figure 10.1(b): after clicking on | Information | the Information screen is displayed.
- Figure 10.2(a): after clicking on | Continue | the Enter Data screen is displayed, and the user enters 1000 for litres and selects High Safety Required .
- Figure 10.2(b): after clicking on | Enter | the Results screen is displayed, with the message 'Fuel does not fit in tank.'

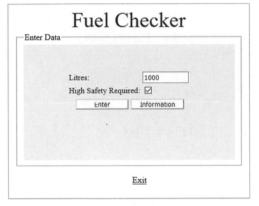

(a) Title: Fuel Checker

(b) Title: Fuel Checker Information

Figure 10.1 Fuel Checker trial run – part 1.

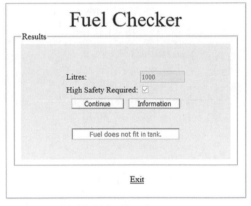

(a) Title: Fuel Checker

(b) Title: Results

Figure 10.2 Fuel Checker trial run – part 2.

- Figure 10.3(a): after clicking on Continue the Enter Data screen is displayed, and the user re-enters 1000 for litres.
- Figure 10.3(b): after clicking on Enter the Results screen is displayed, with the message 'Fuel fits in tank.'
- Figure 10.4(a): after clicking on Continue to return to the Enter Data screen, the user enters xxx for litres, and clicks on Enter . The Results screen is then displayed, with the error message 'Invalid data values.'
- Figure 10.4(b): after clicking on Continue to return to the Enter Data screen, the user clicks on the Exit link at the bottom of the screen. The Goodbye screen is now displayed, with the message 'Thank you for using FuelChecker.'

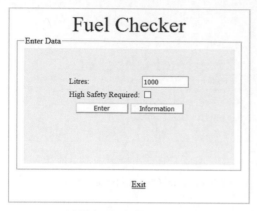

(a) Title: Fuel Checker

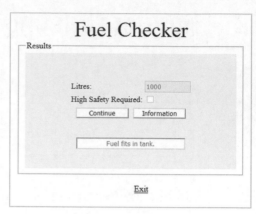

(b) Title: Results

Figure 10.3 Fuel Checker trial run – part 3.

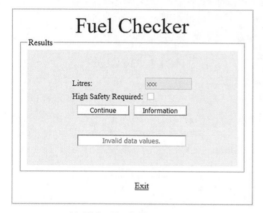

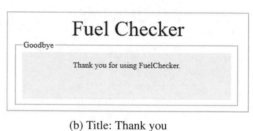

(b) Title: Thank you

(a) Title: Fuel Checker

Figure 10.4 Fuel Checker trial run – part 4.

From these trial runs we can now identify each page displayed by the application, the interface components required for testing, and the data representation being used.

Extracting Information from the Trial Runs

The page titles can be seen in the web browser: they are usually displayed in the tab name and can be easily read from the screen.

A well-designed web page uses *unique* HTML id attributes to identify each element. These trial runs allow the tester to discover the ids required to interact with the input and output elements on each web page. Without these, automated testing is much more difficult.[1]

---

[1] In a test driven design (TDD) environment, tests may be developed as soon as the screen layout has been designed, using ids selected by the graphical user interface (GUI) designer or the tester. The code would then use these ids in order to pass the tests.

Most web browsers include an *inspector* that allows the element id (and other information) to be examined in the web browser.[2] Three examples of this are shown below.

Example 1: Figure 10.5 shows the Element tab displayed by Chrome when the user right-clicks on the input textbox for litres and selects Inspect from the pulldown menu.

Figure 10.5 Inspector – litres input textbox.

The important details of this element for the tester are:

- the html element type (`<input type = "text">`)
- the id (`id = "litres"`)

Example 2: Figure 10.6 shows the inspector information for the Enter button on the same web page.

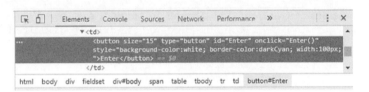

Figure 10.6 Inspector – Enter button.

The important details of this element for the tester are:

- the html element type (`<button type = "button">`)
- the id (`id = "Enter"`)

Example 3: Figure 10.7 shows the inspector information for the body element.

Figure 10.7 Inspector – body element.

---

[2] Alternatively, the page source may be viewed in the browser.

In cases where displayed text is not within a container with an id, then a higher-level container may be used.[3] For example, the lines of displayed text for the information screen are contained within <p> elements, which are in turn contained within a <span> element with no id. The <span> element is in turn contained with a <div> element which has an id 'body'.

The important details of this element for the tester are:

* the html element type (<div>); and
* the id (id = "body").

Using the inspector, the HTML element type and id of all the necessary web elements are determined, as listed in Table 10.1.

Table 10.1 HTML element information.

Page title	HTML element/type	id
Fuel Checker	<input type = "text">	litres
	<input type = "checkbox">	highsafety
	<button type = "button">	Enter
	<button type = "button">	Info
	<a>	exitlink
Fuel Check	<button type = "button">	goback
Information	<div>	body
Results	<input type = "text" disabled>	litres
	<input type = "checkbox" disabled>	highsafety
	<button type = "button">	Continue
	<input type = "text">	result
	<a>	exitlink
Thank you	<div>	body

The input elements for litres and highsafety are disabled initially. They are then dynamically enabled as required by the application, producing the screens shown in the trial run.

Data Representation

The data representation used for the inputs and outputs is determined by examining the HTML elements and their appearance on the screen.

* The input *highSafety* is a checkbox element. This represents a Boolean value.
* The input *litres* is a text input element (a string). This represents an integer value.

---

[3] HTML elements can be nested, so if the element or container you want to refer to has no id, you can select the higher-level element or container. See www.w3schools.com/html/html_elements.asp for an explanation. An alternative is to search for paragraph elements that contain the required text within the higher-level container.

- The output `result` is a non-editable text element (a string). The text can take one of three possible outputs:

  – "Fuel fits in tank"
  – "Fuel does not fit in tank"
  – "Invalid data entered"

- The output `body` of the information screen is also a non-editable text element (a string). The content of `body` is a complex HTML expression (as shown in Figure 10.7). We are not testing the text formatting is correct, we just need to check that this element contains the correct text. The other HTML elements can be ignored. The correct text contains the two important phrases:

  – "Standard tank capacity: 1200 litres"
  – "High safety tank capacity: 800 litres"

A simple user story test case will use a single data value for each acceptance criterion. In more advanced testing, the analysis can be extended to identify equivalence partitions, boundary values, and combinations for testing.

The analysis is now complete – we have identified each screen displayed by the application, each web element on each screen required for testing, and the data representation used for each of these elements.

10.2.2 Test Coverage Items

Each acceptance criterion (AC) for each user story (US) is a test coverage item (TCI), as shown in Table 10.2.[4] The Test Case column will be completed later as part of our test design review.

Table 10.2 TCIs for Fuel Checker.

TCI	Acceptance criteria	Test case
US1	S1A1	To be completed
US2	S1A2	
US3	S1A3	
US4	S1A4	
US5	S1A5	
US6	S1A6	
US7	S1A7	

Even though US7 reports an error back to the user, it is not an error case in the same sense as in EP testing. Each user story/acceptance criteria is tested separately, so the issue of error hiding does not apply, and we do not need to identify error cases with an asterisk.

[4] We have one user story with seven acceptance criteria. The TCI identifiers US1–7 are arbitrary unique identifiers, with the prefix US selected to indicate that these are user story tests.

10.2.3   Test Cases

In a manner similar to equivalence partition testing, typical data values are selected for the test cases. These may be selected in advance, as shown in Table 10.3, or selected during the development of the test cases. As in the previous test techniques, selecting standard values makes reviewing the completed test cases easier. For application testing, it is not usual to perform the detailed analysis using value lines, which is shown for unit testing in Section 2.2.1.

Table 10.3 Selected input data values.

TCI	Input	Value
US1	litres	"1000"
US2	litres	"400"
US3	litres	"2000"
US4	litres	"1000"
US7	litres	"xxx"

Typical Data Values

There are many possible invalid strings that may be entered for an integer value in US7 – see the discussion in Section 10.4.6.

The expected results (the correct outputs, and their data representation) have already been identified during analysis of the application, as shown in Table 10.4.

Table 10.4 Output data values.

TCI	Output	Value
US1	result	"Fuel fits in tank."
US2	result	"Fuel fits in tank."
US3	result	"Fuel does not fit in tank."
US4	result	"Fuel does not fit in tank."
US5	body	contains "Standard tank capacity: 1200 litres" and "High safety tank capacity: 800 litres"
US6	body	"Thank you for using fuelchecker"
US7	result	"Invalid data values."

Test Case Table

The test data for each test case is specified as a sequence of user actions to be simulated by the automated test. Each TCI is a separate test case.

The development of test data for the first test case is as follows – details such as opening the web page are not necessary here, as the test implementer may chose to reopen the page for each test or not (for efficiency purposes it is better not to).

- After starting the application, enter 1000 into litres.
- Make sure that `highsafety` is deselected.

- Click on Enter, and make sure the application moves to the Results screen.
- Check that Result contains the text `"Fuel fits in the tank."`.

Test case T1 is shown in Table 10.5. The inputs consist of actions: in this example, there are data values to be typed in, checkboxes to be selected/deselected, and buttons to be clicked. The expected results consist of responses by the web application: in this example, there are window titles and displayed text to be verified.

Table 10.5 Test case T1 for user story testing.

ID	TCI covered	Inputs	Exp. results
T1	US1	Enter `"1000"` into litres Deselect `highsafety` Click on Enter	Moved to Results screen Result is `"Fuel fits in tank."`

The data for the other tests is developed the same way, specifying the inputs to the application, and the expected results. See Table 10.6 for the full set of test cases.

Table 10.6 Test cases for user story testing.

ID	TCI covered	Inputs	Expected results
T1	US1	Enter `"1000"` into litres Deselect `highsafety` Click on Enter	Moved to Results screen Result is `"Fuel fits in tank."`
T2	US2	Enter `"400"` into litres Select `highsafety` Click on Enter	Moved to Results screen Result is `"Fuel fits in tank."`
T3	US3	Enter `"2000"` into litres Deselect `highsafety` Click on Enter	Moved to Results screen Result is `"Fuel does not fit in tank."`
T4	US4	Enter `"1000"` into litres Select `highsafety` Click on Enter	Moved to Results screen Result is `"Fuel does not fit in tank."`
T5	US5	Click on Info	Moved to Information screen body contains `"Standard tank capacity: 1200 litres"` body contains `"High safety tank capacity: 800 litres"`
T6	US6	Click on *Exit* link	Moved to Thank You screen body contains `"Thank you for using fuelchecker."`
T7	US7	Enter `"xxx"` into litres Select `highsafety` Click on Enter	Moved to Results screen Result is `"Invalid data values."`

10.2.4   Verification of the Test Cases

The completed test coverage items are shown in Table 10.7. This verifies that each test coverage item is covered, and that there are no unnecessary tests.

Table 10.7 Completed test coverage items table.

TCI	Acceptance criteria	Test case
US1	S1A1	T1
US2	S1A2	T2
US3	S1A3	T3
US4	S1A4	T4
US5	S1A5	T5
US6	S1A6	T6
US7	S1A7	T7

10.3   Test Implementation and Results

TestNG is used to run the tests and collect the results. In order to simulate user input into a web application, and to collect the output for verification, a web automation test library must be used. A good and widely used example is Selenium.[5] This is used in the test implementation as a representative example to demonstrate the principles of test automation for web applications.

10.3.1   Implementation

Only the code for the test methods themselves is shown here. The complete test program requires additional methods to configure Selenium and open the web browser, which are shown in Section 10.4.

Test 1

The implementation of the first test case (T1) is shown in Listing 10.1.

Listing 10.1 Fuel Checker test T1.

```
58    // Tests go here
59
60    @Test(timeOut = 60000)
61    public void test1() {
62       String litres = "1000";
63       boolean highsafety = false;
64       String result = "Fuel fits in tank.";
65       wait.until(ExpectedConditions.titleIs("Fuel Checker"));
66       wait.until(ExpectedConditions.visibilityOfElementLocated(
                By.id("litres")));
67       driver.findElement(By.id("litres")).sendKeys(litres);
```

---

[5] See www.selenium.dev for details.

```
68      wait.until(ExpectedConditions.visibilityOfElementLocated(
            By.id("highsafety")));
69      if (driver.findElement(
            By.id("highsafety")).isSelected()!=highsafety)
70        driver.findElement(By.id("highsafety")).click();
71      wait.until(ExpectedConditions.visibilityOfElementLocated(
            By.id("Enter")));
72      driver.findElement(By.id("Enter")).click();
73      wait.until(ExpectedConditions.titleIs("Results"));
74      wait.until(ExpectedConditions.visibilityOfElementLocated(
            By.id("result")));
75      assertEquals( driver.findElement(
            By.id("result")).getAttribute("value"),result );
76      wait.until(ExpectedConditions.visibilityOfElementLocated(
            By.id("Continue")));
77      driver.findElement(By.id("Continue")).click();
78      wait.until(ExpectedConditions.titleIs("Fuel Checker"));
79    }
```

The stages of development for this code are as follows:

- Web-based tests require a timeout: in case the browser does not respond, or the test hangs indefinitely waiting for a specific response. In this test, a timeout of 60 seconds is selected – the value depends on connectivity and is contextual, and may require a few test runs – line 60.
- First the test makes sure the browser is on the correct screen. Where web page titles are used, this can be best achieved by checking the title – line 65.
- Next the value for litres must be entered. The browser may not have finished rendering the window, so the test must wait for this element to appear, and then it can simulate user entry using sendKeys() – lines 66 and 67.
- Each HTML element used in the test is found by calling the method By.id() – see for example line 67.
- The highsafety checkbox must be deselected. To do this, the current value of the checkbox is checked (line 69), and if it is already selected, then it must be clicked to deselect it – lines 69 and 70.
- Again, the browser may not have finished rendering the window, so the test must wait for the Enter button to appear before clicking it – lines 71 and 72.
- The test must check that the application has moved to the correct screen (title "Results") – line 73.
- The test verifies the expected results: that the attribute value of the textfield result has the expected value, as held in the variable result ("Fuel fits in tank.") – lines 64 and 75.
- The test now waits for the Continue button, clicks on it, and verifies that the application has moved to the Fuel Checker screen – lines 76 and 78.

The results of running test T1 are shown in Figure 10.8.

The time the test was started at and the URL are printed by the test code (see Listing 10.6 for details). Their values will therefore change depending on your configuration and when the test is run. The WebDriver startup and connection information confirms

```
Test started at: 2020-08-28T13:04:28.398050100
For URL: ch10\fuelchecker\fuelchecker.html

Starting ChromeDriver 84.0.4147.30 (48
    b3e868b4cc0aa7e8149519690b6f6949e110a8-refs/branch-heads/4147@
    {#310}) on port 35538
Only local connections are allowed.
Please see https://chromedriver.chromium.org/security-considerations
    for suggestions on keeping ChromeDriver safe.
ChromeDriver was started successfully.
Aug 28, 2020 1:04:31 P.M. org.openqa.selenium.remote.ProtocolHandshake
    createSession
INFO: Detected dialect: W3C
PASSED: test1
===============================================
Command line suite
Total tests run: 1, Passes: 1, Failures: 0, Skips: 0
===============================================
```

Figure 10.8 T1 test results for Fuel Checker.

that the web browser has started properly, and a session for the browser has started. These details are not important to the test result. The test has passed.

Adding Tests 2–4 and 7

Test 1 can be run on its own, but adding further tests requires decisions about how the sequence of tests is to run, and how code duplication can be avoided. Restarting the web application each time is very slow, so it is usual to run the tests in sequence. This requires that each test leaves the application on a selected screen. For this application, it is easiest to always return the application to the Fuel Checker screen at the end of each test. Code duplication can be avoided, as in unit testing, by using parameterised tests.

Test cases T1, T2, T3, T4, and T7 have exactly the same structure , but use different data. This is an opportunity to use a `DataProvider`, as shown in Listing 10.2.

Listing 10.2 Fuel Checker tests T1, T2, T3, T4, T7.

```
70    // Tests go here
71
72    // Test data
73
74    @DataProvider(name = "testset1") // Data for test cases
          T1-T4,T7
75    public Object[][] getdata() {
76       return new Object[][] {
77          { "T1", "1000", false, "Fuel fits in tank." },
78          { "T2", "400", true, "Fuel fits in tank." },
79          { "T3", "2000", false, "Fuel does not fit in tank." },
80          { "T4", "1000", true, "Fuel does not fit in tank." },
81          { "T7", "xxx", true, "Invalid data values." },
82       };
```

```
83     }
84
85     @Test(timeOut = 60000, dataProvider = "testset1")
86     public void testEnterCheckView(String tid, String litres,
               boolean highsafety, String result) {
87       wait.until(ExpectedConditions.titleIs("Fuel Checker"));
88       wait.until(ExpectedConditions.visibilityOfElementLocated(
               By.id("litres")));
89       driver.findElement(By.id("litres")).sendKeys(litres);
90       wait.until(ExpectedConditions.visibilityOfElementLocated(
               By.id("highsafety")));
91       if (driver.findElement( By.id("highsafety")).isSelected()
               != highsafety)
92         driver.findElement( By.id("highsafety")).click();
93       wait.until(ExpectedConditions.visibilityOfElementLocated(
               By.id("Enter")));
94       driver.findElement( By.id("Enter")).click();
95       wait.until(ExpectedConditions.titleIs("Results"));
96       wait.until(ExpectedConditions.visibilityOfElementLocated(
               By.id("result")));
97       assertEquals( driver.findElement(
               By.id("result")).getAttribute("value"),result );
98       wait.until(ExpectedConditions.visibilityOfElementLocated(
               By.id("Continue")));
99       driver.findElement( By.id("Continue")).click();
100      wait.until(ExpectedConditions.titleIs("Fuel Checker"));
101    }
```

Test cases T5 and T6 have different structures, so require individual tests, as shown in Listings 10.3 and 10.4.

Listing 10.3 Fuel Checker test T5.

```
103    @Test(timeOut = 60000)
104    public void test_T5() {
105      // Info -> "Standard tank capacity: 1200 litres" and "High
               safety tank capacity: 800 litres"
106      wait.until(ExpectedConditions.titleIs("Fuel Checker"));
107      wait.until(ExpectedConditions.visibilityOfElementLocated(
               By.id("Info")));
108      driver.findElement(By.id("Info")).click();
109      wait.until(ExpectedConditions.titleIs("Fuel Checker
               Information"));
110      wait.until(ExpectedConditions.visibilityOfElementLocated(
               By.id("body")));
111      assertTrue(
112         driver.findElement(
               By.id("body")).getAttribute("innerHTML").contains(
               "Standard tank capacity: 1200 litres")
113         &&
114         driver.findElement(
               By.id("body")).getAttribute("innerHTML").contains(
               "High safety tank capacity: 800 litres")
115      );
116      wait.until(ExpectedConditions.visibilityOfElementLocated(
               By.id("goback")));
```

```
117     driver.findElement(By.id("goback")).click();
118     wait.until(ExpectedConditions.titleIs("Fuel Checker"));
119     }
```

Listing 10.4 Fuel Checker test T6.

```
121     @Test(timeOut = 60000)
122     public void test_T6() {
123         // exit -> "Thank you for using FuelChecker."
124         wait.until(ExpectedConditions.titleIs("Fuel Checker"));
125         wait.until(ExpectedConditions.visibilityOfElementLocated(
                By.id("exitlink")));
126         driver.findElement(By.id("exitlink")).click();
127         wait.until(ExpectedConditions.titleIs("Thank you"));
128         wait.until(ExpectedConditions.visibilityOfElementLocated(
                By.id("body")));
129         assertTrue(driver.findElement(
                By.id("body")).getAttribute("innerHTML").contains(
                "Thank you for using FuelChecker."));
130     }
```

Making sure that a test leaves the application at the main screen, even if the test fails, requires a method to be run after each test. This is shown in Listing 10.5, which uses the TestNG @AfterMethod annotation to require that returnToMain() is run immediately after each @Test method.[6]

Listing 10.5 The returnToMain() method.

```
58      @AfterMethod
59      public void returnToMain() {
60          // If test has not left app at the main window, try to
                return there for the next test
61          if ("Results".equals(driver.getTitle()))
62              driver.findElement(By.id("Continue")).click();
63          else if ("Fuel Checker
                Information".equals(driver.getTitle()))
64              driver.findElement(By.id("goback")).click();
65          else if ("Thank you".equals(driver.getTitle()))
66              driver.get( url ); // only way to return to main screen
                from here
67          wait.until(ExpectedConditions.titleIs("Fuel Checker"));
68      }
```

The returnToMain() method works as follows:

- If a test fails, it is important to return the application to the Fuel Checker screen. This allows subsequent tests to run correctly – we have defined all our tests to start from the main screen. To handle this, an @AfterMethod method returnToMain() is provided that attempts to achieve this – see lines 59–67.

---

[6] See Chapter 11 for more details.

- If the application is left at the Thank You screen after a failure, there is no link or button for the user to click to return to the main screen. The `@AfterMethod` code reloads the main application URL to handle this – see lines 65 and 66.

10.3.2   Test Results

The results of running these tests against the Fuel Checker application are shown in Figure 10.9. All the tests pass.

```
Test started at: 2020-09-24T19:15:14.618050100
For URL: ch10\fuelchecker\fuelchecker.html

Starting ChromeDriver 84.0.4147.30 (48
    b3e868b4cc0aa7e8149519690b6f6949e110a8-refs/branch-heads/4147@
    {#310}) on port 1388
Only local connections are allowed.
Please see https://chromedriver.chromium.org/security-considerations
    for suggestions on keeping ChromeDriver safe.
ChromeDriver was started successfully.
[1600971316.989][WARNING]: This version of ChromeDriver has not been
    tested with Chrome version 85.
Sep 24, 2020 7:15:18 P.M. org.openqa.selenium.remote.ProtocolHandshake
    createSession
INFO: Detected dialect: W3C


=================================================
    Command line test
    Tests run: 7, Failures: 0, Skips: 0
```

Figure 10.9 Fuel Checker user story test results.

10.4   Application Testing in More Detail

Applications are a type of computer-based system with a user interface. It is useful to first consider system testing in general to better understand the role of application testing.

System testing means verifying that a system as a whole works correctly, and is almost invariably done using black-box tests. Simple white-box coverage (statement and branch) may be measured, and these results used to develop further tests. There are many types of system, and each has its own unique testing challenges. However, all systems are tested over their system interface, and the principles of black-box and white-box testing apply when generating test data.

10.4.1   System Test Model

Software systems are tested over their system interface.

A generic test model for system testing is shown in Figure 10.10. The test tool provides inputs to the test item, and receives outputs from the test item, over the system

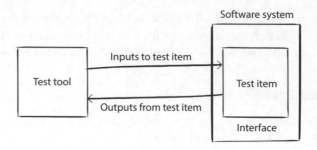

Figure 10.10 System test model.

interface. In some cases the interface will be synchronous, where every input generates an output. In other cases the interface will be asynchronous, where an input may create a sequence of outputs over time, or the test item may spontaneously generate outputs based on timers or other internal events.

10.4.2   Application Test Model

This generic model can be applied to different types of application.

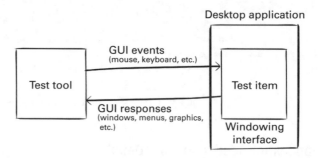

Figure 10.11 Desktop application test model.

A test model for desktop applications is shown in Figure 10.11. The test tool interacts with the desktop application through a windowing interface (e.g. AWT, Swing, or JavaFX in the case of Java) by emulating a user. When a user interacts with the screen, the windowing interface software generates what are referred to as GUI events, and the test tool generate the same GUI events. The responses are in turn delivered back to the test tool via the windowing interface, and these are referred to as GUI responses.

Models for web application testing are shown in Figures 10.12. Web applications use a web browser to provide the user interface, and the communication between the browser and the application running on the web-server is via the hypertext transfer protocol (HTTP) over the network. In Figure 10.12(a) the system is tested via a web browser, and the test tool emulates the actions of a user. In Figure 10.12(b) the system is tested using HTTP directly over the network interface. The test tool in this case must generate the HTTP messages itself. There are utilities and libraries that can be

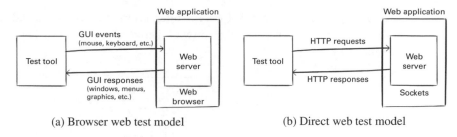

(a) Browser web test model   (b) Direct web test model

Figure 10.12 Web application test model.

used to generate HTTP requests and parse HTTP responses for this purpose (e.g. curl, Beautiful Soup, etc.). This generally executes much faster, and allows testing to be independent of the web browser; however, it is more complex to implement the tests, requiring a deep understanding of HTML and HTTP, and does not guarantee correct operation when running against a web browser. Also, if the application is partially implemented in the browser using JavaScript, then the test tool must support this (which is a substantial task).

10.4.3 System Testing and Integration Testing

System testing and integration testing often take place over the same interface (the system interface). But it is important to note that the purpose of each is different. System tests verify that the system as a whole is working correctly. Integration tests verify that some components (or subsystems) of a system are working correctly together.

Integration Testing

Integration testing takes a number of forms, depending on the software process. In the traditional software process, based on producing layers of software, integration takes places between these layers. Depending on the process, this may take the form of *top-down integration testing*, *bottom-up integration testing*, or *feature testing*, which are explained below. In a modern Agile process, adding new user features typically involves changes to all the layers. Integration testing in this type of process often involves making sure that the old and new user features integrate correctly together – this is sometimes referred to as *testing end-to-end functionality*.

Integration testing may also take place in a way similar to unit testing, where the purpose of the testing is to verify that two software components (usually represented by classes) work correctly together.

Drivers, Stubs, and Mocks

When doing integration testing, the software is often incomplete. This may require the tester to write temporary code to take the place of not-yet-written software. It is a goal to minimise the volume of this temporary software – but it may be necessary for testing. This temporary software is often referred to as drivers and stubs/mocks. The relationship of these to the software being tested (the test item) in shown in Figure 10.13.

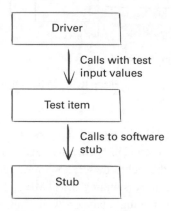

Figure 10.13 Test drivers and stubs.

When the software being tested requires another software component that has not yet been implemented, temporary software (referred to as stubs) is written. This stub software has limited functionality – often it will provide just enough support for the tests to execute. Stubs may also be used to speed up tests by avoiding slow networking calls, or to prevent actual actions taking place (such as sending emails or modifying an active database).

Stubs may include instrumentation (e.g. counters added to the stub code) to measure how much of the temporary code has actually been called, or assertions[7] to verify correct operation. These instrumented stubs are often referred to as *mocks*. Testing with mocks is referred to as *mock testing* or *mocking*, which is supported by many tools.[8]

If the top layer of the software is produced first, then top-down integration testing is used, as shown in Figure 10.14(a). If the bottom layer of the software is produced first, then bottom-up integration testing is used, as shown in Figure 10.14(b).

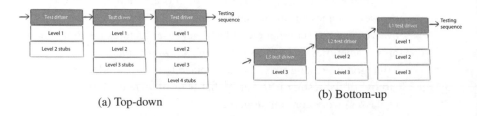

(a) Top-down   (b) Bottom-up

Figure 10.14 Top-down and bottom-up integration testing.

---

[7] See built-in testing in Section 9.4.13.
[8] For example: EasyMock, JMock, JMockit, Mockito, and PowerMock.

In top-down testing, the top layer of software (level 1 in Figure 10.14) is tested first with the underlying layer (level 2) replaced by stubs. At the next stage of testing, the level 2 stubs are replaced by the next layer of software (level 2), and the new underlying layer (level 3) is replaced by stubs. This continues until all the stubs have been replaced by the operational software. All the tests use the top-level interface (which may be an API or a user interface) as presented by level 1. Only one test driver is required, though it may require additions to make sure that the progressive integration with the underlying software is thoroughly tested.

Bottom-up testing is the opposite: it begins with the level 3 test driver testing the lowest layer of software (level 3). Then the next layer is introduced (level 2), and a new test driver written to test this (L2 test driver). This continues until all the levels of the software have been integrated and tested. In contrast to top-down testing, the L3 test driver will use the Level 3 API, but the final L1 test driver will use the level 1 API. No stubs are required, but multiple test drivers must be written.

A hybrid approach, sandwich testing, reduces the number of stubs required by testing just three layers at a time: the focus of testing in this case is the middle layer.

As an alternative to these layered approaches, most modern development processes focus on developing increments of *end-to-end user functionality* – for example, each deliverable feature in the product backlog (see Chapter 13). The order of testing as these features are added incrementally is shown in Figure 10.15.

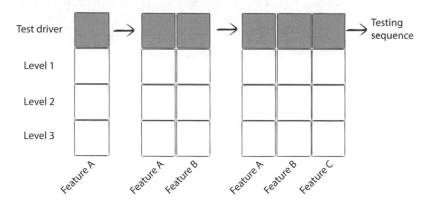

Figure 10.15 Feature integration testing.

In practice, system tests (or application tests) are often used to act as integration tests, with mocks used to verify the integration. Developing tests that thoroughly exercise each interface is time-consuming, and techniques for developing TCIs for integration testing are still being researched – see Chapter 14.

10.4.4   Fault Models for Application Testing

The principle fault model for an application is related to the tasks the user wishes to complete – this leads to the following fault model:

- **User requirements faults:** this occurs where the actual responses from the application do not match the expected responses as specified in the associated user story.

However, it is unusual for the user stories to cover the full functionality of the interface. There is a second level of the design hierarchy to be considered in testing an application. When using an application, a user will navigate between different screens, each screen contains multiple interface elements, and these elements interact with underlying software features. In an MVC (model–view–controller) design, navigation may be associated with the controller, screen contents with the view, and the underlying software features with the model. This leads to three functional fault models for an application:[9]

- **Navigation faults:** this occurs where the navigation between the different interface components (in the form of windows, screens, pages, forms, etc.) does not work correctly. The application may display the wrong screen, or may ignore the user action and do nothing.
- **Screen element faults:** each interactive interface component of the system, with its corresponding inputs and outputs, has expected behaviour. For example, a button should perform some action when clicked, a text input box should accept typing, and a hyperlink should navigate to another page. It is an element behaviour fault when an element does not exhibit the expected behaviour. In the case of a web application, much of the expected behaviour may be implicit and not documented. For example, the designer might assume that a user will type their name into a textbox with the prompt `"Username"` and not specify exactly how the textbox is expected to behave in detail.
- **Software feature faults:** where the software features of the system are documented, these can be tested independently of the user stories. Typically a feature is a set of interactions with the system that result in a particular output. A user story typically involves several features. A feature can be regarded as a method or class, and the black-box techniques of equivalence partition, BVA, and decision tables applied to testing each.

Some of these fault models may overlap: for example, if an HTML anchor link is not implemented correctly, it will not behave correctly when clicked (element behaviour fault), leading to the next screen not being displayed (navigation fault), which may cause the feature being used to not display its outputs (feature fault), and thus the application will not satisfy the acceptance criteria for the associated user story (user requirements fault). User stories attempt to catch most of these faults by testing that the user can complete the required tasks.

---

[9] There are a wide range of appearance- and performance-related fault models which are not included here.

10.4.5   Analysis

The key analysis task in application testing is the analysis of the user interface. In unit testing, a method call requires no analysis: the parameters, their types, and order are all well defined. However, for a user interface, the inputs and outputs are located on a screen, and are represented using text (or other user interface metaphors for the underlying data types). The location of these interface elements may change based on the screen size or orientation, and the user must interact with the application using other interface elements (such as keyboard shortcuts, buttons, links, etc.).

Designing automated tests for an application involves finding a way to (a) locate the required interface elements, and (b) enter/extract data in a way that is compatible with the data representation used. For example, numeric data will often be represented as text on the screen. This involves several transformations:

*   When the user enters a number, each numeric key pressed is interpreted as a digit, and these digits are added to the end of a string displayed as feedback to the user on the screen. This string must then be converted to an integer value for use in the program. The test tool needs to convert integer inputs to strings (or key presses) in order to provide the input.
*   When an integer value is to be shown to the user by a program, then it will first be converted to a text string for display. The test tool needs to retrieve this string, and convert it to an integer, before checking its value.
*   Numeric inputs and outputs may also use different screen elements as metaphors for the value. These may include dials, sliders, pull-down menus, etc. In each case, the test tool must manipulate these screen elements to provide inputs to the program, and must convert from the displayed representation to check the outputs from the program.

The difference between interacting with a software application via its user interface, and calling a method via its programming interface, is discussed below.

Programming Interfaces and User Interfaces

The programming interface for a method to check whether a fuel load will fit in a tank or not is shown in Snippet 10.1.

Snippet 10.1 Software programming interface

```
1    boolean check(int volume, boolean highSafety)
            throws FuelException
```

This programming interface should be interpreted as follows:

*   The input for the volume of fuel is passed in the parameter `volume`.
*   The input for whether the fuel is highly volatile and requires extra space for safety is passed in the parameter `highSafety`.

- The output is returned in the method return value.
- If an error occurs, then the method will raise a `FuelException`.
- The method is identified by its name – in Java the full name includes the package name and the class name: `example.FuelChecker.check()`

Writing a program to interact automatically with this method is straightforward for an experienced programmer, and unless the parameter types are very complex, requires no further analysis.

The user interface for an application that uses this method to check whether a fuel load will fit in a tank or not is shown in Figure 10.16.

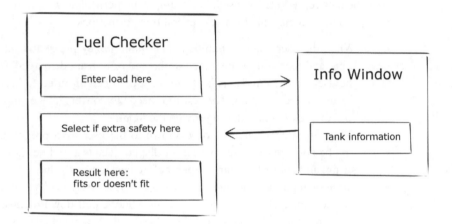

Figure 10.16 Software user interface.

This user interface should be interpreted as follows:

- The inputs for the volume of fuel, and whether extra safety space is required, are located on the screen.
- By convention the prompts for these inputs will be either above or to the left of the entry fields. The prompts may be short and cryptic, as shown in the figure, or long and descriptive.
- The result is shown in a separate field, in this case it is below the entry fields. It may have a prompt, or a title, or may just be identified by context.

The screens may be identified by a title at the top of the page (here we see Fuel Checker and Info Window), by a name external to the screen (for example, web browser tab names), or by content.

The input and output parameters are represented by text on the screen and checkboxes in this example. The question arises of what are the valid representations of numbers as text, and what is the interpretation of the checkbox. These issues are discussed under data representation below.

Writing a test program to interact automatically with this application is complex:

- Interacting based purely on the absolute (x,y) location of each element on the screen can prove problematic. This fails if the layout changes, which is a particular problem for responsive interface design.[10]
- Using the prompt text can also prove problematic. The prompt is usually located by various conventions – for example, the prompt for a dial may be within the element, the prompt for a text box may be to the left of or above the textbox, or even in the textbox in a grey font. It may also prove difficult to locate non-text elements by prompt – for example, a warning message may pop up an icon on the screen, such as a warning flag.

These user interface elements may be easy for a user to locate and interpret, based on prompts, convention, or just experience. But locating them and interpreting the data representation, provide significant challenges for test automation. Unless there is detailed documentation available, specifying the interface in detail, this requires further investigation before black-box techniques can be used to select test data.

An application may use a wide range of on-screen interface elements (pull-down menus, popup menus, sliders, drag-and-drop, keypad gestures, etc.), and even off-screen interfaces such as audio, visual, and haptic interfaces; these are significantly harder to test!

Interacting with HTML Elements

The tester must find a way to locate these elements, and for a web application this is best done (if the pages are well designed) by using the HTML title for each page, and the HTML id for each element. If these are not available, it is a more challenging issue: elements may be identified by their contents (e.g. the text on a button), or in the worst case by their relative or absolute location on the page (or, more accurately, in the currently loaded document object model).

The Selenium library is representative of other web automation tools in that it provides a number of methods to find HTML elements and interact with them.

1. A *By* object is used to represent search criteria. HTML elements may be identified by a number of characteristics: id, classname, css selector, anchor link text, anchor partial link text match, name, tag or xpath.[11]

---

[10] Responsive interfaces will dynamically alter the screen layout to suit the size and orientation of a screen. For example, as a mobile phone is rotated, the position of the screen elements may be modified to suit the new orientation. Sophisticated versions may also alter the contents of the screen, for example removing large logos or summarising text and prompts when displayed on a small screen.

[11] `By.ByXPath()` is very useful where HTML id's are not defined, as elements can be found by their content. However, its use is far from straightforward. Refer to the Selenium documentation at www.javadoc.io/doc/org.seleniumhq.selenium/selenium-api/2.50.1/org/openqa/selenium/By.html for details.

2. The `WebDriver.findElement()/findElements()` methods use `By` to return the first or all matching elements.

Data Representation

Data representation is the other key issue facing the tester. This is demonstrated by an example shown in Figure 10.17, where a text string is used to represent an integer. There are a surprising number of ways in which a string can be formed that can or cannot be converted to an integer in a program – some of the following analysis is Java-specific, and some is common to many languages. The term valid strings is used to indicate strings that can be converted to an integer value by using a single standard Java library call.[12]

```
Strings
├── Valid
│   ├── Decimal string
│   │   └── Examples: "44", "-33"
│   └── Non-decimal string (hex, octal)
│       └── Examples: "0xFFP2", "033", "#bad"
└── Invalid
    ├── Invalid number
    │   └── Examples: "seven", "10+33", "xxx", "45 //comment"
    └── Invalid integer
        ├── Too large (maximum is "2147483648")
        │   └── Example: "300000000000"
        └── Floating point
            └── Examples: "44.0", "44.5", "7.", "7E+2"
```

Figure 10.17 String representations of an integer.

Strings with whitespace (e.g. "␣44␣") cannot be converted by either of these integer conversion methods without pre-processing – typically `String.strip()` might be called first to do this. If an application calls for non-standard integers to be allowed (e.g. in a format not supported by the standard Java string conversion methods), then the programmer must implement custom conversion code, and the tester should test that these integers are handled correctly.

What is important is not what method has been used by the programmer to do the conversion, but what the application should support. Ideally, this will be specified as

---

[12] `Integer.parseInt()` or `Integer.decode()`.

part of the application. Otherwise, the customer may need to be asked, or an interface decision made.

Common-sense is a frequently used approach, but is liable to lead to errors: for example, a programmer may regard the difference between "033" (octal) and "33" (decimal) as obvious, but a customer might well regard this as data corruption.

10.4.6 Test Coverage Items

In basic user story testing, each acceptance criterion is a TCI (as described earlier in the chapter). User applications and their interfaces can be specified using a number of other standard techniques, such as UML use cases[13] and IEEE scenarios.[14] In UML use case testing, each scenario is a TCI; in IEEE scenario testing, the main and alternative scenarios are all TCIs.

User story testing is easily extended by considering not only the acceptance criteria but also the equivalence partitions, boundary values, or combinations of the input values as TCIs. Typically this leads to a few additional normal test cases, and a large number of additional error test cases (as we have seen above, for example, there are many ways of misrepresenting an integer input). A wide range of error test cases is often added to user story testing on an ad-hoc basis – a systematic approach is likely to provide more rigorous testing.

If unit testing has not been performed beforehand, application testing using equivalence partition/BVA/decision tables may be used as a substitute. This is not as rigorous as testing individual methods or classes via their programming interface. If this form of testing is used, then the equivalence partition/BVA/decision tables technique will identify the TCIs (rather than the user stories/acceptance criteria).

Important note: in addition to the user stories agreed with the customer, the tester will probably also identify a large number of extra TCIs using the equivalence partition, BVA, decision tables, and object-oriented (OO) test techniques, and experience-based testing, as discussed previously.

Suggested further readings are presented in Section 14.3.

10.4.7 Test Cases

Each TCI is a test case. Additional test cases may be added to provide a broader range of input values, especially for errors (as seen in the discussion on data representation).

10.4.8 Implementation

The basic structure of a TestNG/Selenium test is outlined in Snippet 10.2.

---

[13] Refer to the Object Management Group standards at www.omg.org for a definition.
[14] ISO/IEC/IEEE 29119-3:2013 Software and systems engineering – Software testing – Part 3: Test documentation.

Snippet 10.2 Basic Test Structure

```
// TestNG import statements
// Selenium import statements

public class WebTestTemplate {

    WebDriver driver;      // used to drive the application
    Wait<WebDriver> wait;  // used to wait for screen
                           //     elements to appear
    String url = System.getProperty("url"); // the URL for
                           // the web application to test

    @BeforeClass
    public void setupDriver() throws Exception {
        // This runs before any other method in the class:
             open web browser
    }

    @AfterClass
    public void shutdown() {
        // This runs after all other methods:
             close the web browser
    }

    // Tests go here

    @Test(timeOut = 20000)
    public void test_Tnnn() {
    }

    // Post test method processing goes here

    @AfterMethod
    public void postMethodProcessing() {
        // Runs after each test method:
            return to a common start screen
    }

}
```

The comments in the code identify the key elements.

Setup and Teardown

Every Selenium test requires a connection to be made to a web browser to run the automated tests, and for the browser to be closed afterwards. The necessary @BeforeClass and @AfterClass methods are shown in Listings 10.6 and 10.7.

Listing 10.6 TestNG/Selenium setup code.

```
33    @BeforeClass
34    public void setupDriver() throws Exception {
35        System.out.println("Test started at:
              "+LocalDateTime.now());
36        if (url == null)
37            throw new Exception("Test URL not defined: use
                  -Durl=<url>");
38        System.out.println("For URL: "+url);
39        System.out.println();
40        // Create web driver (this code uses chrome)
41        if (System.getProperty("webdriver")== null)
42            throw new Exception("Web driver not defined: use
                  -Dwebdriver=<filename>");
43        if (!new File(System.getProperty("webdriver")).exists())
44            throw new Exception("Web driver missing: "+
                  System.getProperty("webdriver"));
45        System.setProperty("webdriver.chrome.driver",
              System.getProperty("webdriver"));
46        driver = new ChromeDriver();
47        // Create wait
48        wait = new WebDriverWait( driver, 5 );
49        // Open web page
50        driver.get( url );
51    }
```

Listing 10.7 TestNG/Selenium shutdown code.

```
53    @AfterClass
54    public void shutdown() {
55        driver.quit();
56    }
```

The code has the following important features:

- The browser is controlled through a Selenium WebDriver.
- Before any tests are run, the Selenium WebDriver must be opened using an @BeforeClass method. In this example, the Chrome browser is used, which requires chromedriver.exe[15] to run – lines 45 and 46.
- It is necessary to wait for items to appear in a browser, as the web browser runs asynchronously from the test program, so a Selenium WebDriverWait object is created – line 48.
- The browser must be triggered to open the web page – line 50.

---

[15] See www.selenium.dev for details.

- When the tests are all finished, the web browser should be closed, using an `@AfterClass` method – lines 53–56.
- The URL is passed as a parameter to the test. This allows different versions of a web application to be more easily tested, as different URLs may be used for each version. The URL parameter is retrieved using `System.getProperty()`, as shown in Snippet 10.2, and then checked for validity on lines 36 and 37 in Listing 10.6.

10.4.9   Interacting with HTML Elements

Each HTML element has its own attributes and behaviour,[16] and these need to be understood to develop effective tests. In this chapter we use the following Selenium methods for interacting with HTML elements:

- `anchor.click()`
- `button.click()`
- `checkbox.click()`
- `checkbox.isSelected()`
- `div.getAttribute("InnerHTML")`
- `element.id`
- `input, type=text, element.getAttribute("value")`
- `input, type=text, element.sendKeys()`
- `page.title`

In practice, frequent reference to the HTML document object model and HTML specifications[17] and the Selenium API documentation[18] is needed to find the necessary API calls, and to ensure that HTML elements are being accessed correctly.

Sometimes a tester may need to perform trials with different Selenium calls or different attributes to make sure the test is working correctly. When developing tests, it can be useful to print different attributes of an element, or the results of different Selenium methods, to the console for inspection.

10.4.10   Test Output Messages

There are two elements of the test output that we have not considered so far:

- logging the time and test item; and
- `WebDriver` startup messages (in this example, ChromeDriver).

Figure 10.18 shows both of these.

It is particularly valuable for application testing (and other system tests) to record the date and time of the test, and also the details of the application being tested

---

[16] Defined by the W3C – see https://dev.w3.org for details.
[17] See www.w3.org for details.
[18] www.selenium.dev/documentation/en.

```
Test started at: 2020-09-24T19:15:14.618050100
For URL: ch10\fuelchecker\fuelchecker.html

Starting ChromeDriver 84.0.4147.30 (48
    b3e868b4cc0aa7e8149519690b6f6949e110a8-refs/branch-heads/4147@
    {#310}) on port 1388
Only local connections are allowed.
Please see https://chromedriver.chromium.org/security-considerations
    for suggestions on keeping ChromeDriver safe.
ChromeDriver was started successfully.
[1600971316.989][WARNING]: This version of ChromeDriver has not been
    tested with Chrome version 85.
Sep 24, 2020 7:15:18 P.M. org.openqa.selenium.remote.ProtocolHandshake
    createSession
```

Figure 10.18 Additional test output messages.

(the test item). In this example the test item is a URL. These are printed by the @BeforeClass method of the test program – see lines 35 and 38 in Listing 10.6.

The ChromeDriver messages show the version running, a warning that only local connections are allowed by Chrome when running under the control of ChromeDriver, and confirmation that ChromeDriver has successfully opened a connection to the Chrome browser.

10.4.11 Record and Playback Testing

An alternative form of automated user interface testing is to record a manual interaction with an application. The user interactions can then be automatically played back to the application, and the recorded responses compared with the responses generated by the application in response to the automated playback. This is especially useful to verify that existing behaviour of the software has not been broken after a change has been made (referred to as regression testing).

These tools generally record the user input automatically, but require the user to identify the important output fields manually (the tool has no way to tell which parts of the screen are important for a correct response and which are not). The data in these important fields can then be recorded automatically. When the test is rerun (playback), the same user input is provided, and the tool checks that the important output fields contain exactly the same values as previously.

Most web-based test tools, such as Selenium,[19] provide such a facility. Simple editors may allow some customisation (for example, date fields may change every time the test is run). But testing stories usually requires a more programmatic approach, as shown in the example in this chapter.

---

[19] Reference the Selenium IDE at www.selenium.dev/selenium-ide.

10.5   Evaluation

In a well-established development process, the classes that implement the fuel checker functionality should have been unit tested in advance. So it is likely that only user-interface-related faults will cause failures of the system test. The limitations of user story testing are explored in the following sections.

10.5.1   Limitations

Some example faults are explored in this section, based on the following faults types:

- Navigation fault: a fault is inserted that prevents the application moving from one screen to another.
- Screen element fault: a fault is inserted into a screen element.
- Software feature fault: a fault is inserted into the software feature to check the fuel load.

The application is implemented in HTML and JavaScript, and can be viewed in the file Fuelchecker.html.

Navigation Fault

A fault is inserted into the navigation from the Results screen to the Exit screen in the Fuel Checker application.

Two extracts from the correct code are shown here. Listing 10.8 shows where the `exitlink` href is set to call the JavaScript `Exit()` function when the Exit hyperlink is clicked on the screen.

Listing 10.8 Exitlink initialisation.

```
74    <li style ="display: inline"><a id="exitlink"
          href="javascript:Exit()"
          style="color:black">Exit</a></li>
```

When the application switches to the results page, the correct code to implement this is shown in Listing 10.9.

Listing 10.9 Correct navigation code.

```
132        document.getElementById("result").value = result;
133
134        document.getElementById("Enter").style.display='none';
135        document.getElementById("Continue").style.display='block';
136        document.getElementById("subhead").innerHTML = "Results";
137        document.getElementById("result").style.display='inline';
138        document.getElementById("litres").disabled = true;
139        document.getElementById("highsafety").disabled = true;
140        document.title = "Results";
```

Listing 10.10 shows the faulty code.

Listing 10.10 Faulty navigation code.

```
132    document.getElementById("result").value = result;
133
134    document.getElementById("Enter").style.display='none';
135    document.getElementById("Continue").style.display='block';
136    document.getElementById("subhead").innerHTML = "Results";
137    document.getElementById("result").style.display='inline';
138    document.getElementById("litres").disabled = true;
139    document.getElementById("highsafety").disabled = true;
140    document.getElementById("exitlink").removeAttribute("href");
           // navigation fault
141    document.title = "Results";
```

On line 140, the `exitlink` href is incorrectly removed during the transition to the Results page. As a consequence, nothing happens when the Exit hyperlink is subsequently clicked on the screen.

The results of running the user story tests against the application with this fault inserted are shown in Figure 10.19.

```
Test started at: 2020-08-28T13:24:31.014562300
For URL: ch10\fault-nav\fuelchecker.html

Starting ChromeDriver 84.0.4147.30 (48
    b3e868b4cc0aa7e8149519690b6f6949e110a8-refs/branch-heads/4147@
    {#310}) on port 8104
Only local connections are allowed.
Please see https://chromedriver.chromium.org/security-considerations
    for suggestions on keeping ChromeDriver safe.
ChromeDriver was started successfully.
Aug 28, 2020 1:24:33 P.M. org.openqa.selenium.remote.ProtocolHandshake
    createSession
INFO: Detected dialect: W3C
PASSED: testEnterCheckView("T1", "1000", false, "Fuel fits in tank.")
PASSED: testEnterCheckView("T2", "400", true, "Fuel fits in tank.")
PASSED: testEnterCheckView("T3", "2000", false, "Fuel does not fit in
    tank.")
PASSED: testEnterCheckView("T4", "1000", true, "Fuel does not fit in
    tank.")
PASSED: testEnterCheckView("T7", "xxx", true, "Invalid data values.")
PASSED: test_T5
PASSED: test_T6
===================================================
Command line suite
Total tests run: 7, Passes: 7, Failures: 0, Skips: 0
===================================================
```

Figure 10.19 Test results for navigation fault.

All the tests have passed – this particular link is never used after the Results page is displayed in the user stories. Navigation testing can be used to ensure that every link, or other action that should cause a page transition, works on every screen.

Screen Element Fault

A fault is inserted into the handling of the screen element `highsafety` in the Fuel Checker application – it is disabled when it should be enabled when returning back to the main screen. Listing 10.11 shows a snippet of the correct code.

Listing 10.11 Correct screen element code.

```
150     document.getElementById("Info").style.display='block';
151     document.getElementById("Enter").style.display='block';
152     document.getElementById("Continue").style.display='none';
153     document.getElementById("result").style.display='none';
154     document.getElementById("litres").disabled = false;
155     document.getElementById("highsafety").disabled = false;
156     document.title = "Fuel Checker";
157     document.getElementById("subhead").innerHTML = "Enter
            Data";
```

When the Continue button is clicked, the application returns to the main screen with the `highSafety` checkbox re-enabled – line 155. The user can now select/deselect the checkbox as required for the next data entry.

Listing 10.12 shows the code with a fault inserted.

Listing 10.12 Faulty screen element code.

```
150     document.getElementById("Info").style.display='block';
151     document.getElementById("Enter").style.display='block';
152     document.getElementById("Continue").style.display='none';
153     document.getElementById("result").style.display='none';
154     document.getElementById("litres").disabled = false;
155     document.getElementById("highsafety").disabled = true;
            // Screen element fault
156     document.title = "Fuel Checker";
157     document.getElementById("subhead").innerHTML = "Enter
            Data";
```

When the Continue button is clicked, the applications returns to the main screen with the `highSafety` checkbox disabled – line 155. The user is now unable to select/deselect the checkbox as required for the next data entry.

The results of running the user story tests against the application with this fault inserted are shown in Figure 10.20.

Four of the tests have failed. The tests T1, T2, T3, and T4 use the `highsafety` button after returning to the main screen, and as the faulty code does not re-enable this button, the tests fail. Tests T5 and T6 do not use the `highsafety` button. Test T7 uses the `highsafety` button, but does not rely on it working properly. High-impact faults like this are likely to cause multiple user story tests to fail, but more subtle faults may not be found by simple user story tests.

Software Feature Fault

When a user interacts with an application, they generally use one or more features to achieve their tasks (as documented in the user stories). The Fuel Checker application has three software features:

```
Test started at: 2020-08-28T13:35:51.590660100
For URL: ch10\fault-elem\fuelchecker.html

Starting ChromeDriver 84.0.4147.30 (48
    b3e868b4cc0aa7e8149519690b6f6949e110a8-refs/branch-heads/4147@
    {#310}) on port 25965
Only local connections are allowed.
Please see https://chromedriver.chromium.org/security-considerations
    for suggestions on keeping ChromeDriver safe.
ChromeDriver was started successfully.
Aug 28, 2020 1:35:54 P.M. org.openqa.selenium.remote.ProtocolHandshake
    createSession
INFO: Detected dialect: W3C
PASSED: testEnterCheckView("T7", "xxx", true, "Invalid data values.")
PASSED: test_T5
PASSED: test_T6
FAILED: testEnterCheckView("T1", "1000", false, "Fuel fits in tank.")
java.lang.AssertionError: expected [Fuel fits in tank.] but found [
    Invalid data values.]
        at example.FuelCheckerWebStoryTest.testEnterCheckView(
            FuelCheckerWebStoryTest.java:97)

FAILED: testEnterCheckView("T2", "400", true, "Fuel fits in tank.")
java.lang.AssertionError: expected [Fuel fits in tank.] but found [
    Invalid data values.]
        at example.FuelCheckerWebStoryTest.testEnterCheckView(
            FuelCheckerWebStoryTest.java:97)

FAILED: testEnterCheckView("T3", "2000", false, "Fuel does not fit in
    tank.")
java.lang.AssertionError: expected [Fuel does not fit in tank.] but
    found [Invalid data values.]
        at example.FuelCheckerWebStoryTest.testEnterCheckView(
            FuelCheckerWebStoryTest.java:97)

FAILED: testEnterCheckView("T4", "1000", true, "Fuel does not fit in
    tank.")
java.lang.AssertionError: expected [Fuel does not fit in tank.] but
    found [Invalid data values.]
        at example.FuelCheckerWebStoryTest.testEnterCheckView(
            FuelCheckerWebStoryTest.java:97)
===================================================
Command line suite
Total tests run: 7, Passes: 3, Failures: 4, Skips: 0
===================================================
```

Figure 10.20 Test results for screen element fault.

1. check a fuel load;
2. display the tank sizes; and
3. exit.

A fault is inserted into the check a fuel load feature, so that the correct parameter values are not passed from the user interface code to the software feature code.

The data is converted correctly from a text string to an integer, but an incorrect multiplication is included so that the wrong data value is used.

Listing 10.13 shows the original, correct code. The string variable `lss` is read from the litres element, and is converted to an integer using `parseInt(lss,10)`.

Listing 10.13 Correct software feature code.

```
104    var lss = (document.getElementById("litres")).value.trim();
105    if (lss == parseInt(lss,10))
106       ls = parseInt(lss,10);
107    else
108       ls = "Invalid";
```

Listing 10.14 shows the faulty code. After the data conversion to an integer has correctly taken place, a multiplication factor of 10 is incorrectly introduced, causing the wrong data values to be used in the check a fuel load feature.

Listing 10.14 Faulty software feature code.

```
104    var lss = (document.getElementById("litres")).value.trim();
105    if (lss == parseInt(lss,10))
106       ls = parseInt(lss,10)*10; // Fault: incorrect
                multiplication
107    else
108       ls = "Invalid";
```

The results of running the user story tests against the application with this fault inserted are shown in Figure 10.21.

Two of the tests fail. The software feature still works for some input values, but not for others. In many cases, this type of fault can create very subtle changes in behaviour that would not be caught by a simple user story test.

10.5.2   Strengths and Weaknesses

Testing that the acceptance criteria for the user stories are met provides an assurance that the basic functionality works for the user.

User story tests are unlikely to find all of the navigation, screen element, and software feature faults in an application – they will only find those faults that are exposed by the user stories and acceptance criteria that are documented for the application.

10.6   Key Points

- Systems are tested over their system interface, which is usually significantly more complex than passing parameters to a method.
- Application testing is a form of system testing.
- Testing applications (web-based, desktop-based, or mobile apps) over their GUI requires some form of unique identifiers so that the required interface elements can be referenced for input and output.

```
Test started at: 2020-08-28T15:43:45.978844200
For URL: ch10\fault-feat\fuelchecker.html

Starting ChromeDriver 84.0.4147.30 (48
    b3e868b4cc0aa7e8149519690b6f6949e110a8-refs/branch-heads/4147@
    {#310}) on port 24601
Only local connections are allowed.
Please see https://chromedriver.chromium.org/security-considerations
    for suggestions on keeping ChromeDriver safe.
ChromeDriver was started successfully.
Aug 28, 2020 3:43:49 P.M. org.openqa.selenium.remote.ProtocolHandshake
    createSession
INFO: Detected dialect: W3C
PASSED: testEnterCheckView("T3", "2000", false, "Fuel does not fit in
    tank.")
PASSED: testEnterCheckView("T4", "1000", true, "Fuel does not fit in
    tank.")
PASSED: testEnterCheckView("T7", "xxx", true, "Invalid data values.")
PASSED: test_T5
PASSED: test_T6
FAILED: testEnterCheckView("T1", "1000", false, "Fuel fits in tank.")
java.lang.AssertionError: expected [Fuel fits in tank.] but found [Fuel
    does not fit in tank.]
        at example.FuelCheckerWebStoryTest.testEnterCheckView(
            FuelCheckerWebStoryTest.java:97)

FAILED: testEnterCheckView("T2", "400", true, "Fuel fits in tank.")
java.lang.AssertionError: expected [Fuel fits in tank.] but found [Fuel
    does not fit in tank.]
        at example.FuelCheckerWebStoryTest.testEnterCheckView(
            FuelCheckerWebStoryTest.java:97)


===================================================
    Command line test
    Tests run: 7, Failures: 2, Skips: 0
===================================================
```

Figure 10.21 Test results for software feature fault.

- Web-based testing over a browser requires browser support, to allow automated tests to simulate user input, and read the output.
- User story testing will probably not provide extensive testing of error cases, or find all the faults in an application.

10.7   Key Differences between Unit Testing and Application Testing

As this chapter demonstrates, application testing is a far more complex activity than unit testing. Essentially, the user interface inserts an additional translation layer between the user and the code, and the complexities are associated with manipulating this correctly to simulate the actions of a user. The key differences in testing are as follows:

- Locating the inputs:

  - In unit testing, the inputs are located by their position in the method/function call (though some other languages also support named parameters). The inputs may also be class attributes, or accessed from an external resource such as a file, database, or physical device.
  - In application testing, the inputs are located as elements on the screen, and may be presented using various analogues (such as a slider for a number). Trial runs of the application are used to identify these. In a well-designed application, they have unique identifiers, at least with regards to each screen, but otherwise the absolute or relative position on the screen may be the only way to locate them. As for unit testing, the input may also come from external sources.

- Locating the outputs:

  - In unit testing, the outputs may be returned by the method/function call, or may be side-effects (i.e. class attribute changes, or sent to an external resource).
  - In application testing, the outputs are represented in the same way as the inputs as elements on the screen, and may be presented over many screens. The same issues apply as for the application inputs in terms of locating them. As for unit testing, the outputs may also be sent to external resources (for example, a database).

- Automating the tests:

  - In unit testing, automated implementation is usually straightforward: locate a set of input values, call the method/functions, get the return value (actual results), and check against the expected results.
  - In application testing, each input element must be located separately, possibly on different screens, and manipulated correctly to represent the input value. The application functionality must then be triggered, sometimes via a simple button press but often requiring more manipulation of screen elements. The output must then be located and extracted from the screen, and then interpreted to generate the actual result before the task of comparing them against the expected results can be performed.

10.8   Notes for Experienced Testers

The experienced tester will usually develop the test code directly from the user stories and acceptance criteria. They will run the application at the same time in order to find the HTML ids and element types as required, and mentally determine the typical data values to use. However, it will be essentially impossible to review the tester's work without the reviewers redoing all the analysis. In order to alleviate this, the tester may note down reasons for picking the typical values as comments in the test code. Additional tests will usually be written to cover potential data representation problems, especially for input data errors. Additional tests will also be developed based on the tester's experience (see Section 1.7.3) in order to try to overcome some of the weaknesses in basic user story testing.

The time spent on developing and executing tests is usually closely related to the value of the application. This is based on the risk of failure as discussed in Chapter 1. On an e-commerce website for a small company selling low-value items to a few customers, the code probably will not be unit tested. The basic user stories of listing the items, adding them to a shopping cart, checking out, and viewing the order status will probably be tested manually with no formal documentation. At the other extreme, a website for a bank will probably have all the code unit tested. And there will probably be extensive automated application testing (including user story testing, and some of the other approaches discussed) to make sure that the bank's customers are unlikely to experience problems.

11   Test Automation

Manual testing is slow, error-prone, and hard to repeat. Software testing needs to be fast, accurate, and repeatable. The solution is test automation. This chapter provides insight into the process of automated testing and relates to the test design techniques discussed in previous chapters.

11.1   Introduction

Software testing needs to be *fast*, so that it can be performed frequently without a time penalty. It needs to be *accurate*, so that the test results can be relied on as a quality indicator. And it needs to be *repeatable* to allow for regression testing, where the same tests may be run many times for different software versions.

This is particularly true for modern *agile* development approaches, where small increments of functionality are added and tested in a rapid cycle.

Some of the testing tasks that can be automated relatively easily are:

- execution of tests;
- collection of test results;
- evaluation of test results;
- generation of test reports; and
- measurement of simple white-box test coverage.

Some of the testing tasks that are more difficult to automate are:

- generation of test coverage items and the data for test cases;
- measurement of black-box test coverage; and
- measurement of complex white-box test coverage;

Unit test execution is invariably automated. This is implemented by writing code that calls the required methods with the specified test input data, and compares the actual results with the expected results.

Application tests are more *difficult* to automate. In manual testing, the correctness of the output on the screen can be left to the tester's judgement. Automated testing requires the details of how the expected results are displayed to be known.

Application tests are also more *complex* to automate, as they depend on the details of the system interface: inputs are provided and results collected via the system interface. It generally takes extra time to develop automated application tests. Not only do the tests themselves have to be implemented, but there is an additional and complex program interface library to be used. In general there is a shift from manual to automated application testing. A rule-of-thumb is that if a test is to be executed more than twice, it is worthwhile using test automation.

Automated tests can be grouped into collections (which are also referred to as test sets or test suites), and the results automatically collated into a report. The report includes an overall summary of the test result (pass or fail). It may also include statistics on the tests that have been run. It will also include a test incident report on each failure, providing exact details on why the test failed in order to assist in locating the fault.

In this chapter, automated unit testing is examined in more detail, using TestNG[1] as an example test framework (as used in Chapters 2–6). Automated application testing is also examined in more detail, based on TestNG to manage the tests, and Selenium[2] to interface the tests with web-based applications. It must be emphasised that these are just example test tools, representative of the typical features to be found in test automation tools.

11.1.1 Interpreting Test Results

Automated testing may generate a number of different test results:

- passed – the test has passed;
- failed – the test has failed;
- skipped – the test was not run (for example if some setup failed to execute properly prior to the test); and
- not selected – the test was in the test collection, but deselected for execution.

It is important to differentiate between tests that failed and tests that were skipped. Tests are usually skipped because the test setup failed: perhaps the class file for the code being tested was not in the expected location, or the web driver was the wrong version for the web browser in use. Skipped tests generally require a response by the tester to rerun them.

11.1.2 Documenting Automated Tests

When designing tests, the test documentation produced includes: analysis results, the test coverage items (TCIs), and the test cases/test data. The test case identifiers should be referenced in the test method names or in the data fields for parameterised tests.

When automating software tests, there are two choices for where to store the test documentation: in separate files (perhaps using word processing and spreadsheet tools, or a database in a larger organisation), or to store it as comments in the test programs.

---

[1] See https://testng.org.
[2] See www.selenium.dev.

Note that all the tests within a file must have unique identifiers (in this book they are numbered using a simple hierarchy). Each test can then be uniquely identified using the test item and the test identifier: for example `giveDiscount()` test T1.3. This allows a specific test to be rerun in order to replicate the failure as part of the debugging process, and also for it to be re-executed to verify that a fault has been correctly fixed.

It is useful to maintain an edit history of the test file (this could be automated under a version control system, such as Git). There is no need to limit a file to one particular type of test: a test file might include tests derived using multiple techniques (e.g. equivalence partition, boundary value analysis (BVA), decision tables). Or, alternatively, each might be put into its own file. Often, black-box and white-box tests are separated into different files, as the black-box tests remain valid even if the implementation changes, but the white-box tests do not. Test runners, such as TestNG, generally provide a number of ways to select different test methods for execution from different test classes.

11.1.3   Software Test Automation and Version Control

It is critical that test reports include an identifier that uniquely states the software being tested (its name, version, variant, etc.). This means that the report can be interpreted in the correct context, and any debugging and fixes applied to the correct version (or variant) of the software. It also enables the verification that the fixes have been made to that specific version (or variant).

For a class, the identifier is generally the version number from the version control system. For complete systems, this is generally the build number from the build procedure (or it may be the release *tag*, or the date for revision control systems similar to Git).

11.2   Test Frameworks: TestNG

In this book, TestNG is used as a representative unit test automation framework. Other frameworks have similar features – this book does not provide a full description of TestNG, but rather uses TestNG to introduce and explain typical features required for automated testing. Only a limited subset of the TestNG features are described in this book. Refer to the TestNG documentation online for full details.[3]

TestNG consists of a set of Java classes that automate the execution of software tests, collect and evaluate the test results, and generate test reports. TestNG tests are executing using a *test runner*.

---

[3] https://testng.org.

11.2.1   A Detailed Look at a TestNG Example

The source code for a sample TestNG test class is shown in Listing 11.1.

- The test class imports the required support from the TestNG libraries (see the import statements referring to *org.testng* in the code), and uses the @Test annotation before each test method.
- Each test method must have one or more assertions – if an assertion fails, then the test fails and halts execution immediately. Otherwise, the test passes.
- The class Demo has the methods setValue(int), add(int), and getValue(). The methods getValue() and setValue() are getters and setters for the attribute value; add() adds the passed parameter to the attribute value.

Listing 11.1 Example TestNG source code/DemoTest.java.

```
1   package example;
2
3   import static org.testng.Assert.*;
4   import org.testng.annotations.*;
5
6   public class DemoTest {
7
8       @Test
9       public void test1() {
10          Demo d = new Demo();
11          d.setValue(56);
12          d.add(44);
13          assertEquals( d.getValue(), 100 );
14      }
15
16  }
```

The key features of a TestNG test method, as shown in test1() in the example, are as follows:

- An object to be tested is created. In our example, an instance of the class Demo – line 10.
- The object is initialised, or put into the right state for testing. In our example by initialising the object with the value 56 – line 11.
- The method under test is now called. In our example, we call the method add() with the input test data value 44 – line 12.
- The output data is now collected. In our example by calling getValue() – line 13.
- Finally, the actual result (output value) is compared with the expected result by using the TestNG assertEquals() method. In our example the expected result is the value 100 – line 13.

The output from running this test is shown in Figure 11.1.

```
PASSED: test1


=================================================
    Command line test
    Tests run: 1, Failures: 0, Skips: 0
=================================================



=================================================
Command line suite
Total tests run: 1, Passes: 1, Failures: 0, Skips: 0
=================================================
```

Figure 11.1 Test results for DemoTest.

The standard output[4] from TestNG includes the following:

* The test result for each test method run.
* The test result for each set of tests run together – in this book we are using the command line to run the tests, and TestNG reports these under *Command line test*. Here it shows the number of tests that were run, the number of tests that failed, and the number of tests that were skipped.
* A summary of the entire test suite – multiple sets of tests can be collected into a suite, as we will see later in the chapter. As the tests are run from the command line, the default suite name is *Command line suite*. Previously in the book, for simplicity, only these test suite results have been shown.

Elsewhere in the book, only the entire test suite results are shown.

TestNG supports a number of assertion methods – the most commonly used ones are `assertEquals()`, `assertTrue()`, and `assertFalse()`.

If the assertion passes, then execution continues to the next line in the method. If the assertion fails, then the test method terminates with an exception, causing the test to fail. This is why it is not a good idea to have multiple tests in a single test method: if one fails, then the subsequent tests are not run. This does not apply to parameterised tests – see Section 11.5.

The test methods are identified by a TestNG Test Runner, which uses Java Reflection to find all the methods in the test class with the `@Test` annotation, and then calls them in turn, trapping exceptions and keeping counters for the numbers of tests run, tests passed, and tests failed. TestNG comes with a default command-line test runner, but TestNG tests can also be run within an IDE such as Eclipse. TestNG test execution can also be managed using an XML file, which is passed to the test runner – see Section 11.3.1.

---

[4] For most of the examples in this book, the level of detail is set using TestNG log level 2.

11.3 Organising Automated Test Code

The best way to organise your test class files, and to ensure that all the code is tested, is to have a test class for every program class. For example, class Demo in file Demo.java would have a test class DemoTest in file DemoTest.java. You can use any naming convention you like; however, in this book we use the convention of adding the word *Test* after the class name.

In the test classes, individual tests are implemented as methods. In TestNG, each test method must be public and identified as a test method by using the Java annotation (@Test) (see the example in Section 11.2.1). It is recommended that each test method implement an individual test for two reasons:

1. The method terminates as soon as a test fails. This means that any subsequent tests, in the same method, will not be executed. So, if you put multiple tests into a single method, the test results cannot indicate whether just one test failed, or a number of tests failed.
2. It is easier to find a fault if you know exactly which test failed.

The way to group multiple tests together is to put one test per method, and group the test methods into suites of tests, sometimes referred to as *test sets*. To increase flexibility, test suites may themselves be grouped into larger test suites. Note that parameterised tests contain more than one test case per test method (see Section 11.5).

11.3.1 Organising TestNG Tests with an XML File

An XML file can be passed as a parameter to the TestNG runner. This can organise the test methods into suites and tests[5] with test classes and test methods. An example is shown in Listing 11.2.

Listing 11.2 Sample XML file/example.xml.

```
1  <?xml version="1.0" encoding="UTF-8"?>
2  <!DOCTYPE suite SYSTEM "http://testng.org/testng-1.0.dtd" >
3
4  <suite name="Suite1">
5    <test name="standardTest">
6      <classes>
7        <class name="example.DemoTest">
8          <methods>
9            <include name="test1" />
10         </methods>
11       </class>
12     </classes>
13   </test>
14   <test name="extraTest">
15     <classes>
16       <class name="example.DemoTestExtra">
```

---

[5] The TestNG terminology is slightly different from the standard IEEE terminology that is used elsewhere in the book.

```
17            <methods>
18              <include name="test2" />
19              <include name="test3" />
20            </methods>
21          </class>
22        </classes>
23      </test>
24    </suite>
```

Figure 11.2 shows the complete output of running this. The TestNG parameter *log level* allows the tester to specify the amount of detail to include (1 is least detail and 5 is most). Here the value 3 has been used, which allows us to see exactly which methods were called.

```
===== Invoked methods
    DemoTest.test1()[pri:0, instance:example.DemoTest@6e171cd7]
        1847008471
=====
PASSED: test1


==================================================
    standardTest
    Tests run: 1, Failures: 0, Skips: 0
==================================================


PASSED: test1


==================================================
    extraTest
    Tests run: 1, Failures: 0, Skips: 0
==================================================

===== Invoked methods
    DemoTestExtra.test2()[pri:0, instance:example.
        DemoTestExtra@4f6ee6e4] 1332668132
    DemoTestExtra.test3()[pri:0, instance:example.
        DemoTestExtra@4f6ee6e4] 1332668132
=====
```

Figure 11.2 Test output using sample XML file.

The output shows the test methods called, and the results at each level of the hierarchy defined in the XML file, but it is not straightforward to read. It closely follows the definition in the XML file.

The instance addresses as shown in this high level of detail may be different every time the test is run.

The log level can be set to 1 to restrict the output to show the pass/fail test result for the suite, as shown in Figure 11.3.

Using the XML file as a basis, the tester can then select just particular tests, test classes, or test suites to execute, based on the names in the XML file.

```
PASSED: test1
PASSED: test2
PASSED: test3


===============================================
    extraTest
    Tests run: 3, Failures: 0, Skips: 0
===============================================



===============================================
Suite1
Total tests run: 3, Passes: 3, Failures: 0, Skips: 0
===============================================



===============================================
Suite1
Total tests run: 3, Passes: 3, Failures: 0, Skips: 0
===============================================
```

Figure 11.3 Test output using sample XML file – log level 1.

11.4   Setup and Cleanup Methods

Test automation tools typically support ways to run particular additional methods before and after every test class, or before and after every test method (or collections of test methods) in a test class. This allows objects (or connections to external software, such as servers or databases) to be setup before a test, and cleaned up afterwards.

For example, if an object needs to be shared between all the tests in a class, it can be created before all the tests are run, and re-initialised before every individual test.

TestNG provides annotations to support this. The use of @BeforeMethod is shown in Listing 11.3. The test methods test1() and test2() each execute against individual instances of Demo, as setup() is executed before every test method.

Listing 11.3 Using @BeforeMethod annotation.

```
6   public class DemoTestM {
7
8     public Demo d;
9
10    @BeforeMethod public void setup() {
11      System.out.println("Creating a new Demo object");
12      d = new Demo();
13    }
14
15    @Test
16    public void test1() {
17      d.setValue(100);
18      assertEquals( d.getValue(), 100 );
```

```
19     }
20
21     @Test
22     public void test2() {
23        d.setValue(200);
24        assertEquals( d.getValue(), 200 );
25     }
26
27  }
```

Executing this test results in the output shown in Figure 11.4 – with only the important lines of the output shown.

```
Creating a new Demo object
Creating a new Demo object
PASSED: test1
PASSED: test2
===================================================
Command line suite
Total tests run: 2, Passes: 2, Failures: 0, Skips: 0
===================================================
```

Figure 11.4 Test output using @BeforeMethod.

A new Demo object is created for each test method – the test results produced by TestNG are all reported at the end of the complete test, not after each test method is run. But the println output is shown immediately, which is why the output lines appear to be out of order.

If the same object is used in every test in a test class, then the single object can be created before any of the tests are run using the @BeforeClass[6] annotation (see Snippet 11.1).

Objects can be cleaned up after all the tests have run using the @AfterClass annotation. By annotating setup() and cleanup() as shown in the example, test1() and test2() would each execute against the same instance of Demo.

Snippet 11.1 Using @BeforeClass and @AfterClass

```
1     @BeforeClass public void setup() {
2        d = new Demo();
3     }
4
5     @AfterClass public void cleanup() {
6        d = null;
7     }
```

TestNG provides a number of annotations to support this, some commonly used examples are:

---

[6] See the TestNG documentation for the full set of annotations.

- @BeforeSuite/@AfterSuite – called before/after a defined *suite* of tests.
- @BeforeClass/@AfterClass – called before the execution of the first test method in a test class/after the execution of the last test method in a test class.
- @BeforeGroups/@AfterGroups – called before/after a defined *group* of tests.
- @BeforeMethod/@AfterMethod – called before/after the execution of every test method.

11.5 Inline Tests vs Parameterised Tests

All test frameworks support the ability to define test methods with inline test data (included as constants inside the method). In TestNG, the @Test annotation is used as shown in Listing 11.4.

Listing 11.4 Inline tests.

```
 6  public class DemoTestInline {
 7    @Test public void test1() {
 8      Demo d = new Demo();
 9      d.setValue(56);
10      d.add(44);
11      assertEquals( d.getValue(), 100 );
12    }
13    @Test
14    public void test2() {
15      Demo d = new Demo();
16      d.setValue(0);
17      assertEquals( d.getValue(), 0 );
18    }
19    @Test
20    public void test3() {
21      Demo d = new Demo();
22      d.setValue(-1000);
23      d.add(-1234);
24      assertEquals( d.getValue(), -2234 );
25    }
26  }
```

The output from running the inline tests is shown in Figure 11.5

```
PASSED: test1
PASSED: test2
PASSED: test3
===============================================
Command line suite
Total tests run: 3, Passes: 3, Failures: 0, Skips: 0
===============================================
```

Figure 11.5 Output from inline tests.

Where different test methods require different code, inline test data may be used without incurring the disadvantages of code duplication. This is shown in Listing 11.4, where the test `method test2()` is slightly different from `test3()`. This is often the case for system tests, where different tests require unique sequences of actions.

Most test frameworks include facilities for parameterised tests. This is invariably used for unit tests, where the same method needs to be repeatedly called with different test data. In TestNG the `dataProvider` parameter is used for this, as shown in Listing 11.5.

Listing 11.5 Parameterised tests.

```
6    public class DemoTestParam {
7      private static Object[][] testData = new Object[][] {
8        { "test1", 56,   44,  100 },
9        { "test2", 0,    0,    0 },
10       { "test3", -1000, -1234, -2234 },
11     };
12     @DataProvider(name = "testset1")
13     public Object[][] getTestData() {
14       return testData;
15     }
16     @Test(dataProvider = "testset1")
17     public void test(String id, int x, int y, int er) {
18       Demo d = new Demo();
19       d.setValue(x);
20       d.add(y);
21       assertEquals( d.getValue(), er );
22     }
23   }
```

With a data provider, the method `test()` is called sequentially with each row of test data in order as follows:

```
test( "test1", 56, 44, 100 );
test( "test2", 0, 0, 0 );
test( "test3", -1000, -1234, -2234 );
```

The output from running the parameterised tests is shown in Figure 11.6

```
PASSED: test("test1", 56, 44, 100)
PASSED: test("test2", 0, 0, 0)
PASSED: test("test3", -1000, -1234, -2234)
===================================================
Command line suite
Total tests run: 3, Passes: 3, Failures: 0, Skips: 0
===================================================
```

Figure 11.6 Output from parameterised tests.

Note the slight difference in output – the name of the parameterised test method and the values of the parameters are shown for each test executed.

Using Iterators

TestNG supports both static and dynamic data providers. Static data providers return a fixed array (or an *Iterator* over a standard collection) and dynamic data providers return a customised *Iterator*, which can generate data on-the-fly.

Dynamic data providers can be written to provide test data that changes based on the test progress, or to support very large data sets. An example is shown in Listing 11.6. Instead of returning an array, the @DataProvider method returns an iterator.

Listing 11.6 @DataProvider with iterator.

```
 9    private static Object[][] testData = new Object[][] {
10        { "test1", 56,  44,  100 },
11        { "test2", 0,    0,   0 },
12        { "test3", -1000, -1234, -2234 },
13    };
14
15    @DataProvider(name = "testset1")
16    public Iterator<Object[]> getData() {
17        return new DataGenerator(testData);
18    }
19
20    @Test(dataProvider = "testset1")
21    public void test(String id, int x, int y, int er) {
22        Demo d = new Demo();
23        d.setValue(x);
24        d.add(y);
25        assertEquals( d.getValue(), er );
26    }
```

Each time the iterator next() method is called, it returns the next row of data. In the example, a pre-intialised array is used, but the data could be dynamically generated within the next method. This is particularly useful for random testing where data may be generated on demand. The supporting DataGenerator class is shown in Listing 11.7.

Listing 11.7 DataGenerator class.

```
28    static class DataGenerator implements Iterator<Object[]> {
29
30        private int index = 0;
31        private Object[][] data;
32
33        DataGenerator(Object[][] testData) {
34                data = testData;
35            }
36
37        @Override public boolean hasNext() {
38            return index < data.length;
39        }
40
41        @Override public Object[] next() {
42            if (index < data.length)
43                return data[index++];
44            else
```

```
45              return null;
46       }
47    }
```

The output from this `DataGenerator` is shown in Figure 11.7.

```
PASSED: test("test1", 56, 44, 100)
PASSED: test("test2", 0, 0, 0)
PASSED: test("test3", -1000, -1234, -2234)
===============================================
Command line suite
Total tests run: 3, Passes: 3, Failures: 0, Skips: 0
===============================================
```

Figure 11.7 Test output for `@DataProvider` with iterator.

11.6   Test Coverage Measurement

Most languages provide automated tools to measure at least statement coverage and branch coverage. These tools can be used to verify that a white-box test actually achieves the coverage it is intended to achieve, and are mainly used in practice to measure the white-box coverage of black-box tests. If only low coverage is achieved, then there are untested components in the code, and achieving higher levels of coverage requires the use of white-box testing techniques. Code coverage can be measured for any type of testing.

For Java there are a number of options. In this book, JaCoCo is used as it is a good example of what can be achieved.

JaCoCo Example

An example of statement and branch coverage results for `giveDiscount()` are shown in Figure 11.8. The code includes Fault 4 (see Chapter 4). The tests used were the equivalence partition tests developed in Chapter 2 – selected to show the different coverage features. The coverage report shows that full statement and branch coverage have not been achieved.

While the tool highlights the lines of source code in color on the screen, we present these using different shades of grey in the book. The details are as follows:

- Some lines of Java source code do not generate any executable code.[7] These lines are not highlighted: lines 1–6, 8, 10, 12, 15, 18, 25, 28, and 30–32.

---

[7] Java statements are converted into executable instructions before a program can be run. Some statements produce no instructions: for example, comments, import statements, and closing braces. Other Java statements may generate multiple instructions.

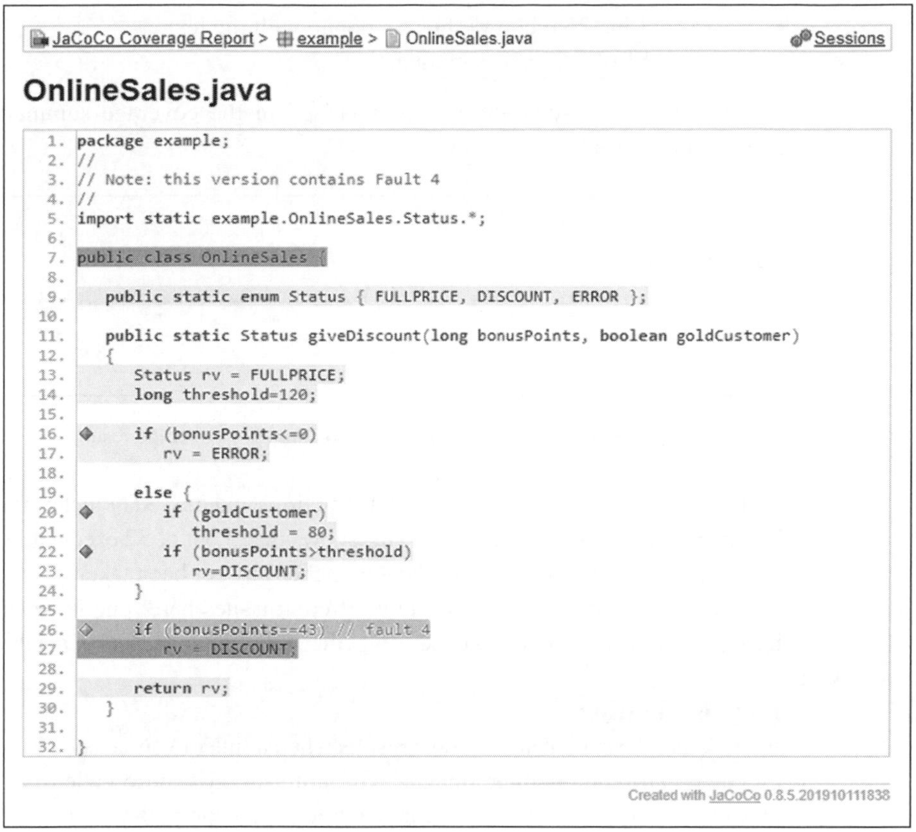

JaCoCo Coverage Report > example > OnlineSales.java Sessions

OnlineSales.java

```
1.  package example;
2.  //
3.  // Note: this version contains Fault 4
4.  //
5.  import static example.OnlineSales.Status.*;
6.
7.  public class OnlineSales {
8.
9.     public static enum Status { FULLPRICE, DISCOUNT, ERROR };
10.
11.    public static Status giveDiscount(long bonusPoints, boolean goldCustomer)
12.    {
13.       Status rv = FULLPRICE;
14.       long threshold=120;
15.
16.       if (bonusPoints<=0)
17.          rv = ERROR;
18.
19.       else {
20.          if (goldCustomer)
21.             threshold = 80;
22.          if (bonusPoints>threshold)
23.             rv=DISCOUNT;
24.       }
25.
26.       if (bonusPoints==43) // fault 4
27.          rv = DISCOUNT;
28.
29.       return rv;
30.    }
31.
32. }
```

Created with JaCoCo 0.8.5.201910111838

Figure 11.8 Example JaCoCo source code coverage results.

- Most lines have been fully executed.[8] These are highlighted in light grey (or green on the screen): lines 9, 13, 14, 16, 17, 20–23, and 29. This means that the equivalence partition tests executed these lines.
- Line 26 has been partially executed, and is shown in a medium grey (yellow on the screen). This means that there are branches on this line, and at least one of them has not been taken. In this case, the branch from line 26 to line 27 has clearly not been taken.
- Lines 7 and 27 are in red: this indicates that they have not been executed. Java has created a default constructor that has not been called (line 7). The tests have not executed line 27.
- The diamonds in the left margin indicate lines that contain branches. In this example, this indicates lines 16, 20, 22, and 26. Hovering the cursor on the diamond gives additional information:
  - Lines 16, 20, and 22 (green) show popups with the text:
    All 2 branches covered.

[8] All of the binary instructions on that line of source code have been executed.

−   Line 26 (yellow) shows a popup with the text:

> 1 of 2 branches missed.

The coverage results are also summarised in the coverage summary report, as shown in Figure 11.9.

Element	Missed Instructions ⬦ Cov. ⬦	Missed Branches ⬦ Cov. ⬦	Missed ⬦ Cxty ⬦	Missed ⬦ Lines ⬦	Missed ⬦ Methods ⬦
⬥ OnlineSales()	▬ 0%	n/a	1 1	1 1	1 1
⬥ giveDiscount(long, boolean)	▬▬▬ 93%	▬▬ 87%	1 5	1 11	0 1
Total	5 of 32 84%	1 of 8 87%	2 6	2 12	1 2

JaCoCo Coverage Report > example > OnlineSales   Sessions

OnlineSales

Figure 11.9 Example JaCoCo summary coverage results.

The key figures here are the missed instructions and missed branches for the method being tested: `giveDiscount()`. This shows that 5 out of 32 executable instructions have not been executed, and 1 of the 8 branches has not been taken.

Note that there are two completely different issues here: one is whether the tests have passed or not, and the second is whether full coverage has been achieved.

Lazy Evaluation

Interpreting the statement coverage results when a line of source code is only *partially* executed can require some thought. An optimisation feature called *lazy evaluation* may cause only some of the Boolean conditions in a complex decision to be executed.

In Java, the conditional-or (||) and conditional-and (&&) operators are guaranteed to be evaluated left-to-right, and the right-hand operand is only evaluated if necessary.[9]

11.7   Timeouts

In general, it is good practice to ensure tests do not continue to run for too long – for example, due to an infinite loop or a deadlock in the code. This may be less relevant for unit testing, but is critical for application testing.

In TestNG, the `timeOut` parameter is used. The test method `test1()` in Listing 11.8 fails if the test takes more than 1000 milliseconds to execute.

Listing 11.8 Test with timeout.

```
6  public class InfiniteTest {
7
8     @Test(timeOut = 1000)
9     public void test1() {
```

[9] See J. Gosling, B. Joy, G. Steele, G. Bracha, A. Buckley, and D. Smith. *The Java® Language Specification, Java SE 11 Edition*. Oracle, 2018.

```
10        assertEquals( Infinite.mul2(10), 20 );
11    }
12
13 }
```

Faulty code with an infinite loop in shown in Listing 11.9.

Listing 11.9 Code with an infinite loop.

```
3 class Infinite {
4        // return x * 2
5        public static int mul2(int x) {
6              while (x > 0)
7                  x = (x * 2) - x;
8              return x;
9        }
10 }
```

Running the test with a timeout against this fault code results in a test failure, as shown in Figure 11.10. If no timeout was included, the test would not terminate.

```
FAILED: test1
org.testng.internal.thread.ThreadTimeoutException: Method example.
    InfiniteTest.test1() didn't finish within the time-out 1000
===================================================
Command line suite
Total tests run: 1, Passes: 0, Failures: 1, Skips: 0
===================================================
```

Figure 11.10 Test timeout failure.

11.8 Exceptions

Most Java test frameworks use exceptions to report a test failure. Therefore, if a method being tested is expected to raise an exception, this must be handled differently (both to prevent the test failing incorrectly, and also to verify that the exception is correctly raised).

A simple example is shown in Listing 11.10 – the method `DemoWithE.add(x)` throws an exception if `x` is not greater than 0.

Listing 11.10 Exception-raising code.

```
5 class DemoWithE {
6    int value = 0;
7    public void setValue(int value) { this.value = value; };
8    public int getValue() { return value; }
9    // Only add values greater than 0
10   public void add(int x) throws IllegalArgumentException
```

```
11    {
12            if (x < 1) throw new IllegalArgumentException("Invalid
                  x");
13        value += x;
14    }
15 }
```

A test for this method must verify that (a) an exception is not raised when x is valid, and (b) that an exception is raised when x is invalid. When an unexpected exception is raised, such as when an assertion fails, then the test fails. To notify TestNG that an exception is expected, parameters to the @Test annotation are used, as shown in Listing 11.11.

Listing 11.11 Test with exception handling.

```
7  public class DemoTestWithE {
8
9     DemoWithE d = new DemoWithE();
10
11    @Test
12    public void test1() {
13            d.setValue(0);
14        d.add(44);
15        assertEquals( d.getValue(), 44 );
16    }
17
18    @Test(expectedExceptions = IllegalArgumentException.class)
19    public void test2() {
20            d.setValue(0);
21        d.add(-44);
22        assertEquals( d.getValue(), 44 );
23    }
24
25 }
```

On line 18, the test parameter expectedExceptions is used to notify TestNG that an exception should be raised, and to fail the test if it is not raised.

The result of running this test is shown in Figure 11.11.

```
PASSED: test1
PASSED: test2
===============================================
Command line suite
Total tests run: 2, Passes: 2, Failures: 0, Skips: 0
===============================================
```

Figure 11.11 Test result with expected exceptions.

The tests both pass. If test1() had raised an exception from assertEquals() failing, then the test would have failed. If test2() had not raised an exception, then that test would have failed.

For the equivalence partition, BVA, and decision tables test techniques, exceptions should be treated as another output (expected results) from the code: a method cannot both return a value and raise an exception.

11.9 Inheritance Testing

When a subclass inherits from a superclass, it inherits the *responsibilities* of the superclass. This means that to test the subclass, it must be run not only against the subclass tests, but also against the superclass tests. Running against the superclass tests is referred to as *inheritance testing* and ensures that the inheritance has been correctly implemented.

The key problem with inheritance testing is running a set of tests designed for one class against a different class. Obviously the different class must be compatible (i.e. inherited).

In the standard template we have used (see Snippet 11.2) this is not possible. The class to be tested is hard-coded into the test class.

Snippet 11.2 Test code for class XXX

```
1   // Test for class XXX
2   @Test
3   public void test() {
4       XXX x = new XXX();
5       x.doSomething( input0, input1, input2 );
6       assertEquals( x.getResult(), expectedResult );
7   }
```

On line 4 the test item is created inside the test class: the test can only be run against an object of class XXX.

If we now have a new class to test, which inherits from this class, we need to run these existing tests against the new class (assuming that it is a true subclass that fully supports all the superclass behaviour[10]). A cut-and-paste approach is shown in Snippet 11.3.

Snippet 11.3 Running XXX tests against YYY using cut-and-paste

```
1
2   // Inheritance test for class YYY
3   @Test
4   public void test() {
5       XXX x = new YYY();
6       x.doSomething( input0, input1, input2 );
7       assertEquals( x.getResult(), expectedResult );
    }
```

This works, but has a number of serious limitations:

- The obvious problem, as with all cut-and-paste approaches, is that any changes to the XXX test code do not automatically get propagated to the YYY test code.

[10] The Liskov Substitution Principle defines this as a strong relationship: the subclass is fully substitutable for the superclass.

Also, it is probably in a different Java file. This is a particular problem in modern development methods, where classes are refactored and added to on a regular basis.

• There is a second, less obvious problem. If a third class ZZZ inherits from YYY, then you need to copy the XXX and YYY tests into the ZZZ test class. This results in an explosion of copied code, and is very likely to lead to mistakes and untested code.

However, there are some strengths in this approach, which we need to consider when designing alternate approaches:

1. It is very clear what tests are being run against which class in the class hierarchy
2. It is possible to select which tests are to be run for inheritance testing. The tester may wish to not run some test cases either for performance reasons, or because the subclass is not fully Liskov substitutable and the tests are not applicable.
3. If the YYY constructor takes different parameters from the XXX constructor, it is easy to handle – the correct parameters can just be passed to the YYY constructor.

We will use two classes, Shape (Listing 11.12) and Circle (Listing 11.13), to demonstrate two possible approaches to inheritance testing: passing the class name as a parameter to the test, and inheriting the tests.

Listing 11.12 Source code for class Shape.

```
3   class Shape {
4       String name = "unknown";
5       String getName() { return name; }
6       void setName(String name) { this.name = name; }
7   }
```

Listing 11.13 Source code for class Circle.

```
3   class Circle extends Shape {
4       int radius = 0;
5       int getRadius() { return radius; }
6       void setRadius(int radius) { this.radius = radius; }
7   }
```

The class inheritance hierarchy is shown in Figure 11.12.

11.9.1   Using the Class Name

A test for class Shape is shown in Listing 11.14 – instead of hard-coding the class to be tested, the class name is passed as a parameter, and a factory method[11] is used to create the object to test.

---

[11] A factory method can be used instead of a constructor to create an object. The factory method must call a suitable constructor.

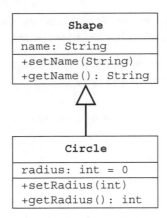

Figure 11.12 UML diagram for Shape and Circle.

Listing 11.14 ShapeTest – by name.

```
 9  public class ShapeTest {
10
11      // Factory method to create a Shape
12      public Shape createShape() throws Exception {
13          String cn = System.getProperty("classname");
14          Class<?> c = Class.forName(cn);
15          Shape o =
                  (Shape)(c.getDeclaredConstructor().newInstance());
16          System.out.println("Running Shape test against instance
                  of "+o.getClass());
17          return o;
18      }
19
20      @Test
21      public void test_demo() throws Exception {
22          Shape o = createShape();
23          o.setName("Test name 1");
24          assertEquals( o.getName(), "Test name 1" );
25      }
26
27  }
```

This test uses a factory method to create the test item, rather than calling the constructor directly. This allows objects of different classes, as required, to be returned by the factory method.

Important lines in the test are:

- Line 13 gets the class name, which is passed as a Java property rather than as a command line parameter; as with TestNG the test class does not have a main() method to pass parameters to.
- Line 14 finds the class associated with the (full) class name.
- Line 15 instantiates an object of that class by calling the constructor indirectly via the newInstance() method.

- Line 16 prints out the test name and the class name, providing a record in the test log of what class was tested (as this test can be run against different classes).

This mechanism allows the Shape tests to be run against an instance of class example.Shape, as in Figure 11.13.

```
Running Shape test against instance of class example.Shape
PASSED: test_demo
===================================================
Command line suite
Total tests run: 1, Passes: 1, Failures: 0, Skips: 0
===================================================
```

Figure 11.13 Running ShapeTest on a Shape.

It also allows the Shape tests to be run against an instance of class example.Circle, as shown in Figure 11.14.

```
Running Shape test against instance of class example.Circle
PASSED: test_demo
===================================================
Command line suite
Total tests run: 1, Passes: 1, Failures: 0, Skips: 0
===================================================
```

Figure 11.14 Running ShapeTest on a Circle.

The main disadvantage of this approach for inheritance testing is that it requires the tester to explicitly run the tests for a class against every superclass in the class hierarchy. The advantage is that the tester can easily select the test classes to execute.[12]

11.9.2   Inheriting Superclass Tests

An alternative approach is to make ShapeTest work as an inherited test. There are many ways to do this – one of the simplest is to use a factory method, which can be overridden by subclass tests. An example is shown in Listing 11.15.

Listing 11.15 Inheritable ShapeTest.

```
 9  public class ShapeTest {
10
11    // Factory method to create a Shape
12    Shape createInstance() {
13      return new Shape();
14    }
15
16    @Test(groups = {"inherited","shape"})
17    public void test_shape() throws Exception {
```

---

[12] The tests for class Circle are not shown here.

```
18      Shape o = createInstance();
19      System.out.println("Running Shape test against instance
            of "+o.getClass());
20      o.setName("Test name 1");
21      assertEquals( o.getName(), "Test name 1" );
22    }
23
24  }
```

Important lines in the test are:

- Lines 12–14 define a factory method that return a Shape object.
- Line 13 instantiates a Shape by calling the constructor.
- On line 18, the factory method is called to create a Shape.

The results of running ShapeTest (on a Shape) are shown in Figure 11.15.

```
Running Shape test against instance of class example.Shape
PASSED: test_shape
===================================================
Command line suite
Total tests run: 1, Passes: 1, Failures: 0, Skips: 0
===================================================
```

Figure 11.15 Running inheritable ShapeTest.

A CircleTest class can now be developed to test the Circle class as shown in Listing 11.16. By extending ShapeTest, the class CircleTest will inherit the test_shape() method (and, critically, its annotation).

Listing 11.16 CircleTest inherits ShapeTest.

```
9   public class CircleTest extends ShapeTest {
10
11      // Factory method to create a Circle
12      Circle createInstance() {
13        return new Circle();
14      }
15
16      // Shape tests are run automatically
17      // New circle tests go here
18      @Test(groups = {"inherited","circle"})
19      public void test_circle() throws Exception {
20        Circle o = createInstance();
21        System.out.println("Running Circle test against instance
            of "+o.getClass());
22        o.setRadius(44);
23        assertEquals( o.getRadius(), 44 );
24      }
25
26  }
```

Class CircleTest has two test methods. It inherits the method test_shape(), and it defines the method test_circle().

As a result of this, when `CircleTest` is run as a TestNG test, the following occurs:

* The test method `testShape()` shown in Listing 11.15, lines 17–22, is inherited from the `ShapeTest` class. TestNG finds this inherited method and runs it as a test.
* The method `testShape()` calls `createInstance()` – Listing 11.15, line 18 – but as the test is running in `CircleTest` context, the method `CircleTest.createInstance()` is called.[13] This returns an object instance of class `Circle` – lines 12–14.
* This causes `shapeTest()` to be run against a `Circle`.

In contrast, when the test `shapeTest()` was run in `ShapeTest` context, the method `ShapeTest.createInstance()` is called, which returns an object instance of class `Shape`, as shown in Listing 11.15.

The result of this is that both the shape tests and the circle tests are run against a `Circle`. This technique works automatically in a deep inheritance hierarchy, as each subclass test inherits all the superclass tests in the hierarchy.

The results of running `CircleTest` are shown in Figure 11.16.

```
Running Circle test against instance of class example.Circle
Running Shape test against instance of class example.Circle
PASSED: test_circle
PASSED: test_shape
===============================================
Command line suite
Total tests run: 2, Passes: 2, Failures: 0, Skips: 0
===============================================
```

Figure 11.16 Running `CircleTest` with inheritance.

There are two issues that can be addressed:

1. the order of testing – it may be desired to do inheritance testing first;
2. test selection – perhaps the tester does not want to run all the `ShapeTest` methods against a `Circle`.

TestNG, and other frameworks, provide a number of mechanisms to support these issues. Examples are shown in the following sections.

Inheritance Test Ordering

There are a number of ways to enforce ordering, but specifying dependencies is probably the simplest. Test method dependencies can be used to enforce ordering, causing the inherited `Shape` tests to be executed prior to the new `Circle` tests (see Listing 11.17).

---

[13] See Gosling et al., *The Java® Language Specification*.

Listing 11.17 ShapeTest with dependencies.

```
9  public class CircleTest extends ShapeTest {
10
11    // Factory method to create a Circle
12    Circle createInstance() {
13      return new Circle();
14    }
15
16    // Shape tests are run automatically
17    // New circle tests go here
18    @Test(dependsOnMethods = {"test_shape"})
19    public void test_circle() throws Exception {
20      Circle o = createInstance();
21      System.out.println("Running Circle test against instance
              of "+o.getClass());
22      o.setRadius(44);
23      assertEquals( o.getRadius(), 44 );
24    }
25
26  }
```

The results of running this version of CircleTest are shown in Figure 11.17.

```
Running Shape test against instance of class example.Circle
Running Circle test against instance of class example.Circle
PASSED: test_shape
PASSED: test_circle
===================================================
Command line suite
Total tests run: 2, Passes: 2, Failures: 0, Skips: 0
===================================================
```

Figure 11.17 Running CircleTest with dependencies.

The Shape tests run before the Circle tests. The test method dependency notifies TestNG to call test_shape() before it calls test_circle(). This works well with further tests in the test hierarchy. If a new subclass test depends on test_circle(), then test_circle() inherits the dependency on test_shape(). As a result, all the inherited methods will be run from the top of the hierarchy downwards, in the required order.

11.9.3   Inheritance Test Selection

As discussed previously, there may be reasons to exclude some of the inheritance tests. Three common reasons for this are where a tester wants to exclude all the inheritance tests, where the performance is too slow to run all the tests every time in a deep hierarchy, or where some subclasses in the hierarchy are not fully Liskov substitutable.

There are a number of ways to select a subset of tests. Using test groups is probably the simplest approach. Listings 11.18 and 11.19 demonstrate an example.

Listing 11.18 `ShapeTest` with groups.

```
9   public class ShapeTest {
10
11    // Factory method to create a Shape
12    Shape createInstance() {
13      return new Shape();
14    }
15
16    @Test(groups = {"inherited","shape"})
17    public void test_shape() throws Exception {
18      Shape o = createInstance();
19      System.out.println("Running Shape test against instance
              of "+o.getClass());
20      o.setName("Test name 1");
21      assertEquals( o.getName(), "Test name 1" );
22    }
23
24  }
```

Listing 11.19 `CircleTest` with groups.

```
9   public class CircleTest extends ShapeTest {
10
11    // Factory method to create a Circle
12    Circle createInstance() {
13      return new Circle();
14    }
15
16    // Shape tests are run automatically
17    // New circle tests go here
18    @Test(groups = {"inherited","circle"})
19    public void test_circle() throws Exception {
20      Circle o = createInstance();
21      System.out.println("Running Circle test against instance
              of "+o.getClass());
22      o.setRadius(44);
23      assertEquals( o.getRadius(), 44 );
24    }
25
26  }
```

The test groups to be run can be selected at runtime (passed as a parameter to TestNG). This can be used to control the order of execution. If the group shape is specified on the first test run, then all the tests in group shape are run. Then if the group circle is specified on the following test run, then all the tests in group circle are run next. If group inherited is specified, then all the tests will be run in no particular order.

Two examples are now shown. Running the tests in group `circle` results in the output shown in Figure 11.18. Running the tests in group `inherited` results in the output shown in Figure 11.19.

```
Running Circle test against instance of class example.Circle
PASSED: test_circle


===============================================
Total tests run: 1, Passes: 1, Failures: 0, Skips: 0
===============================================
```

Figure 11.18 Test results for group `circle`.

```
Running Circle test against instance of class example.Circle
Running Shape test against instance of class example.Circle
PASSED: test_circle
PASSED: test_shape
===============================================
Command line suite
Total tests run: 2, Passes: 2, Failures: 0, Skips: 0
===============================================
```

Figure 11.19 Test results for group `inherited`.

11.10   Interfacing to Web Applications

Selenium is a popular tool for automating web-based applications. In this book, it is used as a representative example of a library enabling automated web-based application testing. Key features of using the Selenium web driver for testing are presented in the following examples.

WebDriver

WebDriver is a library which can be used with different programming languages such as Java, PHP, Python, Rugby, Perl, and C#. Test code (e.g. Selenium-based tests) can use the WebDriver API to open a browser such as Chrome or Firefox, and then launch a web application (i.e. open a URL). The test code simulates user interactions with the web application. Suitable assertions are inserted into the program to verify that the actual behaviour or output matches the expected behaviour/output. In this book, the Chrome WebDriver is used (as of writing, it was the most up to date). For ease of use, it can be imported into an Eclipse/Java project. A minimal set of the Selenium WebDriver API, which are required to perform basic tests using the Chrome WebDriver,[14] include the following:

---

[14] See https://sites.google.com/a/chromium.org/chromedriver/downloads.

- Loading a page whose URL is specified in the string variable `url`:

```
// webdriver.chrome.driver must be set to full path
//   of the executable file
System.setProperty( "webdriver.chrome.driver",
      "./selenium/chromedriver");
driver = new ChromeDriver();
wait = new WebDriverWait(driver, 30);
driver.get(url)
```

- Verify the page title:

```
assertEquals("<expected name>", driver.getTitle() );
```

- Finding an element on a page by id (finding by name is not recommended):

```
driver.findElement(By.id("<elementid>"))
```

- Simulate data being typed into an input field:

```
driver.findElement(By.id("<elementid>")).
      sendKeys("<input data>");
```

- Get a value from an input field:

```
driver.findElement(By.id("<elementid>")).
      getAttribute("value")
```

- Simulate a user clicking on an element in a page (such as a button, link, checkbox, or menu item):

```
driver.findElement(By.id("<elementid>")).click()
```

- Verify if a checkbox is selected:

```
assertTrue(driver.findElement(By.id("<elementid>")).
      isSelected())
```

- Wait for an element to appear – this is particularly important for web applications, as there can be a significant delay (in the order of several seconds) before the page updates. Reference the Selenium documentation for all the `ExpectedConditions` supported – but note the use of *visibility* rather than *presence* to make sure the web element is actually visible on the screen, rather than merely present in the document object model. For example, to wait for a page to be displayed:

```
wait.until(ExpectedConditions.titleIs("<expected title"));
wait.until(ExpectedConditions.visibilityOfElementLocated(
      By.id("<expected element>")));
```

Note that the system property set is specific to `Chromedriver`: other drivers may support different properties to assist Selenium to locate the driver.

11.11   Interfacing to Desktop Applications

Java GUI desktop applications are usually developed using Java AWT, Swing, JavaFX, or other libraries. As for web applications, the key issues are: (a) how to find the GUI elements to interact with, and (b) how to interact with them.

A typical desktop application test will:

- call the `main()` method in the application to start it running;
- call `Window.getWindows()` to find the application window or call `javax.swing.FocusManager.getCurrentManager()`.`getActiveWindow()` to find the active window after starting the application;
- place all calls that interact with the GUI on the GUI event thread (`Swing.InvokeAndWait()` for a Swing application);
- call `JFrame.getTitle()` to get the title of a window;
- call `Container.getComponents()` recursively to find a component (window, button, textbox, etc.), with `Component.getName()` used to find by name (instead of using the id as in HTML);
- interact with the components: e.g. `JButton.doClick()`, `JTextBox.setText()`, `JTextBox.getText()`.

The key difference when compared to web applications is that the application has full control of the application screen, whereas for a web page the user can return to a *stale* window by typing in the URL or using the browser back button. The tester should reference the API for the GUI library in use for full details.[15]

There are a number of frameworks for Java GUI application testing: these are built on top of the underlying AWT/Swing/JavaFX libraries. There are also many OS-dependent and language-independent frameworks for GUI application testing frameworks. Both proprietary and open-source tools are available. A review of these tools is beyond the scope of this book.

11.12   Interfacing to Mobile Applications

Developing tests for mobile applications is similar to developing tests for web applications.

---

[15] The AWT, Swing, and JavaFX APIs are published by Oracle at https://docs.oracle.com.

Some example tools are:

- selendroid (Selenium for Android) – API as for Selenium, using the selendroid-client libraries.[16]
- iOS Driver on Apple phones – based on Selenium/WebDriver.[17]

Again, there are many such tools, and the reader is recommended to view an up-to-date online comparison of these.

---

[16] See http://selendroid.io.
[17] See https://ios-driver.github.io/ios-driver.

12 Random Testing

12.1 Introduction to Random Testing

Fully automated random testing with no manual input is a goal of the software industry, and is a key research area. However, as discussed in the introduction in Chapter 1, there are three key issues with automated random testing:

1. the test oracle problem – how to tell if the result is correct;
2. the test data problem – how to generate representative random data; and
3. the test completion problem – how to know when to stop generating tests.

This is an active research area, and a discussion of all the up-to-date solutions to these problems is beyond the scope of this book. We will, however, present an introduction to the topic: a simple form of automated random testing using random data in conjunction with manually generated black-box or white-box test coverage items is presented in this chapter.

12.2 Random Data Selection

In this chapter, the same techniques that were covered previously are used to generate the test coverage items (TCIs) (see Chapters 2–9), but instead of creating test cases with specific test data *values*, more general test data criteria are developed. This allows the selection of random values that meet those criteria at runtime. This approach addresses the automated random test problems as follows:

- Manual development of the test coverage items addresses the test oracle problem by including the tester in the process.
- Using test data criteria and random number generators addresses the test data problem as these allow the generation of good test data.
- Limiting the test execution time addresses the test completion problem by offering a strategy for stopping.

The technique is demonstrated through two examples: (1) unit testing and (2) application testing.

12.3   Unit Test Example

The method giveDiscount(), as described in Chapter 2, is used as an example. As a reminder, the specification is reproduced here.

Status giveDiscount(long bonusPoints, boolean goldCustomer)
Inputs
>   **bonusPoints:** the number of bonusPoints the customer has accumulated
>   **goldCustomer:** true for a Gold Customer

Outputs
>   **return value:**
>>   FULLPRICE if bonusPoints $\leq$ 120 and not a goldCustomer
>>   FULLPRICE if bonusPoints $\leq$ 80 and a goldCustomer
>>   DISCOUNT if bonusPoints $>$ 120
>>   DISCOUNT if bonusPoints $>$ 80 and a goldCustomer
>>   ERROR if any inputs are invalid (bonusPoints $<$ 1)

Status is defined as follows:

```
enum Status { FULLPRICE, DISCOUNT, ERROR };
```

The tests developed in this example are based on the equivalence partition tests developed already for this method. All the other black-box and white-box tests could also be used for more comprehensive testing.

12.3.1   Test Coverage Items

The equivalence partition tests for the method giveDiscount() as developed in Chapter 2 will be used to demonstrate the technique. The TCIs are reproduced here for reference – see Table 12.1.

Table 12.1 TCIs for giveDiscount().

TCI	Parameter	Equivalence partition
EP1*	bonusPoints	Long.MIN_VALUE..0
EP2		1..80
EP3		81..120
EP4		121..Long.MAX_VALUE
EP5	goldCustomer	true
EP6		false
EP7	Return Value	FULLPRICE
EP8		DISCOUNT
EP9		ERROR

12.3.2   Test Cases

When developing the test cases, instead of selecting actual data values to represent each equivalence partition, criteria that define that equivalence partition are used instead. These allow specific data values to be selected at random at runtime, based on the criteria. For simple partitions, the criteria will state the minimum and maximum values in the partition. In this example, these criteria are based on the partition boundaries for each TCI, as shown in Table 12.2.

Table 12.2 Equivalence value criteria.

Parameter	Equivalence partition	Criteria
bonusPoints	Long.MIN_VALUE..0	(Long.MIN_VALUE$\leq$bonusPoints) && (bonusPoints$\leq$0)
	1..80	(1<=bonusPoints) && (bonusPoints<=80)
	81..120	(81<=bonusPoints) && (bonusPoints<=120)
	121..Long.MAX_VALUE	(121<=bonusPoints) && (bonusPoints<=Long.MAX_VALUE)
goldCustomer	true	goldCustomer
	false	!goldCustomer
Return Value	FULLPRICE	Return Value==FULLPRICE
	DISCOUNT	Return Value==DISCOUNT
	ERROR	Return Value==ERROR

Using these criteria, random test data can be specified for each test case, as shown in Table 12.3. This is essentially the same as Table 2.9 in Chapter 2 as developed for equivalence partition testing, but for each test case actual data values are replaced by the criteria for generating random values.

Table 12.3 Random equivalence partition test cases for `giveDiscount()`.

ID	TCI covered	Inputs		Exp. results
		bonusPoints	goldCustomer	return value
T12.1	EP2,5,7	rand(1,80)	true	FULLPRICE
T12.2	EP3,6,[7]	rand(81,120)	false	FULLPRICE
T12.3	EP4,[6],8	rand(121,Long.MAX_VALUE)	false	DISCOUNT
T12.4*	EP1*,9	rand(Long.MIN_VALUE,0)	false	ERROR

Some important features are:

1. The shorthand `rand(l,h)` is used to represent a random number between the low-bound (l), and high-bound (h) – inclusive of both values.
2. By using specific error test case(s), the problem of almost all inputs being in error is avoided.

3. `goldCustomer` cannot be random: for some test cases specific values are required to generate the expected results. If all the inputs are Boolean, this technique is unlikely to be of value.

4. T12.4 is an error test case, so it only covers a single input error TCI (EP1).

12.3.3   Test Implementation

The test implementation (see Listing 12.1) is similar to that for equivalence partition testing. As the same test method is used for a large number of random data values, a data provider is used. The data provider returns the criteria required for selecting values, instead of specific values. The criteria are then used in the test method to create the data values.

Listing 12.1 Random equivalence partition test for `giveDiscount()`.

```
18  public class RandomTest {
19
20    private static long RUNTIME = 1000; // Test runtime in
            milliseconds
21
22    // Store the data values in case of test failure
23    long bonusPoints;
24    boolean goldCustomer;
25    boolean failed = false;
26    Status expected, actual;
27    String testId;
28
29    @DataProvider(name = "eprandom")
30    public Object[][] getEpData() {
31      return new Object[][] {
32          { "T12.1",            1L,           80L, true, FULLPRICE},
33          { "T12.2",           81L,          120L, false, FULLPRICE },
34          { "T12.3",          121L, Long.MAX_VALUE, false, DISCOUNT },
35          { "T12.4", Long.MIN_VALUE,    0L, false, ERROR }
36      };
37    }
38
39    @Test(dataProvider = "eprandom")
40    public void randomTest(String tid,long minp, long maxp,
            boolean cf, Status exp) {
41      Random rp = new Random();
42      long endTime = System.currentTimeMillis()+RUNTIME;
43      testId = tid;
44      while (System.currentTimeMillis() < endTime) {
45        bonusPoints = generateRandomLong( rp, minp, maxp );
46        goldCustomer = cf;
47        failed = true;
48        expected = exp;
49        actual =
                OnlineSales.giveDiscount(bonusPoints,goldCustomer);
50        assertEquals( actual, exp );
51        failed = false;
```

```
52        }
53      }
54
55      private static long generateRandomLong( Random r, long min,
                 long max ) {
56        long value;
57        if (min > 0)
58          value = min + (long) (r.nextDouble() * (max - min));
59        else do
60          value = r.nextLong();
61        while ((value < min) || (value > max));
62        return value;
63      }
64
65      @AfterMethod
66      public void reportFailures() {
67        if (failed) {
68          System.out.println("Test failure data for test: "+
                 testId);
69          System.out.println(" bonusPoints="+ bonusPoints);
70          System.out.println(" goldCustomer="+ goldCustomer);
71          System.out.println(" actual result="+ actual);
72          System.out.println(" expected result="+ expected);
73        }
74      }
75
76    }
```

The assertion on line 50 is placed within a loop that generates random values for bonusPoints on line 45. The values for the other inputs are fixed by the equivalence partition test criteria. The loop also limits the execution time on line 44 in order to terminate the test.

If a test fails, the standard test report will only show the inputs to the test method, which are the test data criteria rather than the actual data values. This can make replicating and debugging problems difficult. To address this, and report the actual random data values that caused the failure, the test method saves the input parameter values and the expected results and sets failed to true (lines 45–48). If the test succeeds, then line 51 will be executed, setting failed to false. If the test fails, then failed will remain true and the @AfterMethod method will be called. This prints out the parameters values for a failed test (lines 68–72).

12.3.4 Test Results

Running these tests against the class OnlineSales produces the results shown in Figure 12.1.

All the tests have passed. With the selected value of RUNTIME = 1000 milliseconds in the code, the total test execution time is approximately 4 seconds for the four tests.

```
PASSED: randomTest("T12.1", 1, 80, true, FULLPRICE)
PASSED: randomTest("T12.2", 81, 120, false, FULLPRICE)
PASSED: randomTest("T12.3", 121, 9223372036854775807, false, DISCOUNT)
PASSED: randomTest("T12.4", -9223372036854775808, 0, false, ERROR)
================================================
Command line suite
Total tests run: 4, Passes: 4, Failures: 0, Skips: 0
================================================
```

Figure 12.1 Equivalence partition random test results for
`OnlineSales.giveDiscount()`.

12.4   Application Testing Example

To show the broad applicability of random testing, a random application test example
is shown here, based on the Fuel Checker system described in Chapter 10.

As a reminder, the specification for Fuel Checker is reproduced here:

> A fuel depot wants a web-based system to enable the dispatcher to determine
> whether a load of fuel will fit in a tank or not. Some fuels can fill the tank; others
> require extra space for safety reasons. The tank capacity is 1200 litres without
> the extra safety space, and 800 litres with it.

12.4.1   Analysis

The data criteria for randomising the input are derived from the acceptance criteria
shown in Section 10.2:

S1A1 requires a value for litres that fits in a tank without extra safety. The range of
values is from 1 to 1200.

S1A2 requires a value for litres that fits in a tank with extra safety. The range of values
is from 1 to 800.

S1A3 requires a value for litres that does not fit in a tank without extra safety. The
range of values is from 1201 to some unspecified maximum value.

S1A4 requires a value for litres that does not fit in a tank with extra safety. The range
of values is from 801 to some unspecified maximum value.

As for the random unit testing, instead of selecting individual values to represent
each equivalence partition (shown in Table 10.3), criteria are used for selecting random
values at runtime,[1] as shown in Table 12.4.

---

[1] The random values generated will of course have to be converted to strings to be used as inputs to the
application.

Table 12.4 Data value criteria.

Acceptance Criteria	Input	Data criteria
S1A1	litres	$1 \leq$ litres ≤ 1200
S1A2	litres	$1 \leq$ litres ≤ 800
S1A3	litres	$1201 \leq$ litres $\leq$ Integer.MAX_VALUE
S1A4	litres	$801 \leq$ litres $\leq$ Integer.MAX_VALUE

12.4.2 Test Coverage Items

The user story tests developed in Chapter 10 will be used to demonstrate the technique. The selected TCIs, which include inputs suitable for randomisation, are shown in Table 12.5.

Table 12.5 Random TCIs for Fuel Checker.

TCI	Acceptance criteria	Test case
RUS1	S1A1	
RUS2	S1A2	To be completed later
RUS3	S1A3	
RUS4	S1A4	

12.4.3 Test Cases

The test data is based on the criteria developed for the test coverage items. The criteria are presented instead of actual data values (see Table 12.6).

12.4.4 Test Implementation

The test implementation is based on the tests developed in Chapter 10. Where relevant, specific data values are replaced with lower and upper bounds from the criteria developed for randomising the data. The implementation is presented in Listings 12.2–12.5

Listing 12.2 shows the test startup code, based on that used for application testing in Chapter 11, but with extra attributes to support random testing.

Listing 12.2 Setup for `FuelCheckRandomTest`.

```
25    // Selenium
26
27    WebDriver driver;
28    Wait<WebDriver> wait;
29
30    // URL for the application to test
31
32    String url = System.getProperty("url");
33
```

```
34    // Stored data for test failure reports
35
36    static final long RUNTIME = 10000L; // run each random test
            for 10 seconds
37    Random r_litres = new Random(); // RNG for litres input
38    boolean failed;
39    String litres;
40    boolean highsafety;
41    int counter;
42
43    @BeforeClass
44    public void setupDriver() throws Exception {
45       System.out.println("Test started at: " +
             LocalDateTime.now());
46       if (url == null)
47         throw new Exception("Test URL not defined: use
               -Durl=<url>");
48       System.out.println("For URL: "+ url);
49       System.out.println();
50       // Create web driver (this code uses chrome)
51       if (System.getProperty("webdriver") == null)
52         throw new Exception("Web driver not defined: use
               -Dwebdriver=<filename>");
53       if (!new File(System.getProperty("webdriver")).exists())
54         throw new Exception("Web driver missing: " +
               System.getProperty("webdriver"));
55       System.setProperty("webdriver.chrome.driver",
             System.getProperty("webdriver"));
56       driver = new ChromeDriver();
57       // Create wait
58       wait = new WebDriverWait( driver, 5 );
59       // Open web page
60       driver.get( url );
61    }
62
63    @AfterClass
64    public void shutdown() {
65       driver.quit();
66    }
```

Listing 12.3 shows the additional attributes to support random testing (this is an extract from the previous listing, so the line numbers overlap). These allow the data values to be reported for a failed test.

Listing 12.3 Stored test data values.

```
34    // Stored data for test failure reports
35
36    static final long RUNTIME = 10000L; // run each random test
            for 10 seconds
37    Random r_litres = new Random(); // RNG for litres input
38    boolean failed;
39    String litres;
40    boolean highsafety;
41    int counter;
```

Table 12.6 Random test data criteria for Fuel Checker.

ID	TCI covered	Inputs	Expected results
T12.1	RUS1	Enter string $1 \leq litres \leq 1200$ into litres Deselect `highsafety` Click on Enter Click on Check	 Moved to Check screen `litres` is correct `highsafety` is deselected Moved to Results screen Result is "`Fuel fits in tank.`"
T12.2	RUS2	Enter string $1 \leq litres \leq 800$ into litres Select `highsafety` Click on Enter Click on Check	 Moved to Check screen `litres` is correct `highsafety` is selected Moved to Results screen Result is "`Fuel fits in tank.`"
T12.3	RUS3	Enter string $1201 \leq litres \leq Integer.MAX\_VALUE$ into litres Deselect `highsafety` Click on Enter Click on Check	 Moved to Check screen `litres` is correct `highsafety` is deselected Moved to Results screen Result is "`Fuel does not fit in tank.`"
T12.4	RUS4	Enter string $801 \leq litres \leq Integer.MAX\_VALUE$ into litres Select `highsafety` Click on Enter Click on Check	 Moved to Check screen `litres` is correct `highsafety` is selected Moved to Results screen Result is "`Fuel does not fit in tank.`"

Listing 12.4 shows an extended @AfterMethod code. As in Chapter 11, this ensures the application is displaying the main window even after a failed test. In addition, to support random testing it writes the data values selected for any random test that fails, allowing the failure to be subsequently reproduced for debugging.

Listing 12.4 `@AfterMethod` for `FuelCheckRandomTest`.

```
68    @AfterMethod
69    public void runAfterTestMethod() {
70       System.out.println("Random test loops executed:
            "+counter);
71       counter = 0;
```

```
72          // Process test failures
73          if (failed) {
74            System.out.println(" Test failed on input: litres=" +
                  litres + ", highsafety=" + highsafety);
75          }
76          // If test has not left app at the main window, try to
                return there for the next test
77          if ("Results".equals(driver.getTitle()))
78            driver.findElement(By.id("Continue")).click();
79          else if ("Fuel Checker
                Information".equals(driver.getTitle()))
80            driver.findElement(By.id("goback")).click();
81          else if ("Thank you".equals(driver.getTitle()))
82            driver.get( url ); // only way to return to main screen
                from here
83          wait.until(ExpectedConditions.titleIs("Fuel Checker"));
84        }
```

Listing 12.5 shows the data provider and the random test method.

Listing 12.5 Data provider and test method.

```
90     @DataProvider(name = "ECVdata")
91     public Object[][] getEVCdata() {
92       return new Object[][] {
93         { "T12.1", 1, 1200, false, "Fuel fits in tank." },
94         { "T12.2", 1, 800, true, "Fuel fits in tank." },
95         { "T12.3", 1201, Integer.MAX_VALUE, false, "Fuel does
                not fit in tank." },
96         { "T12.4", 801, Integer.MAX_VALUE, true, "Fuel does not
                fit in tank." },
97       };
98     }
99
100    @Test(timeOut = 60000, dataProvider = "ECVdata")
101    public void testEnterCheckView(String tid, int lmin, int
              lmax, boolean hs, String result) {
102      long endTime = System.currentTimeMillis() + RUNTIME;
103      failed = true;
104      highsafety = hs;
105      while (System.currentTimeMillis() < endTime) {
106        counter++;
107        wait.until(ExpectedConditions.titleIs("Fuel Checker"));
108        // generate random litres using normal distribution
109        int n_litres = (int)(((double)lmin + (double)lmax)/2.0 +
110            ((double)lmax - (double)lmin)/6.0 *
                  r_litres.nextGaussian());
111        if (n_litres > lmax) n_litres = lmax;
112        if (n_litres < lmin) n_litres = lmin;
113        litres = Integer.toString(n_litres);
114        // Now do the test
115        wait.until(ExpectedConditions.titleIs("Fuel Checker"));
116        wait.until(ExpectedConditions.visibilityOfElementLocated(
              By.id("litres")));
117        driver.findElement(By.id("litres")).sendKeys(litres);
```

```
118        wait.until(ExpectedConditions.visibilityOfElementLocated(
               By.id("highsafety")));
119        if (driver.findElement(
               By.id("highsafety")).isSelected()!=highsafety)
120          driver.findElement( By.id("highsafety")).click();
121        wait.until(ExpectedConditions.visibilityOfElementLocated(
               By.id("Enter")));
122        driver.findElement( By.id("Enter")).click();
123        wait.until(ExpectedConditions.titleIs("Results"));
124        wait.until(ExpectedConditions.visibilityOfElementLocated(
               By.id("result")));
125        assertEquals( driver.findElement(
               By.id("result")).getAttribute("value"),result );
126        wait.until(ExpectedConditions.visibilityOfElementLocated(
               By.id("Continue")));
127        driver.findElement( By.id("Continue")).click();
128        wait.until(ExpectedConditions.titleIs("Fuel Checker"));
129      }
130    failed = false; // if reach here, no test has failed
131    }
```

Notes on the implementation:

- Attributes for the input parameter values are defined on lines 39–40. A test failure flag is defined on line 38.
- Lines 68–84 shows the @AfterMethod, which is extended to print out the parameters values for a failed random test. Without this, debugging after a failure is extremely difficult.
- An additional value is also reported, a counter for the number of loops achieved for each test in the time available, using the counter (defined on line 41).
- The data provider includes the criteria (for an integer, these are the lower and upper bounds) for litres, instead of specific values. See lines 93–96.
- The parameterised test includes extra input parameters lmin and lmax (line 101) to support the lower and upper bounds for litres for each test.
- Instead of running a single test, a number of loops with different random values are executed, using a timer (line 105) to decide when to complete the random test.
- A random value is selected for litres on lines 108–113. For application testing, values based on actual user inputs are often used, so that testing better matches real-world use. When these statistics are not available,[2] normally distributed values are often used as an approximation. The method Random.nextGaussian() returns a normally distributed value, centered on 0.0, with a standard deviation of 3.0. For a normal distribution, 99% of the values lie within three standard deviations, so the equation on line 109 produces a random number centered in the middle of the range lmin..lmax,

---

[2] Software may record input data values, and with the end-user's permission report these statistics back for use in testing.

and normally distributed. Note that 1% of the values will lie outside this range, and these are moved into the range on lines 111–112.

- The parameter values are recorded on lines 104 and 113 for reporting in case of a test failure.
- The remainder of the test is similar to the application test developed in Chapter 10.
- At the end of each loop, the application is returned to the main screen (lines 127–128), so that subsequent tests can run.

12.4.5   Test Results

The results of running these tests against the application Fuel Checker is shown in Figure 12.2. All the tests have passed. With the selected value of RUNTIME= 10000 milliseconds, the total test execution time is approximately 40 seconds for the four tests.

```
Test started at: 2020-09-09T16:26:40.526107500
For URL: ch12\application-test\fuelchecker\fuelchecker.html
Random test loops executed: 16
Random test loops executed: 16
Random test loops executed: 17
Random test loops executed: 14
PASSED: testEnterCheckView("T12.1", 1, 1200, false, "Fuel fits in tank
    .")
PASSED: testEnterCheckView("T12.2", 1, 800, true, "Fuel fits in tank.")
PASSED: testEnterCheckView("T12.3", 1201, 2147483647, false, "Fuel does
    not fit in tank.")
PASSED: testEnterCheckView("T12.4", 801, 2147483647, true, "Fuel does
    not fit in tank.")
=================================================
Command line suite
Total tests run: 4, Passes: 4, Failures: 0, Skips: 0
=================================================
```

Figure 12.2 Random test results for Fuel Checker web application.

12.5   Random Testing in More Detail

In this chapter only one type of random testing is shown as an introduction to the topic: random input data selection with existing test cases. Ideally the entire testing process would be random and automated, and provide full coverage of the software specification and implementation. This would lead to very comprehensive and low-cost testing. However, there are a number of barriers to this.

12.5.1   Barriers to Full Automation

Three barriers to fully automated random testing are discussed below.

The Test Oracle Problem

Once random data has been automatically selected, and the software executed with this data, the problem is how to verify that the output from the software is correct. For unit tests, this may be the return value. When testing object-oriented (OO) software, this may also include output attributes. For application testing, this includes all the output from the software, which may be delivered to the screen, to databases, to files, as inputs to another system, etc. There are four fundamental approaches to handling the oracle problem:

- Ignore the issue by only requiring that the test completes without crashing the software being tested – this is referred to as stability testing. The test oracle then becomes a generic software utility to verify that the software keeps running after any test input. In principle, this can be applied to all types of testing, but it is usually applied to system testing. For unit or OO testing, this would imply checking that no unexpected exceptions are raised. For a system, it would imply testing that the system keeps running – which may not always be easy to determine.

- Write a program in a higher-level, more abstract language to specify the software requirements, and use that to generate the expected results. This can also be described as an *executable specification*. In a higher-level language the requirements can be stated as what is to happen rather than how it is to be achieved, and the software designed is less likely to be faulty (though it will be slow). A similar solution is to use a second programmer implementing the algorithm separately and use that code as a test oracle.

- Use constraints expressed in a logic-based software specification language (such as Object Constraint Language (OCL), which is part of UML). Instead of calculating the expected results, this approach verifies the actual result against the specification. This technique, however, requires a formal specification for each method implemented in unit testing, or a formal specification of the correct result. It also requires software tools to provide the automated verification. To date, the software industry has not placed much emphasis on this, resulting in a lack of skills and a lack of tools. Examples of research-based solutions are the specification language Java Markup Language (JML) and the OpenJML toolset for Runtime Assertion Checking (RAC).[3]

- Use one of the manual test design techniques in order to develop criteria instead of data values, as shown in the worked examples in this chapter. Any of the equivalence partition, BVA, decision tables, statement coverage, and branch coverage techniques can be used.[4] Random values can then be selected to match the criteria at runtime.

---

[3] See www.openjml.org.
[4] Alternatively, a decision tree can be built, selecting the output first, and then working backwards to develop criteria for each branch in the tree.

The Test Data Problem

The automated generation of test data that thoroughly tests software (be it a unit, a class, or an entire system) is a complex problem. It requires data generation goals to be defined and software libraries that generate data that meets those goals. A stepping stone on the road to full automation is the provision of random object generators, that given a goal will generate a random object for use in unit, OO, or system testing. This can be used in conjunction with manually developed test cases (e.g. equivalence partition), where a goal is selected at random, and then data is generated to match that goal. This can also be used to address the test oracle problem if the goal allows the expected results to be easily determined.

Purely random selection of data values is unlikely to cover all the specification or all the implementation. Research into directed random data generation has focused mainly on white-box coverage, as tools to measure this coverage exist for many languages (for example Directed Automated Random Testing[5]).

For application testing, data generation is often based on statistics of typical customer input data. This allows the tests to mimic actual software usage. As well as helping to find faults, this type of data generation allows the *mean time to failure* (MTTF) to also be estimated in advance of software release. Whereas in principle this can be used for unit testing, it seldom is: the focus on unit testing tends to be more towards complete coverage rather than only coverage of typical inputs.

The Test Completion Problem

Ideally, automated random tests would cover all of the specification and all of the implementation, achieving 100% black-box and 100% white-box coverage. However, as we have seen previously, few tools exist to measure black-box coverage, and not all white-box coverage metrics can be easily measured (such as all-paths coverage).

Approaches to solving this problem tend to be based on pragmatism:

- Number of loops is the simplest completion criterion. Run a certain number of random tests, selecting this number to suit the development process. This can be an iterative process, and may sometimes result either in a lost opportunity to run more tests in the time available, or the need to terminate the random testing run midway in order to meet a project's deadlines.
- Time is a more sophisticated metric. Allow random tests to run for a specific length of time that suits the development process. This may lead to variations in coverage.
- Use existing white-box coverage tools. For example, run random tests until 100% statement and branch coverage have been achieved. This will often result in non-terminating tests, and is usually used in conjunction with time as a completion measure.

---

[5] Refer to P. Godefroid, N. Klarlund, and K. Sen. DART: Directed Automated Random Testing. In *Proc. ACM SIGPLAN Conf. Programming Language Design and Implementation*. ACM, 2005. for details.

12.5.2   Overview of Other Types of Random Testing

There are a number of other approaches to random automated testing that are not addressed in detail in this book, including:

- *Stability testing* – there are various forms that test a system to ensure that it does not hang or crash, for any input. These test techniques (and support tools) do not use the specification to determine if the output is correct, but rather verify the stability of the system to randomly selected inputs.

  - *Undirected random testing* – the user interface is scanned for interactive components, one is selected at random, and then an interaction is selected at random (such as a click, text entry, swipe, and so on) and executed. The test attempts to cause the system to crash. Normally, the completion criteria is based on time.

  - *Directed random testing*[6] – white-box coverage criteria, such as statement or branch coverage, are measured dynamically during testing. Once random tests stop producing additional coverage, then analysis of the code takes place, to try to identify input data that will increase the coverage. This may take the form of symbolic execution, or may be based on statistical or machine learning approaches. The goal is typically to maximise the code coverage, maximise the number of crashes, and minimise the length of the input sequences. It can be used for desktop, mobile, and web-based applications, though determining whether a web-based application has crashed can be challenging. The completion criteria are usually coverage and/or time-based, as it may take a long time to achieve the required coverage, if it is even possible.

  - *Fuzz testing* – existing good data is corrupted at random, and provided as input to the system. The goal is to crash the system with invalid input. The completion criteria is usually time. This technique may be used in conjunction with directed random testing.

- *Stress testing* – the goal is to ensure the system continues to operate correctly when overloaded with inputs. Existing tests may be chosen at random and executed at the highest rate achievable, often running a large number of tests in parallel to maximise the load. This ensures that the system operates correctly, even when overloaded. Alternatively any random tests may be used as input, ensuring the system does not hang or crash when overloaded. Special test

---

[6] For example: Android Monkey (https://developer.android.com/studio/test/monkey) and Sapienz, which is described in K. Mao, M. Harman, and Y. Jia. Sapienz: Multi-objective automated testing for Android applications. In Proc. 25th Int Symp. Software Testing and Analysis. ACM, 2016.

configurations are often used, as this form of testing may place unacceptable load on servers or networks in use for other purposes.

- *Decision trees and random testing* – the goal is to resolve the test oracle and data selection problems, and to ensure that the system operates correctly for randomly selected inputs. The test oracle problem is solved by selecting a test *output* at random, and then using specification-based rules to select appropriate test *inputs*. This approach does not work for all forms of specifications, but is well suited to those where it is straightforward to run the specification back-wards. A decision tree is used (1) to select the output at random, and then (2) to implement the rules to create random inputs. This can be used in conjunction with directed random testing, ensuring coverage of both the specification and the implementation.

- *Automated test case generation from specifications* – there is active research to develop test cases using various approaches such as analysis, evolutionary algorithms, and machine learning. This approach has the potential to solve all three random test problems, providing systems that can automatically generate tests with no user intervention.

12.6   Evaluation

The results of running automated random tests against Fault 6, and a new Fault 10, in `OnlineSales.giveDiscount()` are used to demonstrate the limitations of the technique.

12.6.1   Limitations

Some of the limitations of random testing are explored by looking at its effectiveness against Fault 6 and Fault 10.

Random Equivalence Partition Testing with Fault 6

Fault 6 was introduced in Listing 6.3 by a complete redesign of the method, intro-ducing faults that were unlikely to be found by equivalence partition, BVA, decision tables, statement coverage, or branch coverage testing.

The results of running the random equivalence partition tests against the code with Fault 6 are shown in Figure 12.3.

The fault is detected, and the input data values that caused the test failure are displayed.

Random EP Testing with Fault 10

Random testing is probabilistic and does not always find every fault. Two additional lines have been added that result in faulty execution if `bonusPoints` has the value 965423829 (see line 39 in Listing 12.6).

```
Test failure data for test: T12.1
   bonusPoints=20
   goldCustomer=true
   actual result=DISCOUNT
   expected result=FULLPRICE
PASSED: randomTest("T12.2", 81, 120, false, FULLPRICE)
PASSED: randomTest("T12.3", 121, 9223372036854775807, false, DISCOUNT)
PASSED: randomTest("T12.4", -9223372036854775808, 0, false, ERROR)
FAILED: randomTest("T12.1", 1, 80, true, FULLPRICE)
java.lang.AssertionError: expected [FULLPRICE] but found [DISCOUNT]
================================================
Command line suite
Total tests run: 4, Passes: 3, Failures: 1, Skips: 0
================================================
```

Figure 12.3 Test results for Fault 6.

Listing 12.6 OnlineSales.giveDiscount() with Fault 10.

```
24   public static Status giveDiscount(long bonusPoints, boolean
            goldCustomer)
25   {
26     Status rv = FULLPRICE;
27     long threshold = 120;
28
29     if (bonusPoints <= 0)
30       rv = ERROR;
31
32     else {
33       if (goldCustomer)
34         threshold = 80;
35       if (bonusPoints > threshold)
36         rv = DISCOUNT;
37     }
38
39     if (bonusPoints == 965423829) // Fault 10
40       rv = ERROR;
41
42     return rv;
43   }
44
45 }
```

The results of running the equivalence partition tests against the code with Fault 10 are shown in Figure 12.4.

The fault is not detected. There is in fact a very low probability that the fault will be detected: approximately 1 in 2^{63}.

12.6.2   Strengths and Weaknesses

Random testing is used as an approximation of exhaustive testing. By covering a wide range of values at random, rather than using a single value in each test, the probability of finding faults in the software is increased.

```
PASSED: randomTest("T12.1", 1, 80, true, FULLPRICE)
PASSED: randomTest("T12.2", 81, 120, false, FULLPRICE)
PASSED: randomTest("T12.3", 121, 9223372036854775807, false, DISCOUNT)
PASSED: randomTest("T12.4", -9223372036854775808, 0, false, ERROR)
================================================
Command line suite
Total tests run: 4, Passes: 4, Failures: 0, Skips: 0
================================================
```

Figure 12.4 Test result for Fault 10.

In this case, as equivalence partition testing has been used as the basis for randomisation, only faults that can be found by equivalence partition testing can be discovered. It is unlikely that faults related to a single data value will be found, but faults related to a range of values within an equivalence partition have a higher chance of being found with random testing. Using decision tables, statement coverage, or branch coverage[7] test data increases the chance of each of these finding faults by using a wider selection of input values.

Strengths

- Limited or no manual intervention is required to run the tests. This holds the potential for a significant improvement in software quality.
- A large number of tests can be run in a limited time.
- Stability testing has proven very successful in finding situations in which software hangs or crashes, and has been an important element in improving this aspect of software quality.

Weaknesses

- Most existing tools only perform stability testing, and therefore do not verify the correct operation of the software, which must be tested separately.
- The test oracle, data selection, and test completion problems are still largely unsolved.
- Effective techniques require full software specifications. These are time-consuming to develop, and many developers are not experienced in producing these using formal languages (e.g. OCL).

12.7   Key Points

- There are three key problems with fully automated random testing: the test oracle problem, the test data problem, and the test completion problem.

---

[7] Using randomisation with BVA is unlikely to be effective as the boundary values are fixed values.

- Random data selection can be used with any of the black-box and white-box test techniques by selecting test data criteria rather than test data values, and then selecting test data values at runtime that match the criteria. In this case the test oracle is manual.
- Fully random data selection can be used with a simple test oracle (the software does not crash) for stability testing.
- There are a number of approaches for determining test completion: simple and pragmatic approaches consist of specifying a fixed number of loops, or a fixed amount of time for test execution. More advanced techniques include measuring code coverage at runtime.

12.8 Notes for the Experienced Tester

Generating random tests is probably one of the most effective ways for the experienced tester to create large numbers of tests quickly. The stability of an application can be tested by generating random input actions and checking that the application does not crash. The tests created using equivalence partitions, BVA, decision tables, statement coverage, and branch coverage for unit testing, OO testing, or application testing can be used to expand the breadth of data values used. By using input data which is statistically representative of real-world data, collected from execution of the application by real customers, an estimate of the mean time between failures (MTBF) can be derived. Safety tests can often be developed by adding *invariants* to represent the safety criteria for an application or a class, writing code to check for these (periodically or after every method call), and simulating random inputs. Instead of checking that the output of each method is correct, this form of testing verifies that the effect of the method is correct with respect to the safety criteria.

13 Testing in the Software Process

The activity of testing can be approached in two ways. The first is to wait until all the code has been written and then to test the finished product all at once. This is referred to as 'Big Bang' development. On the surface, it is an attractive option to developers because testing activities do not hold back the progress towards completing the product. However, it is a risky strategy as the likelihood that the product will work, or even be close to working, can be very low, and is particularly dependent on program complexity and program size. Additionally, if tests do reveal faults in the program, it is much more difficult to identify their source.

A more modern approach is to test the software while it is being developed. This is referred to as 'incremental' development. Individual modules, or software features, are tested as they are written. This process continues as additional software increments are produced until the product is completed. While this may delay the release of the final product, it should produce one with higher quality, and allows interim versions to be produced earlier. Also, incremental development is more responsive to changing user requirements.

The incremental approach thus includes testing as part of the development process. Every stage of development relates to a specific stage of testing as shown from left to right in Figure 13.1.

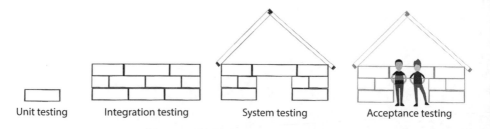

Unit testing   Integration testing   System testing   Acceptance testing

Figure 13.1 The stages of incremental testing.

In unit testing, individual components are tested. In integration testing, the interaction between these components is tested. In system testing, a complete system is tested against its specification. In acceptance testing, a user validates that the system meets their needs.

This chapter describes the activities required to plan software testing, and examines how software testing fits into different models of the software development process.

13.1   Test Planning

The time and resources required for software testing can be of a scale similar to those required for developing the software. The testing activity therefore needs to be planned and managed in a similar way. A typical test plan would include such information as:

- items to be tested;
- tasks to be performed;
- responsibilities;
- schedules; and
- required resources.

IEEE standard 29119[1] provides a formal framework within which a test plan can be prepared and executed. It defines three levels of test documentation:

1. Organisational test documentation: these documents define the organisational test policy and test strategy.
2. Test management documentation: these documents define the pre-test and post-test management documents consisting of test plans and test completion reports.
3. Dynamic test documentation: Prior to the test being run, this documentation defines the test environment and the test data. After the test has run, this defines the test execution documentation, including incident reports and test status reports.

In reality, only a very large or mission-critical project would use the full standard: most projects would use a subset, tailored for the project.

13.2   Software Development Life Cycle

The software development life cycle is a structured plan for organising the development of a software product. There are several models for such processes, each describing approaches to a variety of tasks or activities that take place during the process. The need for such planning arose with the growth in size and complexity of software projects. Unstructured approaches were found to result in cost overruns, late deliveries, and uncertainties regarding quality. By adopting a plan for the development, it was intended to create a repeatable and predictable software development process that would automatically improve productivity and quality.

All models for development include software testing as part of the process, but differ on the emphasis it is given. The next sections discuss some of the models and the role software testing has within them.[2]

---

[1] ISO/IEC/IEEE 29119-3:2013 Software and systems engineering – Software testing – Part 3: Test documentation.
[2] See I. Somerville. *Software Engineering*, 10th ed. Pearson, 2016. for a more detailed discussion on software engineering and process models.

13.3   The Waterfall Model

This model visualises the software development process as a linear sequence of software development activities: requirements, design, implementation, verification, and maintenance. The idea behind the waterfall model is to spend time early on making sure that requirements and design are correct, saving time and effort later. Thus, no time will be wasted creating a design from inaccurate requirements or writing code based on a faulty design. Furthermore, there is an emphasis on documentation that keeps all knowledge in a central repository and can be referenced easily by new members joining the team. The model is often criticised for showing no visible progress until the very end, and for not being flexible to changes.

Figure 13.2 shows a simplified model[3] centred around the testing activity.

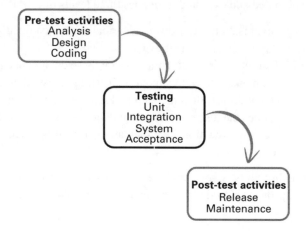

Figure 13.2 A tester's view of the waterfall model.

This is categorised into three groups of activity: pre-test activities, testing, and post-test activities:

- Pre-test activities consist of analysis of the user requirements, followed by the design of the system, and coding.
- Testing consists of unit testing, integration testing, system testing, and acceptance testing of the system.
- Post-test activities consist of release of the software/product, and the subsequent maintenance after the software has been deployed.

All the planning is done at the beginning, and once created it is not to be changed. There is no overlap between any of the subsequent phases. Often, anyone's first chance to 'see' the program is at the very end once the testing is complete and the software is released.

---

[3] This is a simplification of the standard waterfall diagram, as it focuses on the testing activity.

For example, the requirements may need to change during the project or a better approach to the design may become obvious during the coding phase. Additionally, it can be time-consuming to produce all the associated documentation. From a testing viewpoint, all the tests are carried out once the software is completed. This can cause a number of problems. First, budgetary or time pressure on the project at this stage could result in insufficient or incomplete testing being carried out. This could be further exacerbated by much testing being done on the program as a whole rather than systematically progressing from unit testing to application or system testing. Second, if testing exposes design faults in the program, it is too late to do a redesign in this process, and the only option is to try to fix the problems in the code, which is followed by more testing. If some faults are difficult to trace, it could result in many iterations back and forth between fixing and testing. Lastly, customers may request changes once they have received the product, which may lead to a long maintenance phase.

13.4   The V-Model

The V-model visualises the software development process as a relationship between the specification and associated testing activities of software development. The idea behind the V-model is to increase the focus on testing. Each activity leads to two outputs: a specification of the next activity, and the criteria for testing the activity has been correctly executed later in the process. It is called the V-model for two reasons: the focus on the verification and validation of the software product, and the shape of the process.

Figure 13.3 shows a viewpoint of the V-model[4] that groups the pre-coding and post-coding activities, to emphasise these relationships.

This diagram is categorised into three groups of activity: pre-testing software creation, coding, and software testing. Pre-testing software creation includes requirements gathering, analysis, high-level design and detailed design activities, each of which produces the documentation shown in the diagram. After coding, software testing begins, based on this documentation. Each document is associated with a pair of matching phases in the model, representing the associated creation and testing activities:

- Requirements gathering produces the user requirements specification, which is both the input to analysis and the basis for acceptance testing.
- Analysis produces the software requirements specification, which is both the input for the high-level design of the software and the basis for system testing.
- High-level design produces the software design specification, which is both the input for the detailed design of the software and the basis for integration testing.
- The detailed design activity produces the detailed design specification. This is used to write the code, and also is the basis for unit testing.

---

[4] This is a particular viewpoint of the standard V-model diagram, emphasising the relationships.

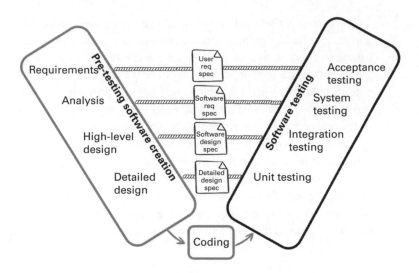

Figure 13.3 A tester's view of the V-model.

The advantages of the V-model are that it is simple and easy to manage due to the rigidity of the model, and that it encourages verification and validation at all phases: each phase has specific deliverables and a review process. Unlike the waterfall model, it gives equal weight to testing rather than treating it as an afterthought.

13.5   Incremental and Agile Development

In many software projects it is impossible to arrive at a stable, consistent set of user requirements at the beginning of the project. The waterfall model and the V-model of development do not provide an adequate framework for this situation, and an approach based on incremental or Agile models can provide much better results. Agile software development is associated with the Agile Manifesto,[5] which outlines four key components:

1.   individuals and interactions over processes and tools;
2.   working software over comprehensive documentation;
3.   customer collaboration over contract negotiation; and
4.   responding to change over following a plan.

Like other incremental development methods, Agile methods emphasise building releasable software quickly in short time frames. Unlike other incremental methods, Agile development measures these time frame in days or weeks rather than months.

---

[5] K. Beck, M. Beedle, A. van Bennekum, et al. *Manifesto for Agile Software Development*. The Agile Alliance, 2001.

Agile development encourages a high degree of collaboration between the software engineers. There are a number of guidelines to provide control over an Agile project:

- Testers should participate in the requirement 'negotiation' process that usually occurs between developers and customers. This includes asking questions, identifying if requirements are untestable, and other issues.
- Testers should immediately translate requirements into test cases serving as documentation for the upcoming iteration. Testers and developers should collaborate in automating those test cases.
- Testers should be informed immediately when requirements change so that they can modify their test cases.

13.5.1   Incremental Development

The incremental model begins with a simple implementation of a part of the software system. Each increment enhances the product until the final version is reached. A test-centric illustration of the process is shown in Figure 13.4.

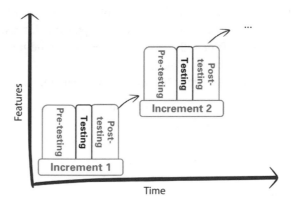

Figure 13.4 A tester's view of incremental development.

In this diagram, each increment is considered from the viewpoint of three phases: pre-testing, testing, and post-testing. In each increment, the testing consists of regression testing (to ensure the new increment has not broken any previously working software), and the testing of the new features added. The progressive release of tested software increments means that interim versions of the software become available much earlier in the development process. The quality of the final product is expected to be higher due to increased testing and the opportunity for a customer to view early releases of the product.

A major advantage of the incremental model is that the product is written and tested in smaller pieces. This reduces risks associated with the process and also allows for changes to be included easily along the way. Additionally, by adopting an incremental model the customer or the users of the product have to be involved in the development from the beginning. This means the system is more likely to meet their needs and the users are more committed to the system because they have watched it grow. Thus, another advantage of the incremental approach is an accelerated delivery of customer services: important new functionality has to be included with every iteration so that the customer can monitor and evaluate the progress of the product. Two primary disadvantages are that it can be difficult to manage because of the lack of documentation, in comparison to other models, and continual changes to the software can make it difficult to maintain as it grows in size.

13.5.2   Extreme Programming

Extreme programming (XP) was an early approach to Agile software development, which emphasises code reviews, continuous integration, and automated testing in iterations. It favours ongoing design refinement (or *refactoring*) in place of a large initial design phase, in order to keep the current implementation as simple as possible. It favours real-time communication, preferably face-to-face, over written documents, leading to less documentation compared to the waterfall method. Working software is seen as the primary measure of progress. The methodology also emphasises team work: managers, customers, and developers are all part of a team dedicated to delivering quality software. Programmers are responsible for testing their own work; testers are focused on helping the customer select and write functional tests, and on running these tests on a regular basis.

The XP process values encourage developers to:

- continuously *communicate* with customers and fellow programmers;
- keep their design *simple* and clean;
- get *feedback* from early software testing; and
- deliver a system to customers as early as possible and implement changes as suggested, so developers respond with *courage* to changing requirements and technology.

Figure 13.5 presents a test-centric diagram of the XP process[6] that highlights the testing activities.

User stories are written by the customers, providing the user requirements specifications. They are in the format of about three sentences of text written by the customer using non-technical language. The user stories are the basis for the software requirements, which are used to plan releases of the software. They are also used to produce test scenarios that drive the acceptance testing for each release. A release of the software consists of multiple iterations, each of which lasts typically 1–3 weeks. Each iteration can be considered as containing pre-testing, testing, and post-testing activities.

---

[6] The standard diagram focuses on release planning and software increments – see www.extremeprogramming.org/map/project.html.

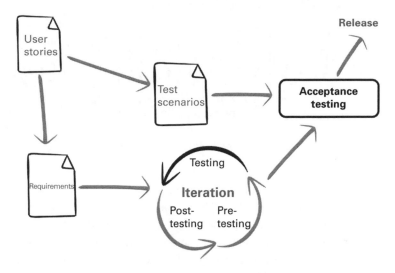

Figure 13.5 Testing in extreme programming.

Testing is a key part of XP. Unit tests are implemented before the code is written. Doing this helps the developer to think deeply about what they are doing. The requirements are defined fully by the tests. Another benefit is that the code, influenced by the existing unit tests, is expected to be easier to understand and to test. When a fault is fixed, new tests are created to ensure it has been fixed correctly.

13.5.3   Scrum

Scrum is a process for managing complex software projects and is a technique of Agile software development. It is similar to XP but there are a number of differences:

- Scrum teams work in iterations called sprints. These can last a little longer than XP iterations.
- Scrum teams do not allow changes to be introduced during the sprints. XP teams are more flexible with changes within an iteration as long as work has not started on that particular feature already.
- In Scrum there is more flexibility for additional stakeholders to influence the ordering of implementing features. XP implements features in a priority order decided essentially by the customer.
- In Scrum it is up to the team to organise themselves and adopt the practices they feel work best for themselves. In XP, unit testing and simple design practices are built in.

Figure 13.6 shows the Scrum process with a focus on the testing activities.[7]

---

[7] The standard Scrum process diagram focuses on the product backlog and the Scrum sprint cycles – see www.scrum.org/resources/scrum-framework-poster.

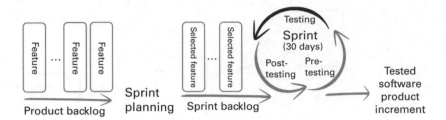

Figure 13.6 Testing in the Scrum process.

The diagram starts with the product backlog, which is a prioritised list of all the required product features. Scrum teams take on as much of the product backlog as they think they can turn into an increment of product functionality within a 30-day iteration or sprint, forming the sprint backlog. A sprint consists of the pre-testing, testing, and post-testing activities for each selected feature in the sprint backlog. The testing approach depends on the team, and is not strictly prescribed as in XP, but will usually consist of unit testing, regression testing, etc. There are daily Scrum meetings as part of each sprint, not highlighted in this diagram as they are not strictly test-related. The selected features are also used to create acceptance tests, which are used to verify the tested software product increment for each sprint.

This approach has proven successful, as the testing team collaborates closely with the developers from the start of the project.

13.6   Process-Related Quality Standards and Models

There are a number of other models and quality-related standards that the tester should be aware of. In general, they address testing as a part of the larger quality assurance (QA) process. A key model is the ISO 9000/25000 series of standards. The ISO 9000/25000 series of standards are a significant concern for companies developing software and systems for public tender – they provide state bodies with an assurance that the software is being developed in a professional manner.

14 Wrap Up

This chapter summarises the test techniques presented in the book, takes a reverse look at the testing process to explain the dependencies of the test activities, and finishes with some recommended further reading and a look at research directions.

14.1 Summary

This book has introduced the reader to the following essential testing material:

- An introduction to testing (Chapter 1), covering:
    - The importance of software quality;
    - The theory of testing that implies exhaustive testing;
    - Exhaustive testing and why it is not feasible;
    - The role of test heuristics;
    - Static and dynamic testing; and
    - Fault models.

- A description of the basic test activities (Chapter 1):
    - Test design, consisting of:
        - analysis of the requirements (and the source code, to a lesser degree);
        - development of test coverage items;
        - development of test cases and test data; and
        - verification of the test design.
    - Test implementation, with a focus on test automation (Chapter 11);
    - Reviewing the test results.

- A description of three black-box test techniques: equivalence partitions, boundary value analysis, and decision tables for combinations (Chapters 2, 3, and 4, respectively):
    - Equivalence partitions involves selecting representative values from ranges of inputs and outputs that represent equivalent processing. It can be considered as testing with typical values.

- Boundary value analysis involves selecting the lower and upper edge values from these ranges. It can be considered as testing with extreme values.
- Decision tables involves selecting combinations of input values that should cause different processing or different outputs. It can be considered as testing for all possible situations.

- A description of three white-box test techniques: statement coverage, branch coverage, and all paths coverage (Chapters 5, 6, and 7, respectively):

  - Statement coverage involves selecting input values to ensure that all statements in the tested code are executed. It is the simplest form of white-box testing.
  - Branch coverage involves selecting input values to ensure that all branches in the tested code are taken. It is a stronger form of testing than statement coverage.
  - All paths testing involves selecting input values that ensure that all the end-to-end paths through the code being tested are taken.

- An overview of unit testing and application testing (Chapters 8 and 10).

  - Unit testing involves calling a method or function with selected input values, and comparing the output (the actual results) to the expected results.
  - Application testing involves emulating a user interacting with an application and making sure that every user story meets its acceptance criteria.

- An introduction to techniques for testing object-oriented software (Chapter 9). Three essential techniques are discussed:

  - Testing in class context: how to test methods and attributes that interact with each other in a class.
  - Inheritance testing: testing that inherited behaviour functions correctly.
  - State-based testing: testing the state-based behaviour of a class.

- An introduction to random testing (Chapter 12). Random testing poses three key challenges.

  - The test data problem: how to generate valuable random data.
  - The test oracle problem: how to calculate the expected output for random inputs.
  - The test completion problem: how to know when to end random testing.

- An overview of key test automation topics, with representative examples (Chapter 11).

  - Unit testing, using TestNG;
  - Test coverage measurement, using JaCoCo;
  - Automated application testing, using Selenium.

- A look at testing in the software process (Chapter 13). This chapter clarifies the positioning of testing in the larger context of software development:

  – A look at where testing fits into the standard software development models; and
  – A look at some specific development processes and the role of testing in each.

14.2   A Reverse Look at Testing

The approach used in this book has followed the test development activities in order, each producing outputs for the next activity. In this section, we will complement this by considering software testing from the opposite perspective: with a *reverse* look. By considering what is required at each step, the reader can develop a deeper understanding of the need for this ordering of the activities. This argument will also provide some motivation for documenting the outputs of each step, as a component in the development of high-quality software.

14.2.1   A Test Implementation

Snippet 14.1 shows a simple, automated black-box unit test using equivalence partitions[1] to test a method `TestItem.categorise()`. The specification for this method is shown later.

Snippet 14.1 Sample test implementation

```
@Test public void test1() {
    TestItem ti = new TestItem();
    AssertEquals( 100, ti.categorise(23, true) );
}
```

There are three data values in the code: 100, 23, and true. There is also the name of the test method: `test1()`. Where do these come from? Let us examine the previous activity.

14.2.2   Test Cases

The data values come from the specification of the required test cases – a test case for this test is shown in Table 14.1.

The test case ID (`test1`) has been assigned by the tester using an appropriate naming scheme. But where do the Input values in the test case (`23` and `true`) come from? Where does the Expected Results value (`100`) come from? And where do the

---

[1] For more on equivalence partitions, refer to Chapter 2.

Table 14.1 Test data for `TestItem.categorise()`.

ID	TCI covered	Inputs		Exp. results
		p1	p2	
test1	a,b,c	23	true	100

TCI (test coverage item) Covered identifiers (a, b, and c) come from? Again, we examine the previous activity.

14.2.3   Test Coverage Items

The TCI Covered and data values, shown in Table 14.1 are derived from the TCIs shown in Table 14.2. Each test coverage item has a unique identifier (the TCI), and defines an equivalence partition for a parameter.

Table 14.2 Test cases (equivalence partitions) for `TestItem.categorise()`.

TCI	Parameter	Equivalence partition
a	p1	0..100
b	p2	true
c	expected results (return value)	100

The test coverage item identifiers have been assigned by the tester, again using a suitable naming scheme. The values in the test cases of 23, true, and 100 have been selected by the tester from the equivalence partitions shown. But where do the three equivalence partitions shown come from? Again we refer to the previous activity.

14.2.4   Test Analysis

An analysis of the software specification identifies the partitions for the input parameters shown in Table 14.1, and the partitions for the return value (or output) shown in Table 14.4.

The test coverage items shown previously use the partitions [0..100] for p1, [true] for p2, and [100] for the expected results (return value).

Note: Table 14.4 shows the return values (0, 100, 101). Each of these represent a single-valued partition for the return value.

Where do these parameters, and their associated partitions come from? They come from the software specification.

Table 14.3 Input equivalence partitions for `TestItem.categorise()`.

Parameter	Equivalence partition

p1	`(*) Integer.MIN_VALUE..-1`
	`0..100`
	`101..Integer.MAX_VALUE`

p2	`true` `false`

Table 14.4 Output equivalence partitions for `TestItem.categorize()`.

Parameter	Equivalence partition

Return value	`0`
	`100`
	`101`

14.2.5   The Software Specification

The equivalence partitions are derived from an analysis of the functional specification of the software. The specification is shown below using Javadoc notation.

`public int categorise(int p1, boolean p2)`
Determine which group the value `p1` is in.
Inputs
   p1: the value being analysed
   p2: a Boolean value (or flag) used to enable/disable the categorisation
Outputs
   return value:
      `0` if `p1` is negative
      `100` is `p1` is in the range `0..100` and `p2` is `true`
      `101` otherwise

14.2.6   Discussion

If we examine the sequence of activities and output produced, we can see that, for black-box testing, the tester requires, in this order:

1.   The specification to analyse. In the case of white-box testing, the analysis would require the source code as well as the specification.
2.   The results of analysing the specification (identifying the equivalence partitions).
3.   The TCIs (which define *what* needs to be tested).
4.   The test cases with test data (which define *how* to do the tests).
5.   The test implementation (which is executed to perform the tests).

Except for software with high quality requirements, it is unusual to document the outputs of the test design process to the level of detail shown in this book. Normally, much of the work is done in the tester's mind. It is, however, almost impossible to review a test to ensure it is correct without some documentation of the analysis, TCIs, test cases, and test data. Whether the outputs are written down or not, the tester must perform the same work. While learning how to test, it is excellent practice to write down the output of every activity in the process.

14.3   Further Reading

In this book, we have focused on what we regard as the absolutely essential techniques that the software tester must understand. There are therefore many topics that are covered only briefly, or not at all. This section provides some suggested works providing a deeper understanding of topics covered in the book, and also suggested works that cover additional topics not covered in the book. The focus is on books that describe the principles of specific testing techniques and how to apply them in practice – many books that cover software testing at a higher level, or that are focused on specific tools or environments, are not included.

There are many books and papers on software testing. In this section we provide an annotated list of recommended texts, ones which we have found useful in preparing this book. The list starts with more general works that discuss the software process and how testing fits into this, and ends with more specific works that address particular techniques or aspects of testing. We only provide a small number of selected, key texts in each area; this is not a comprehensive survey of the software-testing literature.

Full details to access these readings are provided in the Bibliography.

14.3.1   Testing in the Software Process

The standard software engineering textbooks include *Software Engineering a Practitioners Approach* (Pressman) and *Software Engineering* (Sommerville). These books all describe the process of software engineering, and provide an overview of software testing and how it fits into the process.

14.3.2   Standards on Software Testing

Probably the most prominent international standard is IEEE/ISO/IEC 29119. This provides a detailed look at software testing from five viewpoints.

- Part 1 defines concepts and definitions.
- Part 2 describes test processes.
- Part 3 discusses test documentation.

- Part 4 defines specific test techniques.
- Part 5 covers keyword-driven testing.

Not every technique in the standard is covered in this book, and not every technique in this book is included in the standard. Three particular topics not covered in the current standard are integration testing, the testing of object-oriented software, and all paths testing. The standard defines a very detailed and rigorous approach to software testing – it is likely that only large organisations with a requirement for high-quality software will use the full standard. There are a number of other related IEEE standards on particular aspects of testing.

The other key standard is the ISO 25000 family of standards. These provide guidelines for software quality requirements and evaluation, and are essentially process related.

14.3.3 Software Testing Techniques

The classic books on software testing techniques are *Software Testing* (Roper) and *The Art of Software Testing* (Myers). The ideas in Roper's book are still relevant today, and this book provides an excellent description of how to actually apply test techniques. Myers presents many interesting ideas, but they often require interpretation by the reader to apply in practice.

The modern classic on the topic is *Introduction to Software Testing,* 2nd edition (Ammann and Offutt). This provides an excellent mathematical foundation for software testing. It is a book best suited to expanding the understanding of the experienced tester.

14.3.4 Testing Object-Oriented Software

There are many books on the subject, but in our opinion by far the best is *Testing Object-Oriented Systems: Models, Patterns, and Tools* (Binder). This has detailed coverage on the topic, and is best treated as a reference book rather than as an introductory textbook. It provides probably the best discussion on using fault models in any software testing book. It also includes a detailed, if slightly out of date, treatment of UML diagrams and how to use them as the source of test data.

14.3.5 Integration Testing

For such an important topic in the modern development environment, there is a disappointing lack of texts on systematic techniques for integration testing. In particular, there is little detailed definition of fault models and how to identify test coverage items and test data. In an Agile process, software is produced in a series of small increments, and as each is added (software integration) it should be tested to make sure it works correctly with the existing code (integration testing). Integration testing is currently addressed as an ad-hoc approach, and is best learned through experience in large software systems.

Two representative books we have selected that address the topic are *Integration Testing from the Tranches* (Frankel) and *Continuous Integration* (Duvall). Frankel has a number of examples, and shows how to use a number of tools, and contains an interesting discussion on integration with external software systems. From a testing viewpoint, Duvall is more focused on how to automate various tests (unit, component, system, functional). Both books contain useful coverage of stubs/mocks and the tools used to test with these.

We suggest this topic to the reader as an important and fruitful area for future research.

14.3.6   Random Testing

There is no up-to-date, comprehensive textbook covering the principles of random software testing.

A detailed introduction to the research can be found in *New Strategies for Automated Random Testing* (Ahmad). The specific technique of DART referenced in the book is discussed in *DART: Directed Automated Random Testing* (Godefroid). An up-to-date survey of adaptive random testing can be found in *A Survey on Adaptive Random Testing* (Huang) – adaptive random testing adapts the test input based on the behaviour of previous tests.

There are many tools for random stability testing for android applications, often referred to as monkey testing, and a number of papers evaluate these – for example, *An Empirical Comparison between Monkey Testing and Human Testing* (Mohammed). Of particular interest to the reader might be the use of this approach by Facebook, as discussed for example in *Sapienz: Multi-objective Automated Testing for Android Applications* (Mao).

14.3.7   Testing for Language-Specific Hazards

Most programming languages are a compromise between simplicity and features. This leads to programming mistakes that are language-specific as the designers of every language make different decisions about these compromises. For example, the same statement in different languages may have different effects, and a programmer moving to a new language is likely to make mistakes. The tester should understand these hazards in order to write language-specific tests.

There are many books written on the topic. For the Java programmer, we find the most detailed book to be *More Java Pitfalls* (Daconta et al.). This book is very useful for the tester, as they identify programming constructs that are likely to cause faults in the code.

The tester should know the term *anti-pattern*, which is used to refer to practices that are not recommended. If an anti-pattern has been used in software, it is more likely to have a fault. The book *AntiPatterns: Refactoring Software, Architectures, and Projects in Crisis* (Brown et al.) is a good introduction to the topic for the tester.

14.3.8 Program Proving

Static verification (or program proving) can be used to mathematically prove the correctness of code using logic, set theory, etc. It has for many years been seen as a powerful adjunct, or even a replacement, for dynamic software testing. However, despite many research advances, there is a lack of commercially supported tools with support for the latest versions of programming languages.

Some of the key, classic texts in the area are *A Method of programming* (Dijkstra and Feijen), *The Specification of Complex Systems* (Cohen), and *Program Specification and Verification in VDM* (Jones).

Much of the more recent work is more easily available via research results, and some relevant websites are listed here, with a focus on more recent results and commonly used languages:

- The Viper toolset, and associated research, supports languages such as Python, RUST, Java, and OpenCL – we recommend this as a starting point for the beginner, especially as there are online tutorials and proof tools available:

    - www.pm.inf.ethz.ch/research/viper.html
    - https://vercors.ewi.utwente.nl

- The JML language and toolset support the Java language, though not currently the latest version of Java

    - www.openjml.org

- Spec# was a very promising project by Microsoft to support the C# language, but unfortunately this is discontinued

    - https://research.microsoft.com/en-us/projects/specsharp

14.3.9 Testing Safety-Critical Software

The quality of safety critical software is of paramount importance, and there is a significant body of work addressing the topic. Some suggested readings are:

- the NIST programme for Automated Combinatorial Testing for Software (ACTS) – www.nist.gov/programs-projects/automated-combinatorial-testing-software-acts
- the seminal NASA paper on MC/DC: *A Practical Tutorial on Modified Condition/Decision Coverage* (Hayhurst), which extends decision/condition coverage by adding the requirement that the effect of the change of each individual condition on the outcome of the decision also be verified.

14.3.10   Going *Off-Piste*

This book presents a *systematic* introduction to software testing – we believe that it is important to understand the essential elements of testing before going *off-piste*. In practice, a software tester may need to exhibit significant innovation to effectively test software systems. We present here a short selection of books that may stimulate ideas that can be used to augment the more structured approaches presented in the book, and provide an insight into the broader role of the software tester.

- *Black-Box Testing* (Bezier) and *The Complete Guide to Software Testing* (Hetzel) are other classic books on software testing. Their approach is somewhat less structured than the other classic books, and we recommend them as useful for considering software testing from a more holistic viewpoint.
- *Testing Computer Software* (Kaner et al.) addresses many issues which are supplementary to those covered in this book. It is divided into three sections: fundamentals, specific testing skills, and managing testing projects and groups. We recommend it for its breadth of coverage.
- *The Software Testing Engineer's Handbook* (Bath and McKay) is a study guide for the ISTQB Test Analyst and Technical Test Analyst Advanced Level Certificates. We recommend this both in preparation for this certification, and as for the previous book, for its breadth of coverage.
- *How Google Tests Software* (Whittaker et al.) gives an excellent idea of the roles of the software tester in an industrial setting. We recommend it for the insights it gives to the reader.

14.4   Research Directions

As in most areas of software engineering, research into software testing is a wide and varied field. This section gives some indications to the reader on where to go for more information.

14.4.1   Conferences

The following list of conferences, while not complete, gives a starting point to the reader for exploring the topic further, and gaining knowledge of the state-of-the-art:

- AITEST International Conference on Artificial Intelligence Testing
- CAST Conference of the Association for Software Testing
- EUROSTAR European Software Testing Annual Conference
- ICSTTP International Conference on Software Testing, Types and Process
- ICSE International Conference on Software Engineering
- ICSQ International Conference on Software Quality
- ICST International Conference on Software Testing, Verification and Validation
- ISSTA International Symposium on Software Testing and Analysis

- QUEST Quality Engineered Software & Testing Conference
- SoCraTEs International Conference for Software Craft and Testing
- STAREAST and STARWEST Software Testing Analysis & Review Conference
- STPCON Software Test Professionals Conference
- VALID International Conference on Advances in System Testing and Validation Lifecycle

14.4.2 Research Topics

A number of indicative research fields, selected from the conferences listed, are outlined below:

- **Search-based software testing**. Random testing is often used to try to achieve white-box coverage criteria, such as code coverage. Research is directed at search-based techniques to achieve particular coverage criteria.
- **Mutation analysis**. The idea of mutation testing has mainly been applied at the source-code level. Recently, the idea has been applied to test different artefacts, including research into the notation used.
- **Regression test reduction**. Running regression tests is often the most time-consuming testing activity. When software is changed or extended, checking that the existing functionality still works correctly is at least as important as checking that the new functionality works correctly. Research is directed at finding the optimal set of tests to re-run.
- **Model-based testing**. Recent years have seen increasing interest in the use of models for testing software, for example UML. Research includes formal verification of model transformations into code, adding debug support for model-based testing, automatic test data generation based on the models.
- **Automated software verification**. Formal specifications provide the basis for automating testing, either at runtime or statically. These usually take the form of assertions stating pre-conditions, post-conditions, and invariants that must hold for the software to match its specification. Recent research has started to provide working tools that do both static and dynamic evaluation of software against its specification.
- **New technologies**. New software technologies and architectures require the application of test principles in new ways. Examples include research into effective testing for SOA (service oriented architecture), virtualisation, dynamic software systems, GUI (graphical user interface), cloud computing, and artificial intelligence.
- **Software process and tools**. Testing is a key part of the software process, and tools are critical to its support. Research is active into the relationship between testing and the other process activities, the development of test-driven development processes, and the effectiveness of testing as a quality measure. Good examples of new directions include automated tools for testing Android applications and autonomous vehicles.

Appendix: Running the Examples

All the examples shown in the book are available online at www.cambridge.org/ bierig. They can be run on Windows or Linux, and have been verified on Windows 10 and Ubuntu 18.04. Some small changes may be required to run the examples under MacOS.

Before running any of the examples, you must have the Java JDK installed. All the examples have been verified using the latest LTS (long-term support) version of Java at the time of publication: JDK 11. You must also have TestNG installed. Chapters 5 and 6 require the JaCoCo coverage libraries, and Chapters 10–12 require Selenium. Details of the versions required, and where they were downloaded from, are provided in the file readme.txt in the top-level folder. All the dependencies should be placed in the 'libraries' folder before running the examples.

For simplicity, the examples have been developed to run from the command line. For this to work, you must have the JDK bin folder on your PATH (see the JDK installation instructions for details). You can verify this by typing the commands 'javac –version' and 'java -version'. Both command should complete successfully, and should show the same Java version. You can also run the examples from an IDE (such as Eclipse), but no instructions for this are included.

The top-level folder contains utility scripts (windows batch files) to build and run the examples:

- **readme.txt** provides a complete list explaining each file for that chapter;
- **check-dependencies.bat** checks that the Java compiler is on PATH, and that all the .jar files needed are in the libraries folder;
- **compile-all.bat** compiles all the java files required for the book;
- **run-menu.bat** allows you to run all of the examples; select the chapter and then the figure number.

Each chapter has its own folder, and in each folder there are scripts to compile and run the associated examples. See how these are called from run-menu.bat.

Every Windows batch file (xxx.bat) has a corresponding bash script for use on Linux (xxx.sh).

Bibliography

Ahmad, M. New strategies for automated random testing. PhD Thesis, University of York, 2014.

Ammann, P. and J. Offutt. *Introduction to Software Testing*, 2nd ed. Cambridge University Press, 2017.

Bath, G. and J. McKay. *The Software Testing Engineer's Handbook: A Study Guide for the ISTQB Test Analyst and Technical Test Analyst Advanced Level Certificates 2012*, Rock Nook Computing, 2015.

Beck, K., M. Beedle, A. van Bennekum, et al. *Manifesto for Agile Software Development.* The Agile Alliance, 2001.

Bezier, B. *Black-Box Testing: Techniques for Functional Testing of Software and Systems.* Wiley, 1995.

Binder, R. *Testing Object Oriented Systems: Models, Patterns, and Tools.* Addison-Wesley, 2010.

Brown, W., R. Malveau, H. McCormick, and T. Mowbray. *AntiPatterns: Refactoring Software, Architectures, and Projects in Crisis.* Wiley, 1998.

Cohen, B., W. Harwood, and M. Jackson. *The Specification of Complex Systems.* Addison-Wesley, 1986.

Daconta, M., K. Smith, D. Avondolio and W. Richardson. *More Java Pitfalls.* Wiley, 2003.

Dijkstra, E. and W. Feijen. *A Method of Progamming.* Pearson Education, 1988.

Fowler, M. *UML Distilled.* Addison-Wesley, 2018.

Frankel, N. *Integration Testing from the Trenches.* Leanpub, 2015.

Godefroid, P., N. Klarlund, and K. Sen. DART: Directed Automated Random Testing. In *Proc. ACM SIGPLAN Conf. Programming Language Design and Implementation.* ACM, 2005.

Goodenough, J. and S. Gerhart. Toward a theory of test data selection. *Proc. Int. Conf. Reliable Software*, ACM, 1975.

Gosling, J., B. Joy, G. Steele, G. Bracha, A. Buckley, and D. Smith. *The Java®Language Specification, Java SE 11 Edition.* Oracle, 2018.

Grady, R.B., *Practical Software Metrics for Project Management and Process Improvement.* Prentice-Hall, 1992.

Hayhurst, K.J., D.S. Veerhusen, J.J. Chilsenski, and L.K. Rierson. A practical tutorial on modified condition/decision coverage. Technical report. NASA, 2001.

Hetzel, B. *The Complete Guide to Software Testing.* QED Information Sciences, 1988.

Huang, R., W. Sun, Y. Xu, et al. A survey on adaptive random testing. *IEEE Transactions on Software Engineering.* DOI: 10.1109/TSE.2019.2942921

Liskov, B.H. and J.M. Wing. A behavioral notion of subtyping. *ACM Transactions on Programming Languages and Systems*, Vol. 16, No. 6, 1994.

ISO/IEC 25010:2011 Systems and software engineering – Systems and software Quality Requirements and Evaluation (SQuaRE) – System and software quality models.

ISO/IEC/IEEE 29119-3:2013 Software and systems engineering – Software testing – Part 3: Test documentation.

ISO/IEC/IEEE 29119:2016 Software and systems engineering – Software testing (parts 1–5).

Jones, C. *Program Specification and Verification in VDM*. Springer-Verlag, 1987.

Kaner, C., J. Falk, and H. Nguyen. *Testing Computer Software*. Wiley, 1999.

Kellegher, D. and K. Murray. *Information Technology Law in Ireland*. Bloomsbury Professional, 2007.

Mao, K., M. Harman, and Y. Jia. Sapienz: Multi-objective automated testing for Android applications. In *Proc. 25th Int Symp. Software Testing and Analysis*. ACM, 2016.

Myers, G.J. *The Art of Software Testing*. Wiley, 2004.

NIST. *The Economic Impacts of Inadequate Infrastructure for Software Testing*. NIST, 2002.

Pfleeger, S.L. and J.M. Atlee. *Software Engineering: Theory and Practice*, 4th ed. Pearson Higher Education, 2010.

Pressman, R. and B. Maxim. *Software Engineering: A Practitioner's Approach*. McGraw-Hill, 2014.

Roper, M. *Software Testing*. McGraw-Hill, 1994.

Software Magazine. 2018 Software 500 Companies. Available at: www.rcpbuyersguide.com/top-companies.php.

Sommerville, I. *Software Engineering*, 10th ed. Pearson, 2016.

Vinter, O. and P. Poulsen. Experience-driven software process improvement. In *Proc. Conf. Software Process Improvement* (SPI 96). International Software Consulting Network, 1996.

Whittaker, J., J. Arbon, and J. Carollo. *How Google Tests Software*. Addison-Wesley, 2012.

Listings

Index